# THE SIXTIES

THE AMERICAN RETROSPECTIVE SERIES

# THE
# SIXTIES

### Recollections
### of the Decade from
## HARPER'S MAGAZINE

*With an introduction by Eugene J. McCarthy*
*Edited by Katharine Whittemore, Ellen Rosenbush,*
*and Jim Nelson*

NEW YORK

Published by Franklin Square Press, a division of Harper's Magazine
666 Broadway, New York, N.Y. 10012

First Edition

First printing 1995

Library of Congress Cataloging-in-Publication Data:
The sixties: recollections of the decade from Harper's magazine/edited by
Katharine Whittemore, with an introduction by Eugene J. McCarthy.—1st ed.
p. cm.—(The American retrospective series)
ISBN: 1-879957-20-5 (pbk: alk. paper)
1. United States–History–1961–1969. I. Whittemore, Katharine. II. Harper's
magazine. III. Series.
E841.S54 1995
973.923—dc20
95-19275
CIP

Book design by Deborah Thomas
Cover design by Louise Fili

Manufactured in the United States of America.

This book has been produced on acid-free paper.

# CONTENTS

# INTRODUCTION

## Eugene J. McCarthy

As I was growing up in central Minnesota, in a town of fewer than a thousand, my reading was largely limited to what was available in a modest school library and an even more modest town library. Our family library was limited as well, but fortunately we were always well supplied with magazines: popular ones, practical ones, and also magazines of ideas (as we called them), including *Harper's*.

I became addicted to these magazines, and especially to essayists and their works. This addiction continued through college, through years as a teacher, and as a member of Congress. I still read and re-read the great essayists, particularly the British—Bacon and Swift, Addison and Dryden, Carlyle and Ruskin; the Americans—Washington Irving, Ralph Waldo Emerson, and, later, William Allen White, Elmer Davis, and Walter Lippmann; and the Canadians, such as Stephen Leacock. But the essays that I relish the most are those of E. B. White as they appeared in *Harper's* (under the title "One Man's Meat") and those of Bernard De Voto, who for years wrote "The Easy Chair" column in the magazine.

A good essay should, of course, reflect and express the time in which it was written, but an excellent one will outlive the period to have a shelf life of its own. And as Yeats said of a poem, a good essay should hold an element of surprise, distinguishing it from a tract or article. The individual essays selected for this book by and large fit these standards of excellence.

The decade of the Sixties did not have a clearly marked beginning, other than the numerical one. Its birth was more in the ending of the Fifties, as described by Eric Goldman in the opening essay of this collection, "Good-by to the Fifties—and Good Riddance," published in the January 1960 issue of *Harper's*. Politically, the decade began with the defeat of Richard Nixon. It ended, by mathematical count, with a "new" Nixon in the White House, elected, or rather "sold" as a product of the spin doctors, media advisers, makeup artists, and speechwriters, as Joe McGinniss reports in his essay on the 1968 campaign. The "new" Nixon did not last. By 1972, the old one had resurfaced, in dirty tricks and Watergate. The politics of the Sixties was to end in the resignation of the President and, ultimately, in the vague and halting administrations of Ford and Carter.

The decade's political beginning—the election of John Kennedy— was marked by optimism, with the promise of peaceful growth, tranquillity, and an easing of national and international tensions. That mood was shattered by Kennedy's assassination. It was an act, as Priscilla Johnson McMillan reports in her essay based on an interview with Lee Harvey Oswald, that was neither politically motivated nor based on any personal hatred (or even envy) of John Kennedy. Oswald, Johnson shows us, was not Camus's stranger but something else entirely.

By the end of the Sixties, the early optimism was gone, dispelled by the folly of the Bay of Pigs and the threat, heightened during the Cuban Missile Crisis, of nuclear war. With the arms race and the Cold War in full gear, the United States became increasingly mired in the Vietnam War, the early stages of which are described in the essays by David Halberstam and Ward Just. By 1970, the war had passed beyond the limits of rational control (as Halberstam and Just suggested it might) and was operating on self-generating justification, a momentum fueled by successive presidents who defended their pursuit of the war on the grounds that they were continuing the work of their predecessors.

The Kennedy assassination and the subsequent investigations into it have, since the Sixties, nagged at the nation, and so have the consequences of the Vietnam War. The year 1995 saw one of the war's most prominent, persistent, and forceful advocates, Robert McNamara, confess (the press seemed to prefer the word "reveal," as if it marked a higher order of communication) that he did not believe in the war. Now some who did not support the war (including the current President of the United States) say they have been vindicated, if not absolved of fault or guilt, by McNamara's going public. Others who supported the war or helped to direct it and fight it also claim vindication because of McNamara's report. All might have found shelter in the word that the Nixon Administration employed for the war as it moved into Cambodia: "incursion." Never before had this word been used in reference to military actions. There is no verb form for it; one can "invade," but one cannot "incurse." An incursion is a kind of happening, an existential, amoral act. A Vietnam veteran attending a service at the memorial wall in Washington observed, "It's just like the war. It's not complete." He was right. Like the memorial, the war has no clear beginning or end.

The second major theme of this book of essays is the civil-rights issue, which was also a part of the cultural fabric of the Sixties. Civil rights were not carried into the decade with ringing political statements, or even with leadership or support from editors and commentators. Government and media support was limited. Whatever action was taken by the Eisenhower and Kennedy administrations was reactive: they responded to the states' defiance of court orders and decisions with legal and military force. The passage of civil-rights legislation in the mid-Sixties set the stage for social, economic, cultural, and racial change unmatched since Emancipation, and for conflict more complicated and only slightly less violent than that of a century earlier.

The essays of three writers who attempted to deal with the difficult and troubling years of the civil-rights conflict are included in this book. Walker Percy, white, writes of his home state, Mississippi, as "The Fallen Paradise." He sets the courage of James Meredith and Medgar Evers, whom he calls the "bravest Mississippians in recent years," against all that was personified in the Snopeses and incarnate in many Mississippians, and does not quite despair.

Louis Lomax, black, from Georgia, ventured to "go home" in 1965 to find that he could indeed go home, but to a place very different from that which he had left. In 1965, the same year in which Percy reported on the "tragedy" of Mississippi, Lomax reported that he found "no tension" in Valdosta, his hometown. He discovered that between 1960 and 1965, income per black family had risen from a little over two thousand dollars per year to more than four thousand dollars. The hospital had been integrated, and some progress had been made toward integrating the public schools. He was optimistic. "They," he writes, "the black and the white of my town—are now looking across at each other in estrangement against the day when they might join in frank friendship."

The third essay on civil rights, written by C. Vann Woodward, asks the critical question "What Happened to the Civil Rights Movement?" The year in which the essay was written, 1967, was too early—coming, as it did, shortly after the passage of the last major civil-rights legislation, the Civil Rights Bill of 1966—to answer the question reliably or to project what might happen in the future. Nonetheless, Woodward accurately identified historical, psychological, and social trends that would mark the movement to equal rights in both the North and the South. He foresaw that what he called a "Third Reconstruction" would be, at best, a difficult time for the United States. He was right. The change, though for the better, has been complicated by two developments—one political, the other economic. The political development (and this may seem a contradiction in terms) was a network of programs and policies designed to establish what President Lyndon Johnson labeled "The Great Society." This was to be the completion of the New Deal. It included programs designed to provide opportunities for the poor and the underprivileged, and also, in anticipation of these opportunities, to supplement the income of the poor, to provide them with services, food stamps, rent and housing subsidies, unemployment compensation, education benefits, etc.—all of which served an intermediate good but also distracted the politicians, especially the Democrats, from giving proper attention to the functional and structural disorders in the nation's economy and society. Instead of providing more employment by, say, shortening working time and eliminating overtime so as to provide more jobs (and give parents more time at home), unemployment benefits and home subsidies were offered. Instead of facing the facts of the maldistribution of wealth and of debt, a wholly inadequate response was offered:

adjusting the income tax. Instead of moving to provide some measure of job security in this country, the United States joined the international economic community to compete in a market marked by exploitation on a scale comparable to that accompanying the introduction and growth of the factory system.

The Woodward essay in this collection is probably the most demanding and compelling, as it forces us to face the consequences of our having accepted the exploitation of blacks as slaves (for centuries after the other nations of the Western world had abolished slavery) as well as the exploitation that occurred during the century following the Civil War and Emancipation. If there is a judgment of nations, and we seem to accept that there is—as evidenced by our passing a continuing judgment on both the Japanese and the Germans for their conduct in World War II—then we must accept continuing national responsibility for slavery and its consequences. The conditions, as described by Woodward, were observed by Alexis de Tocqueville in his book *Democracy in America,* published after his visit to this country in 1831. He wrote of the degradation and rootlessness of the slaves, of their awareness of their plight, and of the despair, if not self-hatred and resentment, among them. He found racial prejudice to be even stronger in the free states than in the slave states, and noted that segregation extended even to cemeteries. He predicted the Civil War and foresaw only one of the two possible solutions to the race problem: "The Negroes and the whites," he wrote, "must either mingle completely or they must part."

We have set our course on "mingling," a course that Woodward sees as irreversible and providing no rationale for despair. This "mingling" is of such importance as a test of our democracy that no decision—involving all matters from foreign policy, to economics and trade, to any domestic decision—can be made without weighing its bearing on race relations.

The third distinguishable block of essays in the book is comprised of writing on youth, the younger generation. These essays do not have the character of a "strain," as do the pieces about the Vietnam War and civil rights. They are more like the threads of the "woof" involved with the warp in a weaving. The John Aldridge essay, "In the Country of the Young, Part II," is not optimistic about the potential of the young to make society over. Aldridge doubts whether there will be found persons of the "exceptional mind, imagination, sensitivity, and courage" to do so. The "Country of the Young" he identifies was not a happy one, nor, in a setting in which the young quickly became "young adults," was it an easy one. The young were called upon to make judgments and commitments that their elders refused or failed to make. Prime among these was the judgment on whether to fight or not to fight, but there were other decisions—like the question of whether to march in civil-rights protests—that called on them to exercise not only moral courage but also physical courage; to endure police brutality and face the guns of National Guardsmen; to die, in places like Kent State University and in southern swamps and woods. Sixties America was a variation on a title of a Yeats poem; it was "No Country for the Young."

The distress and anguish of the young is caught in Stephen Minot's essay on draft counseling. Under the threat of Section 12 of the Universal Military Training and Service Act, "Any person . . . who . . . knowingly counsels, aids, or abets another to refuse . . . service in the armed forces . . . shall be punished by imprisonment for not more than five years or a fine of not more than $10,000 or both." Minot, after a counseling session, reports, "I lean back in my seat, nodding, rubbing my aching eyes with both hands. You'll make it, I'm thinking, you'll make it. CO or Canada or jail or wherever [he did not mention the National Guard], you'll make it."

John Simon, in his essay on the plays of Edward Albee, has both the first and last word on "The Sixties." The decade was like an Albee play, without clear beginning or end. It was all in the second act.

The essays included in this collection support the claims of *Harper's* that it provides information, ideas, and observations that help readers get through the clutter and distraction, find meaning, and reach an understanding, not only of the Sixties but also of our time.

# GOOD-BY TO THE FIFTIES— AND GOOD RIDDANCE

### (JANUARY 1960)

## *Eric F. Goldman*

TODAY THE UNITED States may be suffering from a number of perfectly obvious ills but they are all connected with—and worsened by—something that is none too tangible. That something is an atmosphere, a climate of opinion, a habit of reacting.

Where it came from is plain enough. We've grown unbelievably prosperous and we maunder along in a stupor of fat. We were badly scared by the Communists, so scared that we are leery of anybody who even so much as twits our ideas, our customs, or our leaders. We live in a heavy, humorless, sanctimonious, stultifying atmosphere, singularly lacking in the self-mockery that is self-criticism. Probably the climate of the late Fifties was the dullest and dreariest in all our history.

This situation is the more striking because never in history has a nation been more ripe, more begging for mockery, for satire, for wit. Look at this land today: We have a President, an overwhelming public hero, who persists in talking platitudes straight out of the old days of the Rutherford B. Hayes Marching Societies.

We have a Vice President, a front-running candidate for the Presidency, who is widely hailed by our press as a new man, a wonderful new man, because he intermittently stops using slander as a politi-

*1*

cal weapon and has ceased making dogs the subject of his high policy declarations.

We have an opposition party, a powerful opposition party in firm control of both branches of Congress, which for the most part is afraid to oppose on important issues. And there is its latest shining gladiator, Senator Lyndon Johnson—the choice for President of such cognoscenti as Dean Acheson—a leader who most conspicuously demonstrates his statesmanship by a profound sympathy for natural gas and an extraordinary ability to compromise the heart out of basic legislation.

We have mighty business leaders in this country, in Cabinet posts and out. At the time of the Hungarian revolt, one of them, a vice president of a large corporation, offered us his wisdom. He said: "The way to settle that Hungarian situation is to buy those fellows another little country of their own someplace, say in South America." A while ago, when the Sputniks were first going up, the ex-head of General Motors and then Secretary of Defense contributed his definition of basic research: "Basic research is when you don't know what you're doing."

We have an intellectual class in this nation with its own interesting characteristics. Much of it—railing endlessly against conformity and the gray flannel man—daily, more eagerly, seeks gray flannels for itself and daily, more eagerly, wraps tighter about itself a conformity to the Democratic party and to Sigmund Freud.

We have a popular journalism that, with a perfectly straight face, talks on and on about the new American home and its principle of togetherness. Pursuing this theme, one of the most widely read magazines asks, in words that continue to baffle me: "Why did you marry your wife? Only because she was a woman?"

We have other mass media, the great radio and television networks. Endlessly delivering themselves of paeans to the majority will and to freedom of speech, they quiver and reach for the blue pencil at the anticipation of twenty-eight letters from some minority religious or racial group, not to speak of the National Council of Women Chiropractors.

## PIETY IN THE JUKEBOXES

WE HAVE A solemn national fetish too: a deeply held assumption that the people are wise and informed, and because they are wise and informed they should continue to have a jugular hold on the all-important decisions of today's foreign policy. Early in 1959 a Los Angeles newspaperman got a little worried about the wisdom of the people and he went out in the city with his own polling question: "Do you think the Mann Act deters or helps the cause of organized labor?"

Twelve percent told the reporter to take his nonsense and go away; they knew what the Mann Act said. About half the people questioned promptly proved they had no idea what the Mann Act said but that did not stop them from having loud, firm opinions. Here are some of them: "We're strictly against that Act in our family. Poppa doesn't get paid enough as it is." Or: "My husband's in the union and I'm for anything that helps the workingman."

Matter of fact, we have a *vox populi* which has developed a still more interesting characteristic: it has learned to talk out of both sides of its mouth almost effortlessly and without a tremor of embarrassment. When the Russians showed how far ahead they were in the missiles field, a thousand voices in the United States cried out that America was done with sneering at the eggheads; we were going to have real schools, yes siree, and real respect for learning.

The same press which described this vast national penance also reported—usually without even so much as a groan—how community after community was cutting down school bond issues; the action of the University of Idaho, which blithely gave an honorary Doctor of Laws to one Dario Louis Toffenetti, of Toffenetti's restaurants, for "promoting better health in the world with the genuine Idaho baked potato"; and the words of the new Dean of the College at, of all places, the University of Chicago, who proclaimed that the University was ending its overemphasis on brains. Chicago was now eager, the Dean went on, for the student of "beauty and brawn . . . the ordinary American boy, who will only make a million in later life, the ordinary girl, who wants a husband . . ."

And we also have here in America, over the whole of this land, a

*3*

kind of creeping piety, a false piety and religiosity which has slithered its way to astounding popularity. The bookstores offer such volumes as *Go with God* or *The Power of Prayer on Plants* or *Pray Your Weight Away.* To continue on the higher levels, in 1956 the Reverend Dr. John Sutherland Bonnell, minister of the Fifth Avenue Presbyterian Church in New York City, ran an ad in the *New York Times.* "For a spiritual lift in a busy day," the ad said, "DIAL-A-PRAYER. Circle 6-4200. One minute of inspiration in prayer." Three years later, Circle 6-4200 continues to answer. Try it sometime. I tried it and I will say this much—it does not exceed one minute.

But to come down from these higher levels. Recent jukebox hits include "I've Got Religion," "Big Fellow in the Sky," and—my favorite—"The Fellow Upstairs." Not long ago the Ideal Toy Company established rapport with its era. In response to "the resurgence of religious feeling and practice in America today," the firm announced, it was producing a doll which, when you stroked it, went down in a kneeling position.

*Modern Screen* magazine ran a series called "How the Stars Found Faith." The articles included Piper Laurie's account of a day during her visit to Korea, when she was riding back through the enemy patrols. And Piper wrote:

"I felt wonderful because I knew, somehow I just *knew* there were not four of us, but five of us going back in that jeep: And guess who the fifth passenger was. It was good old God."

Arthur Godfrey and Jane Russell have spoken up too. Godfrey declared: "Don't tell me about science and its exact explanation of everything. Some things are bigger. God is the difference. He gets around." Jane Russell added: "I love God. And when you get to know Him, you find He's a Livin' Doll."

## WHAT HAPPENED TO THE CLOWNS?

OH MY GOD (or perhaps in our beatific era I should say oh my goodness), where are the guffaws in this country, the purifying wit and humor, the catharsis of caricature, the outcries against all this unmitigated nonsense? They come here and there in a few publications or broadcasts, a few weary voices, a few groans or a few bright shafts, but for the most part the scene is unruffled and unrufflable. Our faces are straight, our thoughts are doggedly constructive, our ramparts are high and wide against the man who belly-laughs. Sometimes I think the real menace to America is not Communism at all. Sometimes I think we are just going to bore ourselves to death.

This is not only a dreary situation; it is a downright dangerous one. It is hardly necessary to point out that as long as there have been human beings, laughter has been the most certain release from comfortable certitudes, the greatest protection from inanity and hypocrisy, the surest spur to fresh, imaginative thinking.

Even the American 1920s were justified, if they were justified at all, by the men of laughter. While the smog of Aimee McPherson, mahjongg, and Warren Gamaliel Harding lay thick over the nation, a band of inspired heretics frolicked away. There was a Fiorello La Guardia kicking up his heels in Congress; a Sinclair Lewis and a Will Rogers, each in his own way subjecting the scene to a persistent irreverence; an H. L. Mencken, endlessly clowning and cannonading, more than ready to explain that he continued to live in America for the same reason that people like to go to zoos. The program of these men was hardly positive; it was never intended to be. But they also serve who only speak the rollicking negative—particularly in eras of positive, so very positive thinking. Without these and similar Americans of the 1920s, the national mind could never have been kept flexible enough to permit the sweep of adventurous thinking in the 1930s.

In some eras laughter is not only effective but close to essential. These periods come when a nation, having solved an important problem, is anxious to put on its slippers and relax and yet is worried by a different and dangerous situation. The solution of the problem produces self-satisfaction; the dangerous situation brings fear. Both the fear and self-satisfaction help lock men's minds against fresh ideas, a locking that can be loosed only by the acid of mockery and satire.

Certainly the American decade of the Fifties—having at least temporarily conquered poverty at home and yet frightened by the world situation—was just such an era. It had a special characteristic which makes the freeing of minds all the more important. An international revolutionary movement brandishing weapons of annihilation is something new in history, something new in the most fundamental sense of the word. More than any previous problem in the American experience, the situation calls for genuine pioneering in ideas and techniques.

Every passing day only makes it more obvious that the problem is not being met—and cannot be met—by mere adaptations of old ideas, by weary extrapolations on the weary doctrines of liberalism or conservatism, Kennanism or Taftism. Its solution requires thorough break-aways; the ground must be cleared of confusing and distracting carry-overs from the past, even from the immediate past. And that ground can be cleared only by the beneficent destructiveness of skepticism, of caricature, and of laughter. If the 1920s, with its men of the persistent cocked eyebrow, made possible the freshness of the 1930s, the coming decade could render the future a similar service that happens to be far more urgently needed.

Perhaps we are about to produce such a note. Now and again evidence appears that a good many of the most gifted minds in the oncoming generation are in a mood of Menckenism. (I say the mood of Mencken because of course it was this and not any specific ideas of his or his confreres which counted and would count.)

But if the oncoming generation does not soon present us with the wondrous gift of laughter, somebody better had. The American civilization which we all cherish could go down either with a whimper or a bang, as the poet's phrase suggests. It could also end with us just sitting solemnly on our lawn chaises, overfed, oversanctified, and overbearing, talking a suicidal stuffiness.

# ON BROADWAY AND OFF
## A MIDSEASON VIEW OF THE CURRENT PLAYS
### (MARCH 1963)

## *John Simon*

BUT THE MOST darkly dazzling play of 1962 is Edward Albee's *Who's Afraid of Virginia Woolf?* It is, by implication, a dance of death on the grave of Western culture as we know it; explicitly, it is a violent denunciation of many of today's marital relationships, amusingly bitchy at the surface but murderously vicious underneath. Still deeper down, the two married couples of the play are held together by a pathetic, grinding need of each partner for the other; but the author seems to suggest that this cowardly need at the bottom scarcely justifies the layers of virulent cruelty with which it is overlaid—that the game is not worth the candle, or, more precisely, the blowtorch.

# OSWALD IN MOSCOW

(APRIL 1964)

## *Priscilla Johnson McMillan*

ON A FROSTY November evening four years ago, I sat in my Moscow hotel room while a twenty-year-old American explained in a soft Southern accent his desire to defect to Russia. With his pale, rather pleasant features and his dark flannel suit, the young man looked like any of a dozen college boys I had known back home. His name was Lee Harvey Oswald.

I had sought him out a few hours earlier on the advice of an American colleague in Moscow. A boy named Oswald was staying at my hotel, the Metropole, my friend remarked casually. He was angry at everything American and impatient to become a Soviet citizen. "He won't talk to any of us," my colleague added, suggesting that, as a woman, I might have better luck.

An American defector was always good copy for a reporter in Moscow, and I had knocked, rather timidly, at Oswald's room late that afternoon. After what I had been told, I fully expected to be turned away. Instead the young man who opened the door readily assented to an interview. He promised with a smile that he would be at my room at nine o'clock in the evening.

He came at nine and stayed until two or three in the morning. Throughout our conversation he sat in an armchair, sipping tea from a green ceramic mug. More tea bubbled softly on a tiny electric burner in the corner. Except for a small gesture of one hand or an occasional tightening of the voice, Oswald's manner was unemphatic. His words seemed chosen to rule out even a hint of emotion. Yet in the notes I made as we talked I find, years later, the repeated marginal reminder to myself, "He's bitter."

In spite of his conventional appearance, I found Oswald, from the outset, extraordinary. From experience I knew just how formidable the long trip from the United States to Moscow can be, even if the traveler has money and a command of the Russian language. Here was a boy of twenty who, with only the money he had been able to save in less than three years as a Marine Corps private, had come six thousand miles with no thought but to live out his life in a country he had never seen, whose language he knew only slightly, and whose people he knew not at all. It was, I thought, a remarkable act of courage or folly.

I was touched by something homemade about him: the way he had tried, as he told me, to teach himself Russian alone at night in his Marine Corps barracks, using a Berlitz grammar; and how he had been reading economics on his own ever since he had discovered Marx's *Das Kapital* at the age of fifteen. I saw him as a lost little boy and, as such boys often are, rather lonely and proud.

Finally, Oswald impressed me because he was the first and, as it turned out, the only "ideological" defector I met in Moscow. Of the two or three other American defectors I encountered, none claimed to be motivated by a belief in communism. All appeared to be fleeing some obvious personal difficulty, such as an unhappy marriage back home. "My decision is not an emotional one," Oswald insisted. He was acting, he maintained, solely out of an intellectual conviction that Marxism was the only just way of life. For this alone he was memorable. In the months, and years, that followed our conversation, I had thought of him often, hoping one day to write a profile of this highly unusual defector. I never wrote it, however, for I felt that the key to this curious boy had eluded me.

## DISMALLY LONELY

I HAVE SUGGESTED that nothing about Oswald was more striking than his burial of the emotional factor—a denial, almost, that he had any feelings at all. And yet, looking back, I have two conflicting recollections. One is that he was struggling to hide his feelings from himself. The other is of emotion that would not be hidden. It was the counterpoint between the two, I suppose, that gave me a sense that there were gaping chinks in his armor and that he was too frail, psychologically, for what he had set out to do.

Among the feelings Oswald could not conceal was anxiety as to whether Kremlin officials would grant his request for Soviet citizenship, and whether his funds would stretch until he could go to work or become a state-supported student at a Soviet technical institute. Another was anger, directed mainly, at the time, against officials of the U.S. Embassy in Moscow. These officials, Oswald felt, had stalled him when he tried to take an oath renouncing his American citizenship. Here the tension between his feelings and his effort to suppress them became articulate: "I can't be too hard on them. But they are acting in an illegal way."

He also felt strongly about his mother. About his childhood Oswald was reticent to the point of mystery. He would only say that he grew up first in Texas and Louisiana and had then gone for two years to New York City with his mother. He refused even to say what section of the city he had lived in. Of teachers, or of friends he had played with there, he said not a word. Only that, in New York, "I had a chance to watch the treatment of workers, the fact that they are exploited. I had been brought up, like any Southern boy, to hate Negroes." When, at fifteen, "I was looking for a key to my environment, I discovered socialist literature. I saw that the description it gave of capitalist conditions was quite correct. It opened my eyes to the economic reasons for hating Negroes: so that wages can be kept low. I became a Marxist." To me, it was as though Oswald wanted to convince us both that he had never had a childhood, that he had been all his life a machine, calibrating social justice.

About his father he was so evasive that I was nonplussed. "My father," he told me, "died before I was born. I believe he was an insurance salesman." That was all. Not another word could I pry out of him.

He sounded quite different when it came to his mother. She was ill,

*11*

Oswald told me, living in Fort Worth with his brother. "My mother had been a worker all her life," he went on, "having to produce profit for capitalists. She's a good example of what happens to workers in the United States." He refused to specify what work she had actually been doing. I asked whether his mother was disillusioned, like him, or worn-out beyond her years. "That's the usual end of people in the United States, isn't it?" he countered. Then came the denial of his own indignation. "It's the end of everyone, in any country. It's a question of why they end up that way. For whom and under what system they work." In spite of Oswald's effort to depersonalize, to blame his mother's suffering on Marxist "social processes," I felt that here was a bitterness too deep for tears. Shortly after this he remarked: "I cannot live in the United States, so I shall remain here, if necessary, as a resident alien." Earlier he had told me that even if Soviet officials refused to grant his application for citizenship, "I would not consider returning to the United States." Throughout the interview he referred to the Soviet government as "my government."

Since Oswald had traveled thousands of miles to build a new life in Russia, I expected that he would be wasting no time learning all he could about the country. He would be anxious, I assumed, to see how the socialist economic theories he believed in were working out in practice. That was where I had my biggest surprise. The life he was leading in Moscow was a dismally lonely one. Most of each day he spent sitting alone in his hotel room waiting for the telephone to ring. If he thought it was his mother calling from Fort Worth to beg him to come home, he wouldn't answer. Every time it rang, though, he hoped it was some Soviet official calling to announce that his request for citizenship had been granted.

Oswald seemed to feel helpless in the Russian language. "I was able to teach myself to read and write," he said. "But I still have trouble speaking." The only expedition he had taken on his own in nearly a month in Moscow had been a walk to Detsky Mir, a children's department store only two blocks from our hotel. He seemed proud that, in the scramble of Soviet shoppers, he had managed to elbow his way to the fourth-floor buffet and buy himself an ice cream cone. He insisted that he had seen the "whole city of Moscow" and "the usual tourist attractions." But he would not name a single landmark he had actually visited. For all his struggle to get to Moscow and his efforts to stay, he appeared to lack even the curiosity of the ordinary American tourist.

Although Oswald claimed that he had visited Russians in their homes, his vagueness left me uncertain as to whether he had actually struck up a single unofficial friendship. He would only say: "Moscow is an impressive city because the energy put out by the government is all used toward peaceful and cultural purposes. People here are so well off and happy and have so much faith in the future of their country. Material poverty is not to be seen here." These generalizations and, above all, Oswald's own walled-in existence led me to conclude that he was strangely blind. Not only was he not looking at the life all around him. He was making an heroic effort not to see it.

I had a similar surprise when it came to his grasp of Marxist economics. For hours we discussed this; apart from his defection, it was the topic that seemed to interest him most. Worried about him now, I tried to warn him of the disappointment which I felt he might encounter once he came in contact with Soviet life as it really is. I argued that there are poverty and injustice in any country, including the Soviet Union, which is undergoing rapid industrialization. The worker has to be paid less than the value of what he has created if there is to be capital for new investment. Oswald agreed. To him, however, the social system for which this injustice is endured was the crucial thing. Soviet workers, like Americans, he observed, "are paid a wage. But the profit they produce is used to benefit *all* [here he gave one of his rare waves for emphasis] of the people. *They* have an economic system that is not based on credit and speculation." Somehow, after listening awhile, I concluded that his views were rigid and naive, and that he did not know his Marxism very well.

In one sense, however, his outlook seemed to fit that of orthodox Marxism. Not once in all our hours of conversation did Oswald so much as mention a single political leader, not President Eisenhower, nor Fidel Castro, nor then Senator John F. Kennedy, nor Josef Stalin, nor Nikita Khrushchev, nor anybody else. If he saw individual statesmen as either heroes or villains, he certainly gave no sign. On the contrary. For him impersonal Marxist social categories—"exploitation of the worker," the "capitalist system of profits," "militarist imperialism"—were explanation enough of the world's ills.

## Destroying an Abstraction

Since this brings us to the assassination, I am impressed by the terrible irony of that deed, if Oswald was, in fact, the assassin. For Marxism has traditionally rejected assassination as a weapon of political struggle. According to Marxist philosophy, those whom we call leaders only appear to lead. In reality it is they who are led by the historical forces around them. The latter, in turn, are determined by the economic modes of production. Thus, in the view of Lenin, assassination was at best irrelevant. I doubt that Oswald was aware that he was violating Lenin's writings on individual terror when—and if—he pulled the trigger last November 22. I suspect, rather, that he was not Marxist enough to realize that his was the ultimate anti-Marxist act.

I should like to make another observation that is outside my recollections. Oswald's defection to Soviet Russia could, as it happened, have been a dry run for the assassination, if he was—again—the assassin. For both actions he had to acquire a skill: in the one case, Russian, which he had learned imperfectly at the time I met him; in the other, marksmanship, which he evidently mastered much better. Both deeds took months to prepare. For the first he spent, as he told me, two years saving money, learning how to get cheaply to Russia, where to apply for a Soviet visa (Helsinki), and how to go about contacting the proper Soviet officials once he arrived in Moscow. For the later deed he had to purchase a rifle inconspicuously, wait for Kennedy to visit Dallas and for a route to be announced, arrange to station himself along it without arousing suspicion, and so forth. Lee Oswald was a failure at nearly everything he tried. But two supremely difficult feats he did accomplish. I saw two qualities in him that could have been crucial to his success in each: single-mindedness and secretiveness.

"For the past two years," Oswald told me, raising his voice a little, "I have been waiting to do this one thing [defect to Russia]. For two years I was waiting to leave the Marine Corps." Throughout those two years, during which he had been saving money and learning the mechanics of defection, he had been so single-minded that he had even taken care to "form no emotional attachments" to girls, since such attachments might weaken his resolve.

Throughout those two years, moreover, he evidently concealed his intention to defect from all who were closest to him. No one at home suspected which way his ideas were tending even when, at the age of fifteen, he began reading Marxist literature. "My family and my friends in the Marines," he explained, "never knew my feelings about Communism." Yet he had harbored those feelings for five years, and for the past year had been studying Russian at night in a Marine Corps barracks with inquisitive buddies all around him!

If Oswald was secretive about his personal life, refusing even to reveal to me how his mother earned a living, what section of New York City he had lived in, or how many brothers he had, he was equally evasive about the circumstances of his defection. He declined, for example, to say whether he had informed Intourist, the Soviet travel agency, of his intention to remain in Russia, how much he was paying for his room at the Metropole, who, if anyone, back in the United States had advised him on how to go about defecting, what Soviet government agencies he was dealing with in his request for citizenship, or even what books by American Communist authors he had read. While discretion was no doubt appropriate in response to some of these questions, he was, I felt, making mountains of secrecy where other boys might have made a molehill. This tight-lipped, conspiratorial attitude that was already so pronounced when I met him could, however, have been invaluable during the long months preparing for the act of November 22.

To enter again into the realm of speculation, I should like to mention that from the moment he was arrested on November 22 it seemed to me unlikely that Oswald would confess to shooting the President. Unless, of course, his resistance were broken by extraordinary methods. If I understood him at all, I believe that refusal to cooperate with authority, expressed in a refusal to confess, would have been nearly as much a part of the social protest he was trying to make as the act of assassination itself. In my opinion, the two would have gone inseparably together.

Another of the ironies in which this case abounds has to do, it seems to me, with Oswald's attitude toward Kennedy as a man. I believe that Oswald may well have been less jealous of Kennedy's dazzling personal attributes—his wealth and good looks, his happy fortune in general—than many men to whom the idea of shooting the President never even occurred. Oswald was preoccupied with himself, not with other men. The good fortune of others, their riches and fine features, did not define him to himself as poor or ugly. Less than many men did Oswald strike me as "desiring this man's art and that man's scope." I believe that the John Kennedy he killed was not, to him, another human being who was richer and better endowed than he, but a surprisingly abstract being, a soulless personification of authority. (In a scornful aside about Marine Corps officers Oswald indicated to me his contempt for anyone in authority over him.) That Kennedy, perhaps more than any world leader of his time, happened also to wear authority with a gaiety and grace that might well have aroused the envy of others is probably beside the point in assessing the motives of Lee Harvey Oswald.

## THE DESIRE TO STAND OUT

NO MATTER HOW steadfastly he might have resisted the efforts of his inquisitors to break him down, I believe that Oswald yearned to go down in history as the man who shot the President. Even if he would not and could not confess, he had, at least, to be caught. For if there was one thing that stood out in all our conversation, it was his truly compelling need—could it have been a response to some childhood humiliation?—to think of himself as extraordinary. A refusal to confess, expressed in stoic and triumphant silence, would have fitted this need. In some twisted way, it might also have enabled him to identify with other "unjustly" persecuted victims, such as Sacco and Vanzetti and the Rosenbergs.

While in one sense Oswald may have wanted to go down in history with a question mark over his guilt, surely in another sense he had to be marked for all time as the man who killed President Kennedy. Conflicting as these two needs—to be caught, yet not to confess—may appear, in reality they were part of a single compelling desire: the desire to stand out from other men.

To the trained psychiatric eye this desire must, I believe, have been written all over Lee Oswald. It became apparent to me, however, only after I had asked several questions arising from a suspicion I had that, for all his unassuming appearance, Oswald was merely another publicity seeker. How, I asked, did ordinary Russians view his defection? "The Russians I meet," he replied, "don't treat me as any celebrity." Somehow the way he said it made me feel that to himself, Lee Oswald really *was* a celebrity.

Later on, I asked Oswald if he would suggest defection as a way out for other young men who, like himself, might be dissatisfied with conditions back home. "I don't recommend defection for everyone," he warned.

It means, he went on, "coming to a new country, always being the outsider, always adjusting." Lesser men, he seemed to imply, might not be up to it. But he was.

As a means, however, of proving his "differentness," if that is what it was, defection seemed to have failed Lee Oswald. Back in Texas, people forgot all about him. Even among the Russians, he ceased after a while to stand out as a curiosity. To be marked as the extraordinary person he needed to be, he had to perform a yet more memorable, and outrageous, act.

That Oswald did, in fact, see himself as extraordinary came out unexpectedly when I asked him why he had been willing to grant me an interview at all. I expected a simple response. That he was homesick, maybe, and wanted someone to talk to. Instead, he surprised me. "I would like," he replied, "to give the people of the United States something to think about."

# Jazz Notes: Foreigners

### (April 1964)

## Eric Larrabee

IF THE CLASS will please come to order we will discuss, for positively the last time, the Beatles. Of course we owe to Professor Daniel J. Boorstin of Chicago the concept of the pseudo-event, which is an event taking place only in order to be reported in the newspapers, just as we owe to *Time* magazine the notion of the non-book, which is a book published in order to be purchased rather than to be read. Combining these two we arrive at the formulation of a non-phenomenon, which is a phenomenon existing primarily in order to be analyzed by sociologists. The Beatles may be classed as a non-phenomenon.

I do not, to be sure, subscribe to the thesis propounded by Dr. Arthur Buchwald: that if parents would only come out enthusiastically in favor of the Beatles, teenagers would immediately turn against them. This is to neglect the entire range of musicological aspects, such as the important question of Oriental influence in the Beatles' chord structure, or "Port Said" effect, as it is sometimes called, not to mention the enormous problem of historical derivation, or Who Has Been Stealing What from Whom? The merest mention of the terms "Skiffle" or "Kingston Trio" suggests the possibilities here.

By now there is general agreement that the definitive remark about the Beatles was made by the noted student John Birks "Dizzy" Gillespie. Emerging from their dressing room, where he had secured their autographs, he said: "Man, I'm going to take this out and sell it, and buy me some old Count Basie records." But there is some uncertainty as to what this significantly cryptic statement means, since any implication that Basie is responsible for the Beatles would be an impermissible example of guilt by retroactive dissociation.

For myself, I adhere to the view that the Beatles are a final demonstration of the superiority of imported over domestic goods. Putting it another way: If we existed, they would not have to be invented.

# MIAMI NOTEBOOK:
# CASSIUS CLAY AND MALCOLM X

### (JUNE 1964)

## *George Plimpton*

THE PRESS WAS incensed at Cassius Clay's behavior before the Liston fight. You could feel it. They wanted straight answers, and they weren't getting them. Usually, particularly with fighters, the direct question of extreme simplicity—which is of great moment to the sportswriters—will get a reply in kind. "Champ," asks the sportswriter, "how did you sleep last night and what did you have for breakfast?" When the champ considers the matter and says he slept real fine and had six eggs and four glasses of milk, the sportswriter puts down, *"gd sleep 6 eggs 4 gl milk,"* on his pad, and a little while later the statistic goes out over Western Union.

But with Clay, such a question simply served to unleash an act, an entertainment which included poetry, the brandishing of arms and canes, a chorus thrown in—not a dull show by any standard, even if you've seen it a few times before. The press felt that the act—it was constantly referred to as an "act"—was born of terror or lunacy. What *should* have appealed, Cassius surely being the most colorful, if bizarre, heavyweight since, well, John L. Sullivan or Jack Johnson, none of this seemed to work at all. The press's attitude was largely that of the lip-curling disdain the Cambridge police have toward the antics of students heeling for the *Harvard Lampoon.*

One of the troubles, I think—it occurred to me as I watched Clay at his last press conference on February 24 before the fight—is that his appearance does not suit his manner. His great good looks are wrong for the excessive things he shouts. Archie Moore used the same sort of routine as Clay to get himself a shot at both the light-heavyweight and heavyweight championships—self-promotion, gags, bizarre suits, a penchant for public speaking—but his character was suited to it, his face with a touch of slyness in it, and always humor. So the press was always very much in his support, and they had much to do with Moore's climb from obscurity. At his training camp outside San Diego—the Salt Mines it is called, where Cassius himself did a tour at the start of his career—Moore has built a staircase in the rocks, sixty or seventy steps, each with a reporter's name painted in red to symbolize the assistance the press gave him. Clay's face, on the other hand, does not show humor. He has a fine grin, but his features are curiously deadpan when the self-esteem begins, which, of course, desperately needs humor as a softening effect. Clay himself bridled at the resentment he caused. It must have puzzled him to be cast as the villain in a fight with Liston, who, on the surface at least, had absolutely no flair or panache except as a symbol of destructiveness.

Clay made a short, final address to the newspapermen. "This is your last chance," he said. "It's your last chance to get on the bandwagon. I'm keeping a list of all you people. After the fight is done, we're going to have a roll call up there in the ring. And when I see so-and-so said this fight was a mismatch, why I'm going to have a little ceremony and some *eating* is going on—eating of words." His manner was that of the admonishing schoolteacher. The press sat in their rows at the Miami Auditorium staring balefully at him. It seemed incredible that a smile or two wouldn't show up on a writer's face. It was so wonderfully preposterous. But I didn't see any.

IN THE CORRIDORS around the press headquarters in the Miami Auditorium, one was almost sure to run into King Levinsky, a second-rate heavyweight in his prime (he was one of Joe Louis's bums of the month) who fought too long, so that it had affected him, and he is now an ambulatory tie salesman. He would appear carrying his ties, which are labeled with a pair of boxing gloves and his name, in a cardboard box, and he'd get rid of them in jig time. His sales technique was formidable: he would single out a prospect, move down the corridor for him fast, and sweeping an arm around the fellow's neck pull him in close . . . to within range of a hoarse and somewhat wetly delivered whisper to the ear: "From the King? You buy a tie from the King?" The victim, his head in the crook of the fighter's massive arm, would mumble and nod weakly, and fish for his bankroll. Almost everyone had a Levinsky tie, though you didn't see too many people wearing them. When the King appeared around a corner, the press would scatter, some into a row of phone booths set along the corridor. "Levinsky!" they'd say and move off quickly and officiously. Levinsky would peer around and often he'd pick someone *in* a phone booth, set his cardboard box down, and shake the booth gently. You'd see him watching the fellow inside, and then the door would open and the fellow would come out and buy his tie. They only cost a dollar.

Sometimes Levinsky, if he knew he'd already sold you a couple of ties, would get you in the crook of his arm and he'd recount things he thought you ought to know about his career. "Joe Louis finished me," he'd say. "In one round that man turned me from a fighter to a guy selling ties." He said this without rancor, as if Louis had introduced him to a chosen calling. "I got rapport now," he'd say—this odd phrase—and then he'd let you go. Clay came down the corridors after the weigh-in and Levinsky bounded after him. "He's gonna take you, kid," he hollered. "Liston's gonna take you, make you a guy selling ties . . . partners with me, kid, you kin be *partners* with me." Clay and his entourage were moving at a lively clip, canes on high, shouting that they were ready to "rumble," and it was doubtful the chilling offer got through.

At the late afternoon press parties in the bar of the Roney Plaza, the promoters had another fighter at hand—the antithesis of Levinsky—a personable Negro heavyweight, Marty Marshall, the only man to beat Liston. The promoters brought him down from Detroit, his hometown, to impress the writers that Liston wasn't invincible, hoping that this notion would appear in their columns and help promote a gate lagging badly since the fight was universally considered a mismatch. Marshall met Liston three times, winning the first, then losing twice, though decking Liston in the second, always baffling him with an unpredictable attack. Liston blamed his one loss on making the mistake of dropping his jaw to laugh at Marshall's maneuvers, and *bam*, getting it broken with a sudden punch.

Marshall didn't strike one as a comic figure. He is a tall, graceful man, conservatively dressed, a pleasant face with small, round, delicate ears, and a quick smile. Greeting him was a complex matter, because he was attended for a while by someone who introduced him by saying, "Shake the hand that broke Sonny Liston's jaw!" Since Marshall is an honest man and it was a left hook that did the business, his *left* would come out, and one had to consider whether to take it with one's own left or with the right, before getting down to the questions. There was almost always a circle around him in the bar. The press couldn't get enough of what it was to be in the ring with Liston. Marshall didn't belittle the experience (after all, he'd been beaten twice), and indeed some of the things he said made one come away with even more respect for the champion.

"When I knocked him down with that hook in the second fight, he got up angry," said Marshall. "He hit me three shots you shouldn't've thrown at a bull. The first didn't knock me down, but it hurt so much I went down anyway."

"Geezus," said one of the reporters.

"Does he say anything—I mean when he's angry—can you see it?"

"No," said Marshall. "He's silent. He just comes for you."

"Gee*zus*," said the reporter again.

We all stood around, looking admiringly at Marshall, jiggling the ice in our glasses.

One of the writers cleared his throat. "I heard a story about the champion this morning," he said. "He does his roadwork, you know, out at the Normandy Golf Course, and there was this greenskeeper working out there, very early, pruning the grass at the edge of a water hazard, the mist coming off the grass, very quiet, spooky, you know, and he hears this noise behind him and there's Liston there, about ten feet away, looking out of his hood at him, and this guy gives a big scream and pitches forward into the water."

"Yeah," said Marshall. He was smiling. "I can see that."

EACH FIGHTER HAD his spiritual adviser, his *guru* at hand. In Liston's camp was Father Murphy, less a religious adviser than a confidant and friend of the champion's. In Clay's camp was Malcolm X, who was then one of the high officials of the Black Muslim sect, indeed its most prominent spokesman, though he has since defected to form his own black nationalist political movement. For months he had been silent. Elijah Muhammad, the supreme leader, the Messenger of Allah, had muzzled him since November for making intemperate remarks after the assassination of President Kennedy. But he had been rumored to be in Miami, and speculation was strong that he was there to bring Cassius Clay into the Muslim fold.

I was riding in a car just after the weigh-in with Archie Robinson, who is Clay's business manager and closest friend—a slightly built young man, not much older than Clay, one would guess, very polite and soft-spoken—and he asked me if I'd like to meet Malcolm X. I said yes, and we drove across Biscayne Bay to the Negro-clientele Hampton House Motel in Miami proper—a small-town hotel compared with the Babylon towers across the Bay, with a small swimming pool, a luncheonette, a pitch-dark bar where you had to grope to find a chair, with a dance floor and a band which came on later, and most of the rooms in balconied barracks-like structures out back. It was crowded and very lively with people in town not only for the fight but also for an invitation golf tournament.

I waited at a side table in the luncheonette. Malcolm X came in after a while, moving by the tables very slowly. Elijah Muhammad's ministers—Malcolm X was one of them—are said to emulate him even to the speed of his walk, which is considerable. But the luncheonette was not set up for a swift entrance. The tables were close together, and Malcolm X came by them carefully—a tall erect man in his thirties, a lean intelligent face with a long pronounced jaw, a wide mouth set in it which seems caught in a perpetual smile. He was carrying one of the Cassius Clay camp's souvenir canes, and with his horn-rimmed glasses, his slow stately walk, and with Robinson half a step behind him, guiding him, I thought for a second that he'd gone blind. He sat down, unwrapped a package of white peppermints which he picked at steadily, and began talking. Robinson sat with us for a while, but he had things to attend to.

I took notes from time to time, scratching them down on the paper tablecloth, then in a notebook. Malcolm X did not seem to mind. He said he was going to be unmuzzled in March, which was only five days away. He himself wrote on the tablecloth once in a while—putting down a word he wanted to emphasize. He had an automatic pen-and-pencil set in his shirt pocket—the clasps initialed FOI on one (Fruit of Islam, which is the military organization within the Muslim temple) and ISLAM on the other. He wore a red ring with a small crescent.

Malcolm X's voice is gentle, and he often smiles broadly, but not with humor, so that the caustic nature of what he is saying is not belied. His manner is distant and grave, and he asks, mocking slightly, "Sir?" when a question is not heard or understood, leaning forward and cocking his head. His answers are always skilled, with a lively and effective use of image, and yet as the phrases came I kept thinking of Cassius Clay and *his* litany—the fighter's is more limited, and a different sort of thing, but neither of them ever *stumbles* over words, or ideas, or appears balked by a question, so that one rarely has the sense of the brain actually working but rather that it is engaged in rote, simply a recording apparatus playing back to an impulse. Thus he is truly intractable—Malcolm X—absolutely dedicated, self-assured, self-principled, with that great energy . . . the true revolutionary. He does not doubt.

When give-and-take of argument is possible, when what Malcolm X says can be doubted, his assurance and position as an extremist give him an advantage in debate. He appreciates that this is so, and it amuses him. "The extremist," he said, "will always ruin the liberals in debate—because the liberals have something too nebulous to sell, or too impossible to sell—like the Brooklyn Bridge. That's why a white segregationalist—what's his name, Kilpatrick—will destroy Farmer, and why William Buckley makes a fool of Norman Mailer, and why

Martin Luther King would lose a debate with me. Why King? Because integration is ridiculous, a dream. I am not interested in dreams, but in the nightmare. Martin Luther King, the rest of them, they are thinking about dreams. But then really King and I have nothing to debate about. We are both indicting. I would say to him: 'You indict and give them hope. I'll indict and give them no hope.' "

I asked him about the remarks that had caused him his muzzling by Elijah Muhammad. His remarks about the assassination had been taken out of context, he said, though it would be the sheerest hypocrisy to suggest that Kennedy was a friend to the Negro. Kennedy was a politician (he wrote down the word on the paper tablecloth with his FOI pencil and circled it)—a "cold-blooded politician" who transformed last year's civil-rights march on Washington into a "crawl" by endorsing the march, joining it, though it was supposed to be a protest against the country's leaders . . . a politician's trick which tamped out the fuse though the powder keg was there. Friend of the Negro? There never had been a politician who was the Negro's friend. Power corrupts. Lincoln? A crooked, deceitful hypocrite, claiming championship to the cause of the Negro who, one hundred years later, finds himself singing "We Shall Overcome." The Supreme Court? Its decision is nothing but an act of hypocrisy . . . nine Supreme Court justices expert in legal phraseology tangling the words of their decision in such a way that lawyers can dilly-dally over it for years—which of course they will continue to do . . .

I scribbled these phrases, and others, on the paper tablecloth, mildly surprised to see the Muslim maxims in my own handwriting. We talked about practicality, which is the weakest area of the Muslim plans, granted the fires of resentment are justifiably banked. Malcolm X was not particularly concerned. What may be illogical or impractical in the long run is dismissed as not being pertinent to the *moment*—which is what the Negro must concern himself with. He could sense my frustration at this. It is not easy to dismiss what is practical. He had a peppermint and smiled.

I changed the subject and asked him what he did for exercise.

"I take walks," he said. "Long walks. We believe in exercise, physical fitness, but as for commercial sport, that's a racket. Commercial sport is the pleasure of the idle rich. The vice of gambling stems from it." He wrote down the word "Promoter" on the tablecloth with his FOI pencil and circled it. "The Negro never comes out ahead—never *one* in the history of sport."

"Clay perhaps."

"Perhaps." He liked talking about Clay. "I'm interested in him as a human being," he said. He tapped his head. "Not many people know the quality of the mind he's got in there. He fools them. One forgets that though a clown never imitates a wise man, the wise man can imitate the clown. He is sensitive, very humble, yet shrewd—with as much untapped mental energy as he has physical power. He should be a diplomat. He has that instinct of seeing a tricky situation shaping up—my own presence in Miami, for example—and resolving how to sidestep it. He knows how to handle people, to get them functioning. He gains strength from being around people. He can't stand being alone. The more people around, the better—just as it takes water to prime a country well. If the crowds are big in there tonight in the Miami Auditorium, he's likely to beat Liston. But they won't be. The Jews have heard he's a Muslim and they won't show up."

"Perhaps they'll show up to see him taken," I said.

"Sir?" he said, with that slight cock of the head.

"Perhaps . . ."

"When Cassius said, 'I am a man of race,'" Malcolm X went on, "it pleased the Negroes. He couldn't eliminate the color factor. But the press and the white people saw it another way. They saw him, suddenly, as a threat. Which is why he has become the villain—why he is booed, the outcast." He seemed pleased with this.

Wasn't it possible, I asked, that the braggart, the loudmouth was being booed, not necessarily the Black Muslim? After all, Clay had been heartily booed during the Doug Jones fight in Madison Square Garden, and that was before his affiliation with the Muslims was known.

"You, *you* can't tell," replied Malcolm X. "But a Negro can feel things in sounds. The booing at the Doug Jones fight was good-natured—I was there—but the booing is now different . . . defiant . . . inflamed by the columnists, all of them, critical of Cassius for being a Muslim."

"And as a fighter?"

"He has tremendous self-confidence," said Malcolm X. "I've never heard him mention fear. Anything you're afraid of can whip you. Fear magnifies what you're afraid of. One thing about our religion is that it removes fear. Christianity is based on fear."

I remarked that the Muslim religion, since it has its taboos and promises and threats, is also based on fear—one remembers that British soldiers extracted secrets from terrified Muslim captives by threatening to sew them up for a while in a pig's skin.

Malcolm X acknowledged that the Muslims had to adapt Islam to their purposes. "We are in a cage," he said. "What must be taught to the lion in a cage is quite different from what one teaches the lion in the jungle. The Mohammedan abroad believes in a heaven and a hell, a hereafter. Here we believe that heaven and hell are on this earth, and that we are in the hell and must strive to escape it. If we can adapt Islam to this purpose, we should. For people fighting for their freedom there is no such thing as a bad device."

He snorted about peaceful methods. "The methods of Gandhi?" Another snort. "The Indians are hypocrites. Look at Goa. Besides, they are the most helpless people on earth. They succeeded in removing the British only because they outnumbered them, out*weighed* them—a big dark elephant sitting on a white elephant. In this country the situation is different. The white elephant is huge. But we will catch him. We will catch him when he is asleep. The mice will run up his trunk when he is asleep.

"Where? They will come out of the alley. The revolution always comes from the alley—from the man with nothing to lose. Never the bourgeois. The poor Negro bourgeois, with his golf clubs, his golfing hat"—he waved at the people in the lunchroom—"he's so much more frustrated than the Negro in the alley; he gets the doors slapped shut in his face every day. But the explosion won't come from him. Not from the pickets either, or the nonviolent groups—these masochists . . . they

*29*

*want* to be beaten—but it will come from the people *watching*—spectators for the moment. They're different. You don't know. It is dangerous to suggest that the Negro is nonviolent.

"There *must* be retribution. It is proclaimed. If retribution came to the Pharaoh for his enslavement of six hundred thousand, it will come to the white American who enslaved twenty million and robbed their minds."

"And retribution, that is in the Koran?"

"Sir?"

"The Koran . . . ?"

He said, "Chapter 22, verse 102."

I put the numbers down, thinking to catch him out; I looked later. The verse reads: *"The day when the trumpet is blown. On that day we assemble the guilty white-eyed (with terror)."*

"These are the things you are teaching Cassius?"

"He will make up his own mind."

He popped a peppermint in his mouth. We talked a little longer, somewhat aimlessly. He had an appointment with someone, he finally said, and he stood up. The noise of conversation dropped noticeably in the luncheonette as he stood up and walked out, erect and moving slowly, holding his gaudy souvenir cane out in front of him as he threaded his way between the tables; the people in the golfing hats watched him go.

I WENT OUT into the lobby of the hotel, just standing around there feeling low. A phrase from Kafka, or rather the *idea* of some phrases from *The Trial* came to me. I looked them up the other day: "But I'm not guilty, said K. It's a mistake. Besides, how can a man be guilty? We're all men. True, said the priest: but that's how the guilty talk."

The lobby was crowded. I didn't feel comfortable. I went out to the street and stood *there,* watching the traffic. The cars came by going at sixty, none of them taxis. I went back to the lobby. The armchairs, not more than four or five, were occupied. I wouldn't have sat down anyway.

Then a fine thing happened. I was talking into the desk telephone, trying to find Archie Robinson, and a Negro, a big fellow, came up and said softly, "Hello, man, how's it?"—smiling somewhat tentatively, as if he wasn't quite sure of himself. I thought he was talking to someone else, but when I glanced up again, his eyes were still fixed on me. "We looked for you in New York when we came through," he said.

I recognized him, the great defensive back on the Detroit Lions, Night Train Lane, a good friend. "Train!" I shouted. I could sense people turn. It crossed my mind that Malcolm X might be one of them. "Hey!" I said. *"Hey!"* Lane looked a little startled. He hadn't remembered me as someone who indulged in such effusive greetings. But he asked me to come back to his room where he had friends, most of them from the golf tournament, dropping in for drinks and beans. I said that would be fine.

We went on back. Everyone we passed seemed to know him. "Hey man," they'd call, and he'd grin at them—a strong presence, an uncomplicated confidence, absolutely trusting himself. He had the room next to mine at the Detroit Lions' training camp (I was out there, an amateur among the pros, trying to play quarterback and write a book about it) and it was always full of teammates, laughing and carrying on. A record player, set on the floor, was always going in his room—Dinah Washington records. He had married her earlier in the year, her ninth or tenth husband, I think. The volume was always up, and if you came up from the practice field late, her voice would come at you across the school grounds. She had died later that year.

His room was small and full of people. I sat quietly. Train offered me some beans, but I wasn't hungry. He said, "What's wrong with you, man?"

"I'm fine," I said.

"Hey!" someone called across the room. "Was that you in the lunchroom? What you doin' talking to that guy X?"

"Well, I was listening to him," I said.

"They were telling around," this man said, "that X had a vision— he seen Cassius win in a *vision.*"

Someone else said that in a fight they'd rather be supported by a

Liston left jab than a Malcolm X vision. A big fine hoot of laughter went up, and Night Train said it was the damnedest co-in-ci-dence but a *horse* named Cassius had won one of the early races at Hialeah that afternoon—perhaps *that* was Malcolm X's vision.

They talked about him this way, easily, matter-of-factly. They could take him or leave him, which for a while I'd forgotten. Malcolm X had said about them: "They all know I'm here in the motel. They come and look at me through the door to see if I got horns . . . and you can see them turning things over in their minds."

THE DAY AFTER he beat Liston, Cassius turned up at a news conference at the Miami Beach Auditorium. The rumor was that he had gone to Chicago for the Muslim celebrations there, and the press was surprised when he appeared—and even more so at his behavior, which was subdued. Since a microphone system had gone out, his voice was almost inaudible. Cries went up which one never expected to hear in Clay's presence: "What's that, Clay? Speak up, Cassius!"

Archie Robinson took me aside and told me that he and Clay had dropped in on the celebrations at the Hampton House Motel after the fight, but it had been too noisy, so they'd gone home. It was quieter there, and they had been up until 4:00 A.M. discussing Cassius's "new image."

I remarked that this was a rare kind of evening to spend after winning the heavyweight championship. I'd met a young singer named Dee Something-or-other who had been waiting for Clay outside his dressing room after the fight. She had some idea she was going to help Cassius celebrate. She was very pretty. She had a singing engagement at a nightclub called the Sir John. Her mother was with her. She was very anxious, and once in a while when someone would squeeze in or out of the dressing room she'd call out: "Tell Cassius that Dee . . ." The girl was calm. "I call him Marcellus," she said. "A beautiful name. I can say it over and over."

The newspapermen waiting to get into the dressing room looked admiringly at her. "Clay's little fox," they called her, using Clay's generic name for girls—"foxes"—which is half affectionate and half suspicious; he feels that girls can be "sly" and "sneaky" and are to be watched warily. When the new champion finally emerged from his dressing room in a heavy press of entourage, photographers, and newspapermen, he seemed subdued and preoccupied. He didn't glance at Dee, who was on her toes, waving shyly in his direction. "Marcellus," she called. The crowd, packed in tight around him, moved down the corridor, the photo bulbs flashing. The mother looked quite put out.

THE LIVING ACCOMMODATIONS for Liston and Clay were as different as their fighting styles. Liston had a big place on the beach, a sixteen-room house next to the Yankees' owner, Dan Topping, reportedly very plush, wall-to-wall carpeting, and each room set up like a golf-club lounge—a television set going interminably, perhaps someone in front of it, perhaps not, and then invariably a card game.

Clay's place was on the mainland, in North Miami, in a low-rent district—a small plain tater-white house with louvered windows, a front door with steps leading up to a little porch with room for one chair, a front yard with more chairs set around and shaded by a big ficus tree with leaves dusty from the traffic on Fifth Street. His entire entourage stayed there, living dormitory-style, two or three to a room. Outside the yard was almost worn bare. There wasn't a neighborhood child on his way home from school who didn't pass by to see if anything was up. Films were shown there in the evening, outside, the children sitting quietly until the film started. Then the questions and the exclamations would come, Clay explaining things, and you could hardly hear the soundtrack. Only one film kept them quiet. That was the favorite film shown two or three times, *The Invasion of the Body Snatchers* . . . watched wide-eyed in the comforting sounds of the projector and the traffic going by occasionally on Fifth Street. When the big moths would show up in the light beam, almost as big as white towels they seemed, a yelp or two would go up, particularly if a body was being snatched at the time, and the children would sway for one another.

The children were waiting for Clay when he drove up from his press conference the day after the fight. So was Malcolm X, a camera slung from his neck; his souvenir cane was propped against the ficus tree. The children came for the car, shouting, and packing in around so that the doors had to be opened gingerly. Clay got out, towering above them as he walked slowly for a chair in the front yard. The litany started almost as soon as he sat down, the children around him twelve deep, Malcolm X at the periphery, grinning as he snapped pictures.

"Who's the king of kings?"

*"Cassius Clay!"*

"Who shook up the world?"

*"Cassius Clay!"*

"Who's the ugly bear?"

*"Sonny Liston!"*

"Who's the prettiest?"

*"Cassius Clay!"*

Sometimes a girl, a bright girl, just for a change would reply *"me,"* pointing a finger at herself when everyone else was shouting *"Cassius Clay,"* or she might shout *"Ray Charles,"* and the giggling would start around her, and others would join in until Clay, with a big grin, would have to hold up a hand to reorganize the claque and get things straightened out. Neither he nor the children tired of the litany. They kept at it for an hour at a time. Malcolm X left after a while. There were variations, but it was essentially the same, and it never seemed to lack for enthusiasm. The noise carried for blocks.

We went inside while this was going on. The main room, with an alcove for cooking, had sofas along the wall. The artifacts of the psychological campaign against Liston were set around—signs that read "settin' traps for the Big Bear," which had been brandished outside his training headquarters, and a valentine, as tall as a man, complete with cherubs, which had been offered Liston and which he had refused. It stood in a corner, next to an easel. Newspapers were flung around— there had been some celebrating the night before—and someone's shoes were in the middle of the room. Souvenir canes were propped up by the side of the stove in the cooking alcove. It was fraternity-house clutter.

I was standing next to Howard Bingham, Clay's "official" photographer. "It was fun, wasn't it?" I asked.

"Oh my," he said. "We have the *best* time here."

He had joined up with Clay after the George Logan fight in California, about Clay's age, younger perhaps, and shy. He stutters a bit, and he told me that he didn't take their kidding lying down. He said: "I walk around the house and sc . . . sc . . . scare people, jump out at them. Or they d . . . doze off on the c . . . couch, and I sneak around and tickle them on the nose, y'know, with a piece of string. Why I was agitating C . . . C . . . Cassius for half an hour once when he was dozing off. And I give the hot f . . . f . . . feet around here, a lot of that. We had a high time."

I asked what Cassius's winning the championship meant for him.

"Well, of course, that must make me the greatest ph . . . ph . . . photographer in the world." He couldn't keep a straight face. "Oh please," he said. His shoulders shook. "Well, I'll tell you. I'm going to get me a mo . . . mo . . . mohair wardrobe, that's one thing."

At the kitchen table Archie Robinson was sorting telegrams, stacked up in the hundreds. He showed me some of them—as impersonal as an injunction, from the long sycophantic messages from people they had to scratch around to remember, to the tart challenges from fighters looking to take Clay's title away from him. Clay wasn't bothering with them. He was going strong outside—his voice rising above the babble of children's voices: "Who shook up the world?"

*"Cassius Clay!"*

I wandered back to his room. It was just large enough for a bed, the mattress bare when I looked there, an armchair, with clothes including his Bear Huntin' jacket thrown across it, and a plain teak-colored bureau which had a large-size bottle of Dickinson's witch hazel standing on it. A tiny oil painting of a New England harbor scene was on one wall, with a few newspaper articles taped next to it, illustrated, describing Clay at his most flamboyant. A training schedule was taped to the mirror over the bureau. It called for "all" to rise at 5:00 A.M. The bedclothes were in a corner. One corner of the mattress was covered with Cassius Clay's signature in a light-blue ink, flowery with the

Cs tall and graceful, along with such graffiti as: "Cassius Clay Is Next Champ"; "Champion of the World"; "Liston Is Finished"; "The Next Champ: Cassius Clay" . . .

Outside, it had all come true. His voice and the answers were unceasing. "You," he was calling to the children, "you all are looking . . . at . . . the . . . champion . . . of . . . the . . . whole . . . wide . . . world."

# THE PARANOID STYLE IN AMERICAN POLITICS

(NOVEMBER 1964)

## Richard Hofstadter

### WHY THEY FEEL DISPOSSESSED

IF, AFTER OUR historically discontinuous examples of the paranoid style, we now take the long jump to the contemporary right wing, we find some rather important differences from the nineteenth-century movements. The spokesmen of those earlier movements felt that they stood for causes and personal types that were still in possession of their country—that they were fending off threats to a still established way of life. But the modern right wing, as Daniel Bell has put it, feels dispossessed: America has been largely taken away from them and their kind, though they are determined to try to repossess it and to prevent the final destructive act of subversion. The old American virtues have already been eaten away by cosmopolitans and intellectuals; the old competitive capitalism has been gradually undermined by socialist and communist schemers; the old national security and independence have been destroyed by treasonous plots, having as their most powerful agents not merely outsiders and foreigners as of old but major statesmen who are at the very centers of American power. Their predecessors had discovered conspiracies; the modern radical right finds conspiracy to be betrayal from on high.

Important changes may also be traced to the effects of the mass media. The villains of the modern right are much more vivid than those of their paranoid predecessors, much better known to the public; the literature of the paranoid style is by the same token richer and more circumstantial in personal description and personal invective. For the vaguely delineated villains of the anti-Masons, for the obscure and disguised Jesuit agents, the little-known papal delegates of the anti-Catholics, for the shadowy international bankers of the monetary conspiracies, we may not substitute eminent public figures like Presidents Roosevelt, Truman, and Eisenhower, Secretaries of State like Marshall, Acheson, and Dulles, Justices of the Supreme Court like Frankfurter and Warren, and the whole battery of lesser but still famous and vivid alleged conspirators headed by Alger Hiss.

Events since 1939 have given the contemporary right-wing paranoid a vast theater for his imagination, full of rich and proliferating detail, replete with realistic cues and undeniable proofs of the validity of his suspicions. The theater of action is now the entire world, and he can draw not only on the events of World War II but also on those of the Korean War and the Cold War. Any historian of warfare knows it is in good part a comedy of errors and a museum of incompetence; but if for every error and every act of incompetence one can substitute an act of treason, many points of fascinating interpretation are open to the paranoid imagination. In the end, the real mystery, for one who reads the primary works of paranoid scholarship, is not how the United States has been brought to its present dangerous position but how it has managed to survive at all.

The basic elements of contemporary right-wing thought can be reduced to three: First, there has been the now-familiar sustained conspiracy, running over more than a generation, and reaching its climax in Roosevelt's New Deal, to undermine free capitalism, to bring the economy under the direction of the federal government, and to pave the way for socialism or communism. A great many right-wingers would agree with Frank Chodorov, the author of *The Income Tax: The Root of All Evil,* that this campaign began with the passage of the income-tax amendment to the Constitution in 1913.

The second contention is that top government officialdom has been so infiltrated by Communists that American policy, at least since the days leading up to Pearl Harbor, has been dominated by men who were shrewdly and consistently selling out American national interests.

Finally, the country is infused with a network of Communist agents, just as in the old days it was infiltrated by Jesuit agents, so that the whole apparatus of education, religion, the press, and the mass media is engaged in a common effort to paralyze the resistance of loyal Americans.

Perhaps the most representative document of the McCarthyist phase was a long indictment of Secretary of State George C. Marshall, delivered in 1951 in the Senate by Senator McCarthy and later published in a somewhat different form. McCarthy pictured Marshall as the focal figure in a betrayal of American interests stretching in time from the strategic plans for World War II to the formulation of the Marshall Plan. Marshall was associated with practically every American failure or defeat, McCarthy insisted, and none of this was either accident or incompetence. There was a "baffling pattern" of Marshall's interventions in the war, which always conduced to the well-being of the Kremlin. The sharp decline in America's relative strength from 1945 to 1951 did not "just happen"; it was "brought about, step by step, by will and intention," the consequence not of mistakes but of a treasonous conspiracy, "a conspiracy on a scale so immense as to dwarf any previous such venture in the history of man."

Today, the mantle of McCarthy has fallen on a retired candy manufacturer, Robert H. Welch, Jr., who is less strategically placed and has a much smaller but better organized following than the Senator. A few years ago Welch proclaimed that "Communist influences are now in almost complete control of our government"—note the care and scrupulousness of that "almost." He has offered a full-scale interpretation of our recent history in which Communists figure at every turn: They started a run on American banks in 1933 that forced their closure; they contrived the recognition of the Soviet Union by the United States in the same year, just in time to save the Soviets from economic collapse; they have stirred up the fuss over segregation in the South; they have taken over the Supreme Court and made it "one of the most important agencies of Communism."

Close attention to history wins for Mr. Welch an insight into affairs that is given to few of us. "For many reasons and after a lot of study," he wrote some years ago, "I personally believe [John Foster] Dulles to be a Communist agent." The job of Professor Arthur F. Burns as head of Eisenhower's Council of Economic Advisers was "merely a cover-up for Burns's liaison work between Eisenhower and some of his Communist bosses." Eisenhower's brother Milton was "actually [his] superior and boss within the Communist party." As for Eisenhower himself, Welch characterized him, in words that have made the candy manufacturer famous, as "a dedicated, conscious agent of the Communist conspiracy"—a conclusion, he added, "based on an accumulation of detailed evidence so extensive and so palpable that it seems to put this conviction beyond any reasonable doubt."

### Emulating the Enemy

The paranoid spokesman sees the fate of conspiracy in apocalyptic terms—he traffics in the birth and death of whole worlds, whole political orders, whole systems of human values. He is always manning the barricades of civilization. He constantly lives at a turning point. Like religious millennialists he expresses the anxiety of those who are living through the last days and he is sometimes disposed to set a date for the apocalypse. ("Time is running out," said Welch in 1951. "Evidence is piling up on many sides and from many sources that October 1952 is the fatal month when Stalin will attack.")

As a member of the avant-garde who is capable of perceiving the conspiracy before it is fully obvious to an as yet unaroused public, the paranoid is a militant leader. He does not see social conflict as something to be mediated and compromised, in the manner of the working politician. Since what is at stake is always a conflict between absolute good and absolute evil, what is necessary is not compromise but the will to fight things out to a finish. Since the enemy is thought of as being totally evil and totally unappeasable, he must be totally eliminated—if not from the world, at least from the theater of operations to which the paranoid directs his attention. This demand for total triumph leads to the formulation of hopelessly unrealistic goals, and since these goals are not even remotely attainable, failure constantly heightens the paranoid's sense of frustration. Even partial success leaves him with the same feeling of powerlessness with which he began, and this in turn only strengthens his awareness of the vast and terrifying quality of the enemy he opposes.

This enemy is clearly delineated: He is a perfect model of malice, a kind of amoral superman—sinister, ubiquitous, powerful, cruel, sensual, luxury-loving. Unlike the rest of us, the enemy is not caught in the toils of the vast mechanism of history, himself a victim of his past, his desires, his limitations. He wills, indeed he manufactures, the mechanism of history, or tries to deflect the normal course of history in an evil way. He makes crises, starts runs on banks, causes depressions, manufactures disasters, and then enjoys and profits from the misery he has produced. The paranoid's interpretation of history is distinctly personal: Decisive events are not taken as part of the stream of history but as the consequences of someone's will. Very often the enemy is held to possess some especially effective source of power: He controls the press; he has unlimited funds; he has a new secret for influencing the mind (brainwashing); he has a special technique for seduction (the Catholic confessional).

It is hard to resist the conclusion that this enemy is on many counts a projection of the self; both the ideal and the unacceptable aspects of the self are attributed to him. The enemy may be the cosmopolitan intellectual, but the paranoid will outdo him in the apparatus of scholarship, even of pedantry. Secret organizations set up to combat secret organizations give the same flattery. The Ku Klux Klan imitated Catholicism to the point of donning priestly vestments, developing an elaborate ritual and an equally elaborate hierarchy. The John Birch Society emulates Communist cells and quasi-secret operation through "front" groups, and preaches a ruthless prosecution of the ideological war along lines very similar to those it finds in the

Communist enemy.* Spokesmen of the various fundamentalist anti-Communist "crusades" openly express their admiration for the dedication and discipline the Communist cause calls forth.

On the other hand, the sexual freedom often attributed to the enemy, his lack of moral inhibition, his possession of especially effective techniques for fulfilling his desires, give exponents of the paranoid style an opportunity to project and express unacknowledgeable aspects of their own psychological concerns. Catholics and Mormons—later, Negroes and Jews—have lent themselves to a preoccupation with illicit sex. Very often the fantasies of true believers reveal strong sadomasochistic outlets, vividly expressed, for example, in the delight of anti-Masons with the cruelty of Masonic punishments.

## RENEGADES AND PEDANTS

A SPECIAL SIGNIFICANCE attaches to the figure of the renegade from the enemy cause. The anti-Masonic movement seemed at times to be the creation of ex-Masons; certainly the highest significance was attributed to their revelations, and every word they said was believed. Anti-Catholicism used the runaway nun and the apostate priest; the place of ex-Communists in the avant-garde anti-Communist movements of our time is well known. In some part, the special authority accorded the renegade derives from the obsession with secrecy so characteristic of such movements: The renegade is the man or woman who has been in the arcanum, and brings forth with him or her the final verification of suspicions which might otherwise have been doubted by a skeptical world. But I think there is a deeper eschatological significance that attaches to the person of the renegade: In the spiritual wrestling match between good and evil which is the paranoid's

---

*In his recent book, How to Win an Election, *Stephen C. Shadegg cites a statement attributed to Mao Tse-tung:* "Give me just two or three men in a village and I will take the village." *Shadegg comments:* "In the Goldwater campaigns of 1952 and 1958 and in all other campaigns where I have served as a consultant I have followed the advice of Mao Tse-tung." "I would suggest," *writes Senator Goldwater in* Why Not Victory?, *that we analyze and copy the strategy of the enemy; theirs has worked and ours has not."*

archetypal model of the world, the renegade is living proof that all the conversions are not made by the wrong side. He brings with him the promise of redemption and victory.

A final characteristic of the paranoid style is related to the quality of its pedantry. One of the impressive things about paranoid literature is the contrast between its fantasied conclusions and the almost touching concern with factuality it invariably shows. It produces heroic strivings for evidence to prove that the unbelievable is the only thing that can be believed. Of course, there are highbrow, lowbrow, and middlebrow paranoids, as there are likely to be in any political tendency. But respectable paranoid literature not only starts from certain moral commitments that can indeed be justified but also carefully and all but obsessively accumulates "evidence." The difference between this "evidence" and that commonly employed by others is that it seems less a means of entering into normal political controversy than a means of warding off the profane intrusions of the secular political world. The paranoid seems to have little expectation of actually convincing a hostile world, but he can accumulate evidence in order to protect his cherished convictions from it.

Paranoid writing begins with certain broad defensible judgments. There *was* something to be said for the anti-Masons. After all, a secret society composed of influential men bound by special obligations could conceivably pose some kind of threat to the civil order in which they were suspended. There was also something to be said for the Protestant principles of individuality and freedom, as well as for the nativist desire to develop in North America a homogeneous civilization. Again, in our time an actual laxity in security allowed some Communists to find a place in governmental circles, and innumerable decisions of World War II and the Cold War could be faulted.

The higher paranoid scholarship is nothing if not coherent—in fact the paranoid mind is far more coherent than the real world. It is nothing if not scholarly in technique. McCarthy's 96-page pamphlet, *McCarthyism*, contains no fewer than 313 footnote references, and Mr. Welch's incredible assault on Eisenhower, *The Politician*, has one hundred pages of bibliography and notes. The entire right-wing movement of our time is a parade of experts, study groups, monographs, footnotes, and bibliographies. Sometimes the right-wing striving for scholarly depth and an inclusive worldview has startling consequences: Mr. Welch, for example, has charged that the popularity of Arnold Toynbee's historical work is the consequence of a plot on the part of Fabians, "Labour party bosses in England," and various members of the Anglo-American "liberal establishment" to overshadow the much more truthful and illuminating work of Oswald Spengler.

## THE DOUBLE SUFFERER

THE PARANOID STYLE is not confined to our own country and time; it is an international phenomenon. Studying the millennial sects of Europe from the eleventh to the sixteenth century, Norman Cohn believed he found a persistent psychic complex that corresponds broadly with what I have been considering—a style made up of certain preoccupations and fantasies: "the megalomaniac view of oneself as the Elect, wholly good, abominably persecuted, yet assured of ultimate triumph; the attribution of gigantic and demonic powers to the adversary; the refusal to accept the ineluctable limitations and imperfections of human existence, such as transience, dissention, conflict, fallibility whether intellectual or moral; the obsession with ineffable prophecies . . . systematized misinterpretations, always gross and often grotesque."

This glimpse across a long span of time emboldens me to make the conjecture—it is no more than that—that a mentality disposed to see the world in this way may be a persistent psychic phenomenon, more or less constantly affecting a modest minority of the population. But certain religious traditions, certain social structures and national inheritances, certain historical catastrophes or frustrations may be conducive to the release of such psychic energies, and to situations in which they can more readily be built into mass movements or political parties. In American experience, ethnic and religious conflict have plainly been a major focus for militant and suspicious minds of this sort, but class conflicts also can mobilize such energies. Perhaps the central situation conducive to the diffusion of the paranoid tendency is a confrontation of opposed interests which are (or are felt to be) totally irreconcilable, and thus by nature not susceptible to the normal political processes of bargain and compromise. The situation becomes worse when the representatives of a particular social interest—perhaps because of the very unrealistic and unrealizable nature of its demands—are shut out of the political process. Having no access to political bargaining or the making of decisions, they find their original conception that the world of power is sinister and malicious fully confirmed. They see only the consequences of power—and this through distorting lenses—and have no chance to observe its actual machinery. A distinguished historian has said that one of the most valuable things about history is that it teaches us how things do *not* happen. It is precisely this kind of awareness that the paranoid fails to develop. He has a special resistance of his own, of course, to developing such awareness, but circumstances often deprive him of exposure to events that might enlighten him—and in any case he resists enlightenment.

We are all sufferers from history, but the paranoid is a double sufferer, since he is afflicted not only by the real world, with the rest of us, but by his fantasies as well.

# GEORGIA BOY GOES HOME

## (APRIL 1965)

## *Louis E. Lomax*

I CAME HOME to Georgia by jet. The flight from New York to Atlanta was uneventful, but as the plane taxied toward the terminal I felt slightly uneasy. Georgia had just gone for Goldwater; Georgia was still Georgia. Walking along the corridor to the main lobby, I heard cracker twangs all about me; these, in my childhood, were the sound of the enemy, so that even now I react when I hear them, and I immediately suspect any white man who has a Southern drawl. Yet I could see no signs telling me where I should eat, drink, or go to the rest room. The white passengers seemed totally unconcerned with me. I could see a change in their eyes, on their faces, in the way they let me alone to be me.

I was on my way to the Southern Airlines counter to confirm my reservation to Valdosta. Suddenly I saw a brown arm waving at me from a phone booth. There, in the booth, was Martin Luther King, Jr. Martin's family and mine had been Negro Baptist leaders in Georgia for almost fifty years; I first got to know him when I was in college and he was in junior high school. Now I was on my way home to Valdosta for *Harper's* to write about the changes in my town and to give a sermon in my uncle's church; Martin was on the way to the island of Bimini to write his Nobel Prize acceptance speech.

Martin and I stood in the lobby and tried to talk, but to no avail. We were continuously interrupted by white people who rushed over to shake his hand and pat him on the back. I could hardly believe that

I was in Atlanta, that these were white people with twangs, and that they were saying what they were saying. Many of them asked for Martin's autograph; a few of them recognized me from television or from the dust jacket of a book and asked me to sign slips of paper. They were an incredible lot: a group of soldiers, five sailors, three marines, a score of civilians including the brother of the present Governor of Georgia, and three Negro girls. One stately old white man walked up to Martin and said, "By God, I don't like all you're doing, but as a fellow Georgian I'm proud of you."

My flight home was several hours away, and I had made a reservation at a motel near the airport. As Martin and I were parting, the loudspeaker announced that the motel bus was waiting for "Dr. Lomax." A Negro porter gathered my baggage and led me to the bus; he put my bags on the ground and I tipped him. A few seconds later I saw the white bus driver, and I knew I had reached a moment of confrontation. It seemed an eternity as I glanced up and down, from the white driver to my baggage; I remembered all those years I had spent serving white people as a bellboy, a shoeshine boy, a waiter. The driver, however, couldn't have cared less about me or my color. He picked up my bags and put them in the bus. This is what the Republic has done to me and twenty million like me—I never felt so equal in all my life when I saw that white man stoop down and pick up *my* bags. "Get right in, sir," he said.

The motel people were the same. They acted as if there had never been such a thing as segregation. I ate and drank where I pleased. Later I had to break away from three white men and their woman companion who latched onto me in the motel dining room and insisted that I party with them until my plane left.

I CAME BACK home to the land tilled and served by my fathers for four generations. Valdostans, like most people, are children of fixity; as individuals and as a tribe they find a crag, a limb, a spot of earth—physical or emotional or both—and they cling on for dear life. They change without growing, and the more they change the more they remain the same. What frightens them, as with most people, is the sudden discovery that what they are—how they have lived all their lives—stands somehow in the path of history and of progress.

One can go home again if he remembers and accepts the land of his birth for what it was, if he understands what that land has become and why. The homecoming is more complete if one admits that he and his land have shaped each other, that from it springs much of both his weakness and his strength. Only as I walked down River Street toward the place I was born did I realize how much of a child of this land I am: its mud squished through my toes as I romped on unpaved streets and alleys; its puritanical somnolence settled over my childhood dreams and all but choked me into conformity. It was on the corner of River and Wells Streets, when I was eight years old, that a white man ordered his bulldog to attack me simply because I was a Negro. Judge J. G. Cranford and his wife lived in the big white house on the corner. They saw the incident from the front porch, and Mrs. Cranford ran into the street to my rescue and drove the man away with shame.

River Street has grown old without changing very much. The weed field that stretched between here and Jackson Street Lane is still a weed field; the old warehouse that sat at the edge of the field is now a surplus food distribution center. The houses are the same houses they were when I was a child.

R. F. Lewes, as I shall call him, lived on this block. The summer before my junior year in college I was a handyman in his shop. Mr. Lewes would entertain his customers with dramatic descriptions of lynchings he had attended. His favorite story was about the night three Negroes were killed in a swamp near the Florida line. Lewes would advise his customers to get to a lynching early and stake out a choice spot on the killing ground. "But if the crowd is already there when you get there," he would add, "get down on your all fours and crawl between their legs so you can get up close to the nigger." One night I was cleaning the store when three of Mr. Lewes's cronies came in. "By God," he said to them, "this has been a rough day. Let's get a pint of moonshine and find some nigger bitches and get our luck changed."

Finally the stories became too much, and one day I threw down my shoeshine rag and went home. (After all, I was almost a junior in college and an official in my campus NAACP.) Lewes's son drove to our house and insisted that I return to work. My grandfather, the minister of the Macedonia First African Baptist Church, flatly said I didn't have to work in a place where my race was abused. R. F. Lewes, Jr., assured Grandfather that he would see to it that his father stopped telling lynch stories while I was in the shop. I had hardly returned to work when Lewes walked up to me and put his arms around my shoulders. "Louis," he said, eyeing me as if I were a wounded animal, "I wouldn't hurt *you!*"

During my visit home I saw Mr. Lewes on the street. He is very old and walks with a stick. A few weeks before, a Negro man had sat on a bench on the courthouse lawn next to him. Recoiling in anger, Lewes began jabbing the Negro in the ribs with his walking stick. The Negro called the police, and they told Lewes that the courthouse bench was for all the people, and either to calm down or move on. Mr. Lewes moved on.

OURS WAS A curious ghetto. Jackson Street Lane was the boundary line between the Negro and white sections along River Street. For one block Negroes lived on the north side of the street; the south side was completely white. To compound the oddness—the kind of thing that keeps the South on the thin edge of insanity—the first two families in our block were white. I remember how their menfolk ran into the street rejoicing the night Max Schmeling defeated Joe Louis.

The two white houses are still there, but I cannot for the life of me account for the white people who had lived in them. They were of another world; I did not know their names, who they were, or what they did. For that matter, I can't recall a single white person in the entire town whom I *really knew* when I was a boy. There were a few white people—R. F. Lewes and the man whose bulldog attacked me— whom I truly feared and, more than likely, hated. There were a few white people, Mrs. Cranford for example, whom I trusted and, perhaps, loved. But whatever understanding I had of all of these people was based on nothing more than surface encounter.

*50*

The house where I was born is torn down, the land covered with brush. The corner grocery store, built by a grocery chain on land leased from my grandfather, is now an eyesore and a public hazard. This land still belongs to us. My Uncle James, now the preacher at the Macedonia Baptist Church, and I are the last of the Lomaxes. Soon we must sit down and decide what to do about the land. Where my grandmother's living room once was, there are wild weeds; thistles cover the place where my grandfather used to retire on Saturday nights to prepare his sermon. There are tall bushes in the potato patch and creeping vines in the bait bed.

There are other changes. The new freeway that runs from Atlanta to Jacksonville has ruined the sucker and catfish hole where Grandfather and I used to fish. The new city hall and its grounds spread over the homesites of more than twenty families, Negro and white. The mud swamp on the Clydesville Road is now the airport, and the Dasher High School from which I was graduated twenty-five years ago is now the J. L. Lomax Junior High School, which is named after my Uncle James.

When I walked these streets as a boy I prided myself in the fact that I knew exactly how many people there were in the town—14,592. (My grandfather used to say that this figure included "Negroes, white people, chickens, cows, two mules, and a stray hound dog.") By 1960 the population had more than doubled, and it is predicted that there may be 75,000 people living here by 1980. Since I was a child the number of people working in agriculture has decreased threefold; the corresponding increase in trades, technical, professional, and government employees is expected to continue.

Despite the occasional new sight, Valdosta, like most American cities and towns, is old and tired and falling down. A few weeks ago, not far from my old home, a chimney fell from a dilapidated building and killed a small child. In October of last year the city manager pleaded with the mayor and the city council for power to initiate a comprehensive housing code. His research showed that 33 percent of Valdosta's housing is either dilapidated or deteriorating, that less than half of the town's dwelling units are owner-occupied, and that only slightly more than five hundred new housing units will be erected during the rest of the 1960s. The city manager wanted to force the owners of deteriorating properties to fix them up, the owners of dilapidated buildings to tear them down under the threat that if they don't the city will. He wanted to do something about the lack of recreational facilities for young people. So far he has not succeeded, but he is still trying.

A referendum that would have levied two bond issues for parks and recreation recently was defeated, with about 10 percent of the registered voters participating. But in October a one-million-dollar school bond issue won the voters' approval, although fewer than two thousand of the city's eight thousand registered women voters bothered to go to the polls. Apathy plagues the town. The people, both Negro and white, seem to have run out of gas. They simply don't care about civic improvements. The referendum for parks and recreation would have given the city two swimming pools. It was defeated by seventeen votes. Yet one night I walked up and down Patterson Street, the white mecca, and saw scores of boys and girls slinking into darkened store alcoves and alleys. Then I went down along South Ashley Street, the Negro section, and saw even more young people darting into back streets, petting in open lots, dancing to funky music in questionable "soda and ice cream parlors."

As FAR AS public accommodations go, Valdosta is an open town. I ate where I chose and went where I pleased, talking with whomever I wished of both races. Like most Southern towns, this one had moments of racial tension during the first days of integrated cafés, lunch counters, and theaters. But a well-disciplined law force invoked the law of the land. While police chiefs in other Southern towns were rousing the white rabble, the Valdosta police chief was traveling through the swamp farmlands on the town's outskirts telling white men who were most likely to get likkered up and come to town to keep calm. The Negroes were told to eat, not just demonstrate, and the whites were warned to keep the peace. They both did just that. Whenever and wherever Negroes have pressed their case there has been compliance with the Civil Rights Act.

This did not happen all by itself. A loosely organized interracial council arrived at reasonable, step-by-step goals. I think the major preventive act took place when the white power structure yielded to demands for Negro policemen. The sight of Negroes whom they knew and trusted policing their community gave Valdosta's Negroes a pride and a sense of personal security they had never had before. My town has not made ugly national and international headlines because the white power structure, led by three key men, took a long look at the turmoil that confronted so many places in the South and decided it would not happen in Valdosta.

E. M. Turner, the seventy-two-year-old editor of the local paper, took the same position with me. I was both astounded and angry. He had been the editor of the paper since I was a child. I had wanted to be a reporter and a writer, to learn the fundamentals of my craft, but I couldn't even get a job as a delivery boy. The first essay I ever wrote won me an honorable mention in a contest sponsored by the paper; they announced that I was a Negro and they misspelled my name. Yet E. M. Turner sat with me now for almost an hour and a half. He traced the rise of Valdosta from a one-crop town that trembled at the thought of the boll weevil to a town which changed its economy to one based on turpentine, pine trees, and resin. He sketched out the semi-industrial era that lies ahead for the town.

Our talk moved on to the race issue. "I've never had any trouble with nigras," Turner said. "I may not like the Civil Rights Bill, but it's the law of the land and it must be obeyed. But let me tell you this," he said. "I talked to my cook; she is a sweet old nigra woman who has been with us for years and she told me she didn't want her grandchildren going to school with white children."

I heard E. M. Turner well, and I thought to myself that I have yet to meet a white man, in the South or the North, whose cook believed in integration. Yet I wondered how, without integrated schools, such a man as Turner expected us to turn out Negroes equally prepared for the American job market. I decided to ask a significant question:

"Would you hire a Negro reporter if he was qualified?"

Turner did not hesitate. "I've never been faced with the issue," he said. "I'm not sure what I would do."

Later that day, when I had a talk with a local businessman, I saw something of the anguish that afflicts many white Valdostans of my age. His brother-in-law lives in Colombia and is married to a Colombian woman darker than most Negroes. The brother wanted to bring his wife to Valdosta for a visit; the proposed visit was, of course, vetoed with vigor. "Lord, how ashamed I am," he told me. "I'm afraid to have my own brother and sister come to my home."

He is a devout member of a Protestant church in Valdosta. His church raises money each month to keep an impoverished Negro church of the same denomination going. "We raise that money," he told me, "to keep the Negroes from coming to our church. I was just horrified when I saw how my fellow white Christians reacted when the question of integrating the two churches came up."

But it was another realization that really troubled him. "Now take you," he said. "I'd like to have you in my home, to sit down to prayer and break bread with my family. My wife feels the same way. But we'd be afraid to invite you."

"I'd invite you to my home," I told him. "I'm not afraid."

"But I'd be afraid to *come*," he shot back, pounding the desk with anger at his world and himself.

"In other words," I said, "there is a sense in which I, a Negro, have more freedom than you have."

"That's true," he replied. "Everything is so confused down here. They wouldn't bother you and your Uncle James if you invited my family to your home. But they would get after *us* if we came." He turned in his chair, dropping me out of his sight as he faced the wall and let his eyes drift toward the ceiling.

"But I did vote for Goldwater," he added, speaking more to himself than to me. "Somebody has just got to stop the Communists from taking over the world."

THE GOLDWATER VICTORY hung like a frightening cloud over the well-meaning white Valdostans who were trying to find a way out of the racial wilderness. One of the men most responsible for Goldwater's carrying Valdosta was George C. Cook, the seventy-three-year-old owner of the radio station. Cook came to town thirty years ago and became a leader in the business community; he has been president of the Chamber of Commerce and has spearheaded the drive to get more industry—"particularly those that will give these nigger women on relief something to do," he explained to me—into Valdosta. He made his station the voice of Goldwater conservatism and the White Citizens' Council. The week before the election, Cook encountered one of Valdosta's most respected Negroes in the post office. "Doctor," Cook said to the Negro, "I want you to go home and call all your friends and tell them to tune in on my station tonight at seven-thirty. We're going to give the niggers and Jews hell tonight and I sure want you and your people to hear it."

I talked with Cook for more than an hour. "Now, I came out for Goldwater, but I ain't no Republican," he said. "I'm a Democrat. That," he went on to say, pounding his chest, "is in here, in my heart. I could no more be a Republican than I could fly. But I just couldn't stomach that Kennedy-Johnson crowd and the way they are taking over the rights of the states and the individual.

"Now, as for this integration business, I don't see what all the hell's about. We never had any trouble with niggers. I was against the Civil Rights Bill but when it became the law of the land I felt we'd better try and live with it. One of my friends called me up and told me he'd gotten word that the niggers were coming to his lunch counter to demonstrate. He said he was going to feed them if they came there. I told him, by God, to feed them niggers and he'd find out that once he fed them, and they had made their point, they would never come back. And you know," he added, bursting into laughter, "that's exactly what happened. Them niggers ate, then they left and ain't a one of them black sonsabitches been back there since.

"Let me tell you something, Louis," he said suddenly. "I lived with niggers all my life; I grew up with them and played with them; there wasn't a bit of trouble. Why, a sweet, old black nigger woman helped raise me; she was as sweet a woman as God ever let live. And if and when I get to heaven I'm going to look up that nigger woman and kiss her on the cheek.

"There ain't going to be no trouble here," he said. "A few young niggers and young white trash might try to start something; then the old heads, nigger and white, will keep things under control. What we need in this town instead of agitation is some new industries with nigger jobs, so these nigger men can feed their families, so these nigger women on relief can make a paycheck. That's what we need to keep Valdosta going. Why, the niggers are pouring into town by the carloads every day, and if we don't find something for them to do we are going to have one hell of a mess in this town before too long. Yes sir, that's what this town needs: nigger jobs, for nigger men and women."

On the subject of jobs, Comer Cherry, a diametrical opposite to Cook among the business community, feels the same way. Cherry has been president of the Chamber of Commerce and the Rotary Club, and a prime mover behind the biracial commission. He is representative of the new thinking among white Valdostans. "The way I see it," he says, "the economy of the nigra community is the root of the problem. Once the nigra can earn a respectable paycheck, most of the agitation will die down."

The median income for a Valdosta white family in 1960 was $4,360; for Valdosta Negro families, $2,364. And there is a chilling prophecy in a recent economic study of the town. The study predicts that by 1980 the median income of Valdosta white families will be $9,500, while the income of Negro families will reach only $4,250—more than twice the present disparity. Comer Cherry and George C. Cook have a point. Somebody, somehow, had better do something about Negro income in Valdosta or there will be real trouble in the future.

I FOUND NO tension whatsoever in the Valdosta Negro community. The Negro masses undulate along the streets, oblivious to what is going on in the Congo, in Red China, or in Mississippi. The county hospital has been completely integrated, and the authorities have shut down the old back entrance marked "colored." Yet despite the fact that the leaders have told local Negroes to use the front door, one witnesses the pathetic spectacle of their going to the same place to find a back way in. What mainly struck me is that there are more of them, and that they are growing in geometric proportions. They are the citizens of "Niggertown," the habitués of juke joints, of pig-foot alley and crumbling shanties. Their children pour into school, only to drop out. Talking with these dropouts one comes away knowing that they never really dropped in. They don't know anything; they can't do anything. Here, among the black masses, is the greatest monument to my town's—the South's—wickedness. It is a society which continues to grind out hundreds, thousands, millions who are totally defeated, who are alienated from that society from the day they are born.

The Valdosta black bourgeoisie serve the black masses. They teach them in school, pull their teeth, prescribe medicine for their livers, tell them about Jesus on Sunday morning, sell them life insurance when they are young, and bury them when they die. That is the way it was thirty-five years ago; that is the way it is now. Their only saving grace—and this is true all over the country—is that they are willing to accept, without recourse to background, any person who can traverse the maze that leads from Shantytown to professionalism. I was born to the black bourgeoisie; I stumbled and floundered for twenty years; and there were grave doubts that I would ever validate my heritage. Yet I had schoolmates who were up from the trash pile; some of them made it, and they are now solid members of the Valdosta Negro middle class.

It would be wrong for me to say that they don't care about the black masses. They do care; they care, at times, almost to the point of nervous breakdown. Their problem, essentially, is the same as that of the concerned white men of Valdosta: the monster created by the Southern way of life is so terrifying, and becoming so gargantuan, that nobody knows what to do or where to start doing it.

Meanwhile, the Valdosta black bourgeoisie are becoming more and more comfortable, their world more and more secure. They are the ones who can afford to dress up and go out for dinner once a week to a previously "white only" restaurant, who can travel during their vacations and take advantage of the integrated motels, hotels, and travel facilities. Yet few of them have actually contributed to the Negro revolution that has made these things possible. The Valdosta black bour-geoisie are largely schoolteachers. Despite their new freedom, they must plod away in schoolrooms that are still separate and unequal; they must keep quiet about integration or be fired.

"I'm doing all I can do and still keep my job," one third-grade Negro teacher told me. "When my principal isn't around, I teach my children that four pickets times nine pickets is thirty-six pickets. I just hope and pray they grow up and get the message."

Part of the tragedy of my town is that there is no real Negro leader-ship to translate to the masses the message this teacher is trying to deliver. Negro leadership in Valdosta is nothing more than ten or twelve men with incomes rooted in the ghetto, who sporadically gath-er to try to muster general support for programs each of them has pre-sented to the town's white fathers when his fellow Negro spokesmen were not looking. A dozen of these Negro leaders—most of whom I have known since childhood—met with me to discuss the plight of the Valdosta Negro and to describe what they planned to do about it. The more they talked the more it became apparent, as one of them had the courage to say, that Negro leadership was about the same as it was when I was a little boy. There is no NAACP in Valdosta, no Urban League. Nobody would dare let Martin Luther King, Jr., preach in their church, and CORE is something they read about in the newspaper and hear about on television. The Negro leaders, such as they are, turn on one another and accuse one another of being dis-loyal, apathetic, and indifferent.

WHAT, THEN, IS the next step forward for Valdosta, not just toward integration, but into the world as it really is?

Although the Negro population is 36 percent, not a single public school is integrated in the town. However, the all-white board of edu-cation is ready to accept Negro pupils into any schools they can estab-lish their legal right to attend. Moreover, the white power structure knows precisely where these schools are, and the white students have been prepared for the probability that their schools will one day be integrated. Even more, the white students have accepted the idea and wish the Negroes would get it over with so everybody concerned can settle down to learning his lessons.

White Valdosta businessmen have jobs waiting for Negroes; these jobs will never be filled until Negro leaders stop fighting one another and draw up a unified job program to place before the biracial commission.

At a state college located in Valdosta, I was told, there were only two Negro students, and these were financed by some of the Negro leaders who met with me. No other Negroes had enrolled in two years. This could be changed if Negro spokesmen would unify and make the right demands. There is an integrated county technical and industrial school on the outskirts of Valdosta that is begging for Negro students. There are all too few Negro applicants. The brunt of the burden, I regret to say, rests with the town's Negro middle class. But they, like so many of their white peers, are consumed by fear.

The Valdosta Negro middle class, then, is on the verge of becoming a tribe; its members are fiercely proud of themselves and their own; they couldn't care less about socializing with white people. At a large party given for me one night, I was able to locate only one Negro friend—a woman—who had a social relationship with a white person. She and a white woman have a "luncheon friendship," largely at the urging of the white woman. Even that almost collapsed when the white woman invited other white women to join.

"The other white women smiled dryly at me," she said, "and I was ready to say, like, forget it. My husband makes more than her husband and I wasn't about to grovel just to have some white lunch dates."

"I know what you mean," a county school principal said. "These phony white liberals are about a bitch. They say they love us, that they want to cement relations, that they want to overcome the fact that there has been no communication between us and them, and then they get in that damn voting booth and . . ."

"Vote for Goldwater," several people shouted.

"You think you got problems," a doctor broke in. "I was walking down Patterson Street a few weeks ago and a white man fell to the sidewalk with a heart attack right in front of me. I forgot he was white and tried to help him. A crowd gathered and became hostile because I was a Negro!"

"Did you go away and let him die?" somebody shouted from the back of the room.

"No," the doctor replied. "I did the best I could for the sonofabitch and sent him off to the hospital." Everyone, of course, laughed.

The party music played, but there was surprisingly little drinking or dancing. I was home; these were my brothers and sisters. They knew me and were glad to see me. We talked of the days when we were children, of our fathers and mothers and grandparents who pushed us so far along the way. We told the "in" jokes. Nobody mentioned white people; nobody wanted or needed them there. We would have stayed all night if it had not been Saturday. But at church the next morning one of the school principals was scheduled to sing a solo. One woman was to play the organ, another the piano. Another school principal was to handle the collection, and I was to deliver the sermon.

THE NEXT DAY I stood in the Macedonia Baptist Church pulpit that has been occupied by a Lomax for more than half a century; some of the people who sat in the congregation had known me before I knew myself. Tribal middle-class pride was running high. Just the Sunday before, Calvin King, one of my younger childhood schoolmates who went on to get his doctorate in mathematics, had been the guest preacher. Uncle James had listened with pride as Calvin told of his travels in the Holy Land, of his work in helping launch a new university in Nigeria.

I told the congregation about my experiences in Africa, behind the Iron Curtain, and in American cities where racial troubles had erupted. White Christianity, I said, had become synonymous with white oppression all over the world, and the black Christians were about all Jesus had left. We were the only ones who could now go about preaching the words of Jesus without being suspected of questionable motives. My plea was that we black Christians become more militant, that we take a courageous stand for human rights, to clarify Christ's name if for no other reason.

It is significant that when I had finished there was a loud congregational "amen." A few white people had come to the service, and one of them was crying. Uncle James issued the invitation for the unchurched to come up and join. But that was not the hour for sinners. Rather, I think, it was a time for the believers to reassess what they were in for.

CHANGE IS COMING. Having seen many of the troubled places of Africa, America, and the Caribbean, I know social dynamite when I see it. But Valdosta will make it peacefully into tomorrow, partly because the whites themselves are slowly changing, partly because the Negroes are not really pushing. Time nudges them both along. They—the black and the white of my town—are now looking across at each other in estrangement against the day when they might join in frank friendship.

# MISSISSIPPI: THE FALLEN PARADISE

## (APRIL 1965)

## *Walker Percy*

*With the collapse of the moderates and the victory of the Snopeses, can it ever be possible for this obsessed and tortured state to emerge from its long nightmare? How is one to explain both its kindliness and its unspeakable violence?*

A LITTLE MORE than one hundred years ago, a Mississippi regiment dressed its ranks and started across a meadow toward Cemetery Ridge, a minor elevation near Gettysburg. There, crouched behind a stone wall, the soldiers of the Army of the Potomac waited and watched with astonishment as the gray-clads advanced as casually as if they were on parade. The Mississippians did not reach the wall. One soldier managed to plant the regimental colors within an arm's length before he fell. The University Grays, a company made up of students from the state university, suffered a loss of precisely 100 percent of its members killed or wounded in the charge.

These were good men. It was an honorable fight and there were honorable men on both sides of it. The issue was settled once and for all, perhaps by this very charge. The honorable men on the losing side, men like General Lee, accepted the verdict.

One hundred years later, Mississippians were making history of a different sort. If their record in Lee's army is unsurpassed for valor and devotion to duty, present-day Mississippi is mainly renowned for murder, church-burning, dynamiting, assassination, night-riding, not to mention the lesser forms of terrorism. The students of the university celebrated the Centennial by a different sort of warfare and in the company of a different sort of General. It is not frivolous to compare the characters of General Edwin Walker and General Lee, for the contrast is symptomatic of a broader change in leadership in this part of the South. In any event, the major claim to fame of the present-day university is the Ole Miss football team and the assault of the student body upon the person of one man, an assault of bullying, spitting, and obscenities. The bravest Mississippians in recent years have not been Confederates or the sons of Confederates but rather two Negroes, James Meredith and Medgar Evers.

As for the Confederate flag, once the battle ensign of brave men, it has come to stand for raw racism and hoodlum defiance of the law. An art professor at Ole Miss was bitterly attacked for "desecrating" the Stars and Bars when he depicted the flag as it was used in the 1962 riot—with curses and obscenities. The truth was that it had been desecrated long before.

No ex-Mississippian is entitled to write of the tragedy which has overtaken his former state with any sense of moral superiority. For he cannot be certain in the first place that if he had stayed he would not have kept silent—or worse. And he strongly suspects that he would not have been counted among the handful, an editor here, a professor there, a clergyman yonder, who not only did not keep silent but fought hard.

What happened to this state? Assuredly it faced difficult times after the Supreme Court decision of 1954 and subsequent court injunctions which required painful changes in customs of long standing. Yet the change has been made peacefully in other states of the South. In Georgia over 39 percent of Negroes of voting age are registered to vote. In Mississippi the figure is around 6 percent.

What happened is both obvious and obscure. What is obvious is that Mississippi is poor, largely rural, and has in proportion the largest Negro minority in the United States. But Georgia shares these traits. Nor is it enough to say that Mississippi is the state that refused to change, although this is what one hears both inside and outside the state. On the contrary, Mississippi has changed several times since the Civil War. There have been times, for example, when dissent was not only possible but welcome. In 1882 George Washington Cable, novelist and ex-Confederate cavalryman, addressed the graduating class at the University of Mississippi:

> We became distended—mired and stuffed with conservatism to the point of absolute rigidity. Our life had little or nothing to do with the onward movement of the world's thought. We were in danger of becoming a civilization that was not a civilization, because there was not in it the element of advancement.

His address was warmly received by the newspapers of the region. It is interesting to speculate how these remarks would be received today at Ole Miss, if indeed Cable would be allowed to speak at all.

Two significant changes have occurred in the past generation. The most spectacular is the total defeat of the old-style white moderate and the consequent collapse of the alliance between the "good" white man and the Negro, which has figured more or less prominently in Mississippi politics since Reconstruction days. Except for an oasis or two like Greenville, the influential white moderate is gone. To use Faulkner's *personae,* the Gavin Stevenses have disappeared and the Snopeses have won. What is more, the Snopeses' victory has surpassed even the gloomiest expectations of their creator. What happened to men like Gavin Stevens? With a few exceptions, they have shut up or been exiled or they are running the local White Citizens' Council. Not even Faulkner foresaw the ironic denouement of the tragedy: not only that the Compsons and Sartorises should be defeated by the Snopeses but that in the end they should join them.

Faulkner lived to see the defeat of his Gavin Stevens—the old-style good man, the humanist from Harvard and Heidelberg—but he still did not despair because he had placed his best hope in the youth of the state. Chick Mallison in *Intruder in the Dust,* a sort of latter-day Huck Finn, actually got the Negro Lucas Beauchamp out of jail while Gavin Stevens was talking about the old alliance. But this hope has been blasted, too. The melancholy fact is that the Chick Mallisons today are apt to be the worst lot of all. Ten years of indoctrination by the Citizens' Councils, racist politicians, and the most one-sided press north of Cuba has produced a generation of good-looking and ferocious young bigots.

The other change has been the emigration of the Negro from Mississippi, reducing the Negro majority to a minority for the first time in a hundred years. At the same time, great numbers of Negroes from the entire South were settling in Northern ghettos. The chief consequence has been the failure of the great cities of the North to deal with the Negro when he landed on their doorstep, or rather next door. Mississippi has not got any better, but New York and Boston and Los Angeles have got worse.

Meanwhile there occurred the Negro revolution, and the battle lines changed. For the first time in a hundred and fifty years, the old sectional division has been blurred. It is no longer "North" versus "South" in the argument over the Negro. Instead there has occurred a diffusion of the Negro and a dilution of the problem, with large sections of the South at least tolerating a degree of social change at the very time Northern cities were beginning to grumble seriously. It seems fair to describe the present national mood as a grudging inclination to redress the Negro's grievances—with the exception of a few areas of outright defiance like north Louisiana, parts of Alabama, and the state of Mississippi.

## Words Without Meaning

It is only within the context of these social changes, I believe, that the state can be understood and perhaps some light shed upon a possible way out. For, unfavorable as these events may be, they are nevertheless ambiguous in their implication. The passing of the moderate and the victory of the Snopeses may be bad things in themselves. Yet history being the queer business that it is, such a turn of events may be the very condition of the state's emergence from its long nightmare.

During the past ten years Mississippi as a society reached a condition which can only be described, in an analogous but exact sense of the word, as insane. The rift in its character between a genuine kindliness and a highly developed individual moral consciousness on the one hand, and on the other a purely political and amoral view of "states' rights" at the expense of human rights led at last to a sundering of its very soul. Kind fathers and loving husbands, when they did not themselves commit crimes against the helpless, looked upon such crimes with indifference. Political campaigns, once the noblest public activity in the South, came to be conducted by incantation. The candidate who hollers "nigger" loudest and longest usually wins.

The language itself has been corrupted. In the Mississippi standard version of what happened, noble old English words are used, words like *freedom, sacredness of the individual, death to tyranny,* but they have subtly changed their referents. After the Oxford riot in 1962, the Junior Chamber of Commerce published a brochure entitled *A Warning for Americans,* which was widely distributed and is still to be found on restaurant counters in Jackson along with the usual racist tracts, mammy dolls, and Confederate flags. The pamphlet purports to prove that James Meredith was railroaded into Ole Miss by the Kennedys in defiance of "normal judicial processes"—a remarkable thesis in itself considering that the Meredith case received one of the most exhaustive judicial reviews in recent history. The "warning" for Americans was the usual contention that states' rights were being trampled by federal tyranny. "Tyranny is tyranny," reads the pamphlet. "It is the duty of every American to be alert when his freedom is endangered."

Lest the reader be complacent about Mississippi as the only state of double-think, the pamphlet was judged by the *national* Jay Cees to be the "second most worthy project of the year."

All statements become equally true and equally false, depending on one's rhetorical posture. In the end even the rhetoric fails to arouse. When Senator Eastland declares, "There is no discrimination in Mississippi" and, "All who are qualified to vote, black or white, exercise the right of suffrage," these utterances are received by friend and foe alike with a certain torpor of spirit. It does not matter that there is very little connection between Senator Eastland's utterances and the voting statistics of his home county: that of a population of 31,020 Negroes, 161 are registered to vote. Once the final break is made between language and reality, arguments generate their own force and lay out their own logical rules. The current syllogism goes something like this: (1) There is no ill-feeling in Mississippi between the races; the Negroes like things the way they are; if you don't believe it, I'll call my cook out of the kitchen and you can ask her. (2) The trouble is caused by outside agitators who are communist-inspired. (3) Therefore, the real issue is between atheistic communism and patriotic God-fearing Mississippians.

Once such a system cuts the outside wires and begins to rely on its own feedback, anything becomes possible. The dimensions of the tragedy are hard to exaggerate. The sad and still incredible fact is that many otherwise decent people, perhaps even the majority of the white people in Mississippi, honestly believed that President John F. Kennedy was an enemy of the United States, if not a communist fellow-traveler.

How did it happen that a proud and decent people, a Protestant and Anglo-Saxon people with a noble tradition of freedom behind them, should have in the end become so deluded that it is difficult even to discuss the issues with them because the common words of the language no longer carry the same meanings? How can responsible leadership have failed so completely when it did not fail in Georgia, a state with a similar social and ethnic structure?

The answer is far from clear, but several reasons suggest themselves. For one thing, as James Dabbs points out in his recent book *Who Speaks for the South?*, Mississippi was part of the wild west of the Old South. Unlike the seaboard states, it missed the liberal eighteenth century altogether. Its tradition is closer to Dodge City than to Williamsburg. For another, the Populism of the eastern South never amounted to much here; it was corrupted from the beginning by the demagogic racism of Vardaman and Bilbo. Nor did Mississippi have its big city which might have shared, for good and ill, in the currents of American urban life. Georgia had its Atlanta and Atlanta had the good luck or good sense to put men like Ralph McGill and Mayor Hartsfield in key positions. What was lacking in Mississippi was the new source of responsible leadership, the political realist of the matured city. The old moderate tradition of the planter-lawyer-statesman class had long since lost its influence. The young industrial interests have been remarkable chiefly for their discretion. When, for example, they did awake to the folly of former Governor Barnett's two-bit rebellion, it was too late. And so there was no one to head off the collision between the civil-rights movement and the racist coalition between redneck, demagogue, and small-town merchant. The result was insurrection.

## DEATH OF AN ALLIANCE

THE MAJOR SOURCE of racial moderation in Mississippi even until recent times has been not Populism but the white conservative tradition with its peculiar strengths and, as it turned out, its fatal weakness. There came into being after Reconstruction an extraordinary alliance, which persisted more or less fitfully until the last world war, between the Negro and the white conservative, an alliance originally directed against the poor whites and the Radical Republicans. The fruits of this "fusion principle," as it is called, are surprising. Contrary to the current mythology of the Citizens' Councils, which depicts white Mississippians throwing out the carpetbaggers and Negroes and establishing our present "way of life" at the end of Reconstruction, the fact is that Negroes enjoyed considerably more freedom in the 1880s than they do now. A traveler in Mississippi after Reconstruction reported seeing whites and Negroes served in the same restaurants and at the same bars in Jackson.

This is not to say that there ever existed a golden age of race relations. But there were bright spots. It is true that the toleration of the Old Captains, as W. J. Cash called them, was both politically motivated and paternalistic, but it is not necessarily a derogation to say so. A man is a creature of his time—after all, Lincoln was a segregationist—

and the old way produced some extraordinary men. There were many felicities in their relation with the Negro—it was not all Uncle Tomism, though it is unfashionable to say so. In any case they lost; segregation was firmly established around 1890 and lynch law became widespread. For the next fifty years the state was dominated, with a few notable exceptions, by a corrupt Populism.

What is important to notice here is the nature of the traditional alliance between the white moderate and the Negro, and especially the ideological basis of the former's moderation, because this spirit has informed the ideal of race relations for at least a hundred years. For, whatever its virtues, the old alliance did not begin to have the resources to cope with the revolutionary currents of this century. Indeed, the worldview of the old-style "good" man is almost wholly irrelevant to the present gut issue between the Negro revolt and the Snopes counterrevolution.

For one thing, the old creed was never really social or political but purely and simply moral in the Stoic sense: if you are a good man, then you will be magnanimous toward other men and especially toward the helpless and therefore especially toward the Negro. The Stoic creed worked very well—if you were magnanimous. But if one planter was just, the next might charge 80 percent interest at the plantation store, the next take the wife of his tenant, the next lease convict labor, which was better than the sharecropper system because it did not matter how hard you worked your help or how many died.

Once again in recent years dissent became possible. During the Depression of the Thirties and afterward there were stirrings of liberal currents not only in the enthusiasm for the economic legislation of the Roosevelt Administration but also in a new awareness of the plight of the Negro. Mississippi desperately needed the New Deal and profited enormously from it. Indeed, the Roosevelt farm program succeeded too well. Planters who were going broke on ten-cent cotton voted for Roosevelt, took federal money, got rich, lived to hate Kennedy and Johnson and vote for Goldwater—while still taking federal money. Yet there was something new in the wind after the war. Under the leadership of men like Hodding Carter in the Delta, a new form of racial moderation began to gather strength. Frank Smith, author of the book *Congressman from Mississippi,* was elected to Congress. Described by Edward Morgan as "a breath of fresh air out of a political swamp," Smith was one of the few politicians in recent years who tried to change the old racial refrain and face up to the real problems of the state. But he made the mistake of voting for such radical measures as the Peace Corps and the United Nations appropriation, and he did not conceal his friendship with President Kennedy. What was worse, he addressed mail to his constituents with a Mr. and Mrs., even when they were Negroes. Smith was euchred out of his district by the legislature and defeated in 1962 by the usual coalition of peckerwoods, super-patriots, and the Citizens' Councils.

But the most radical change has occurred in the past few years. As recently as fifteen years ago, the confrontation was still a three-cornered one, among the good white man, the bad white man, and the Negro. The issue was whether to treat the Negro well or badly. It went without saying that you could do either. Now one of the parties has been eliminated and the confrontation is face to face. "I assert my right to vote and to raise my family decently," the Negro is beginning to say. His enemies reply with equal simplicity: "We'll kill you first."

Yet the victory of the Snopeses is not altogether a bad thing. At least the choice is clarified. It would not help much now to have Gavin Stevens around with his talk about "man's struggle to the stars."

The old way is still seductive, however, and evokes responses from strange quarters. Ex-Governor Ross Barnett was recently revealed as mellow emeritus statesman in the old style, even hearkening to the antique summons of noblesse oblige. A newspaper interview reported that the Governor was a soft touch for any Negro who waylaid him in the corridor with a "Cap'n, I could sho use a dollar." The Governor, it was also reported, liked to go hunting with a Negro friend. "We laugh and joke," the Governor reminisced, "and he gets a big kick out of it when I call him Professor. There's a lot in our relationship I can't explain." No doubt, mused the interviewer, the Governor would get up at all hours of the night to get Ol' Jim out of jail. It is hard to imagine what Gavin Stevens would make of this new version of the old alliance. Unquestionably, something new has been added. When Marse Ross dons the mantle of Marse Robert, Southern history has entered upon a new age. And perhaps it is just as well. Let Governor Barnett become the new squire. It simplifies matters further.

## PUBLIC VS. PRIVATE

THOUGH FAULKNER LIKED to use such words as "cursed" and "doomed" in speaking of his region, it is questionable that Mississippians are very different from other Americans. It is increasingly less certain that Minnesotans would have performed better under the circumstances. There is, however, one peculiar social dimension wherein the state does truly differ. It has to do with the distribution, as Mississippians see it, of what is public and what is private. More precisely it is the absence of a truly public zone, as the word is understood in most places. One has to live in Mississippi to appreciate it. No doubt it is the mark of an almost homogeneous white population, a Protestant Anglo-Saxon minority (until recently), sharing a common tragic past and bound together by kinship bonds. This society was not only felicitous in many ways; it also commanded the allegiance of Southern intellectuals on other grounds. Faulkner saw it as the chief bulwark against the "coastal spew of Europe" and "the rootless ephemeral cities of the North." In any case, the almost familial ambit of this society came to coincide with the actual public space which it inhabited. The Negro was either excluded, shoved off into Happy Hollow, or admitted to the society on its own terms as good old Uncle Ned. No allowance was made—it would have been surprising if there had been—for a truly public sector, unlovely as you please and defused of emotional charges, where black and white might pass without troubling each other. The whole of the Delta, indeed of white Mississippi, is one big kinship lodge. You have only to walk into a restaurant or a bus station to catch a whiff of it. There is a sudden kindling of amiability, even between strangers. The salutations "What you say now?" and "Y'all be good" are exchanged like fraternal signs. The presence of fraternity and sorority houses at Ole Miss always seemed oddly superfluous.

One consequence of this peculiar social structure has been a chronic misunderstanding between the state and the rest of the country. The state feels that unspeakable demands are being made upon it while the nation is bewildered by the response of rage to what seem to be the ordinary and minimal requirements of the law. Recall, for example, President Kennedy's gentle appeal to the university the night of the riot when he invoked the tradition of L.Q.C. Lamar and asked the students to do their duty even as he was doing his. He had got his facts straight about the tradition of valor in Mississippi. But unfortunately, the Kennedys had no notion of the social and semantic rules they were up against. When they entered into negotiations with the Governor to get Meredith on the campus, they proceeded on the reasonable assumption that even in the arena of political give and take—i.e., deals—words bear some relation to their referents. Such was not the case. Governor Barnett did not double-cross the Kennedys in the usual sense. The double cross, like untruth, bears a certain relation to the truth. More serious, however, was the cultural confusion over the word "public." Ole Miss is not, or was not, a public school as the word is usually understood. In Mississippi as in England a public school means a private school. When Meredith finally did walk the paths at Ole Miss, his fellow students cursed and reviled him. But they also wept with genuine grief. It was as if he had been quartered in their living room.

It is this hypertrophy of pleasant familial space at the expense of a truly public sector which accounts for the extraordinary apposition in Mississippi of kindliness and unspeakable violence. Recently a tourist wrote the editor of the Philadelphia, Mississippi, newspaper that, although he expected the worst when he passed through the town, he found the folks in Philadelphia as nice as they could be. No doubt it is true. The Philadelphia the tourist saw is as pleasant as he said. It is like one big front porch.

## A PLACE TO START

HOW CAN PEACE be restored to Mississippi? One would like to be able to say that the hope lies in putting into practice the Judeo-Christian ethic. In the end, no doubt, it does. But the trouble is that

Christendom of a sort has already won in Mississippi. There is more church news in the Jackson papers than news about the Ole Miss football team. Political cartoons defend God against the Supreme Court. On the outskirts of Meridian a road sign announces: "The Largest Percentage of Churchgoers in the World." It is a religion, however, which tends to canonize the existing social and political structure and to brand as atheistic any threat of change. "The trouble is they took God out of everything," said W. Arsene Dick of Summit, Mississippi, founder of Americans for the Preservation of the White Race. A notable exception to the general irrelevance of religion to social issues is the recent action of Millsaps College, a Methodist institution in Jackson, which voluntarily opened its doors to Negroes.

It seems more likely that progress will come about—as indeed it is already coming about—not through the impact of the churches upon churchgoers but because after a while the ordinary citizen gets sick and tired of the climate of violence and of the odor of disgrace which hangs over his region. Money has a good deal to do with it too; money, urbanization, and the growing concern of politicians and the business community with such things as public images. Governor Johnson occasionally talks sense. Last year the Mayor and the business leaders of Jackson defied the Citizens' Councils and supported the token desegregation of the schools. It could even happen that Governor Johnson, the man who campaigned up and down the state with the joke about what NAACP means (niggers, alligators, apes, coons, possums), may turn out to be the first Governor to enforce the law. For law enforcement, it is becoming increasingly obvious, is the condition of peace. It is also becoming more likely every day that federal intervention, perhaps in the form of local commissioners, may be required in places like Neshoba County where the Ku Klux Klan is in control and law enforcement is a shambles. Faulkner at last changed his mind about the durability of the old alliance and came to prefer even enforced change to a state run by the Citizens' Councils and the Klan. Mississippians, he wrote, will not accept change until they have to. Then perhaps they will at last come to themselves: "Why didn't someone tell us this before? Tell us this in time?"

Much will depend on the residue of goodwill in the state. There are some slight signs of the long-overdue revolt of the ordinary prudent man. There must be a good many of this silent breed. Hazel Brannon Smith, who won a Pulitzer Prize as editor of the Lexington *Advertiser*, recently reported that in spite of all the abuse and the boycotts, the circulation of the paper continues to rise. The Mississippi Economic Council, the state's leading businessmen's group, has issued a statement urging compliance with the Civil Rights Act and demanding that registration and voting laws be "fairly and impartially administered for all."

It is not difficult to make a long-range prophecy about the future of the state. The short-term outlook is certainly dark. Most thoughtful Mississippians agree that things are going to get worse before they get better. The vote in the national election, with its bizarre seven-to-one margin in favor of Senator Goldwater, attests to the undiminished obsession with race. It would not have mattered if Senator Goldwater had advocated the collectivization of the plantations and open saloons in Jackson; he voted against the Civil Rights Bill and that was that. Yet there is little doubt that Mississippi is even now beginning to feel its way to what might be called the American Settlement of the racial issue, a somewhat ambiguous state of affairs which is less a solution than a more or less tolerable impasse. There has come into being a whole literature devoted to an assault upon the urban life wherein the settlement is arrived at, and a complete glossary of terms, such as alienation, depersonalization, and mass man. But in the light of recent history in Mississippi, the depersonalized American neighborhood looks more and more tolerable. A giant supermarket or eighty thousand people watching a pro ball game may not be the most creative of cultural institutions, but at least they offer a *modus vivendi*. People generally leave each other alone.

A Southerner may still hope that some day the Southern temper, black and white, may yet prove to be the sociable yeast to leaven the American lump. Meanwhile he'll settle for the Yankee *pax* and be glad of it. I believe a Negro has as much right to be alienated as anyone else. It is at least a place to start.

*75*

# WHAT HAPPENED TO THE CIVIL-RIGHTS MOVEMENT?

(JANUARY 1967)

## C. Vann Woodward

### IT CAME HOME TO THE NORTH

TO CALL THIS a passing "phase," an interruption of a continuous movement, is to miss the historic integrity and distinctiveness of the recent period. It was a period of restitution, an effort to fulfill promises a century old, the redemption of a historic commitment. The appeal to history touched the Great Emancipator's "mystic chords of memory" and evoked a crusading mood charged with romantic sentiment. It was in that mood that the mass marches ("black and white together") were conducted. The objectives were clear and simple and the struggle for fulfillment took place largely in the South, the proper historic (and properly remote) setting for reconstructions. The last major milestone of the crusade was the Voting Rights Act of 1965.

Even before that event, however, problems of a new and disturbingly different character were demanding attention—things like slums, housing, unemployment, deteriorating school and family, delinquency and riots. They were not wrapped in historic sanctions and they were not amenable to romantic crusades and the evangelical approach. They were tough and harsh and brutally raw. What's more, they were national problems, not Southern, though the South faced some of them too. As soon as this came home to the North, the great withdrawal set in. White Congressmen from the Bronx and Chicago set up cries of anguish and dismay as bitter as the familiar chorus from South Carolina and Mississippi. Amid the clamor (North and South together) the Civil Rights Bill of 1966 for open housing and protection of civil-rights workers (combining "Northern" and "Southern" issues) went down in crashing defeat.

How long before the country will be prepared to face up to a Third Reconstruction—which is what a realistic solution of the new national problems really amounts to—remains to be seen. And it is problematical how much of the spent momentum and the old élan of past crusades can be marshaled, and how many veteran leaders can be enlisted to get an entirely new program off the ground. The White House conference of June 1966, which was designed to do just these things, failed of its purpose. Whites and blacks share some of the blame. But public attention was diverted elsewhere. Foreign wars are notorious distracters of public attention—especially when people *want* to be distracted. Veterans of the Second Reconstruction and planners of a Third would do well to face up to the fact that the one is now over and the other is still struggling to be born.

The unhappy interlude, which may be prolonged, would seem an appropriate time for reflection on the remarkable experience through which we have lately passed and such lessons as it might have to teach. In the past, whenever one of these hurricanes of indignation, righteousness, guilt, impatience—or whatever—swept the country, it left things in a state of disarray. The winds came in alternate gusts of love and hate and they left nothing undisturbed. It happened thus in the storm over slavery, and the latest tempest, while not so bloody, has had its effect. An inventory of our mental furniture will bear this out.

THE HISTORY OF the American intellectual community is beset with violent love affairs with other classes. Those of a certain age will be able to recall the one of the Thirties. That one was conducted across class lines and its object was the workingman, but its course was quite as tempestuous as the more recent affair. Such affairs of the heart have been in the romantic tradition that endows the object of love with exalted virtues and sublime attributes and at the same time indulges the lover in dreams of glory and sentimental self-flattery.

The passion was manifest in different forms. The white Southerner, his ardor and devotion suspect from the start, was most given to violent protestation and self-abasement. But in action he was prone to lapse unconsciously into hereditary postures of benevolent paternalism. The white Northerner, the more confident and masterful suitor, was not immune from hereditary posturing himself, and could set forth on his freedom ride humming the "Battle Hymn of the Republic." The Negro intellectual, cast in the curious role of both lover and beloved, was subjected to all the temptations of narcissism or autoeroticism and occasionally succumbed. Some of the whites, overcome with conviction of sin and communal guilt, succumbed to impulses of masochism and begged nothing of the beloved but to be publicly whipped and generally abused. And for a suitable fee there were those who were ready to oblige from the platform, the stage, or the screen.

These impulses, however, were but deviations from the white norm of neo-paternalism, a compound of philanthropy and unconscious condescension. For the underlying assumption was that it was up to the white man to solve "the problem," to lift up the black brother, to redeem the Negro. An incidental dividend that the philanthropist sometimes demanded of the freedom march or the jail-in was an ennobling catharsis, an exercise in self-redemption. So promiscuous was the resulting role confusion that it was hard to say at times whether the actor was playing redeemer or redeemed and whether the underlying purpose of a particular Black Belt march or freedom school was black salvation or white.

The picture was further complicated by the exalted roles the white romantics assigned their black partners. In effect they turned the tables of racial dogma and opted for Negro supremacy. But it was a dubious brand of supremacy, and the flattery, as Robert Penn Warren has pointed out, was shot through with the condescension implicit in the eighteenth-century adoration of the Noble Savage. The savage was extravagantly praised and admired, but he was admired for very particular kinds of virtues. They were the virtues attributed to the natural man, the simple child of nature, untainted by the malaise of civilization and untrammeled by its inhibitions, its compromises, and its instinctual deprivations. The modern Negro, like the Noble Savage, was endowed with the compensatory graces of simplicity, naturalness, spontaneity, and uninhibited sexuality.

The white Southerner, even the more orthodox of the breed, has long been familiar with this projection of yearnings and the type of condescension involved. They have haunted daydreams down the generations and provide the central theme of hundreds of pious folk stories, and some not so pious. They range in degree of sophistication from the legendary virtues of black mammy and the fabulous lubricity of black folk generally to dreams of restored innocence based on the literary model of Huck Finn and Nigger Jim: "Come back to the raft, Huck, honey."

### THE GIFT FOR IMITATION

THE YANKEES CAME to this exercise with a fresher approach. The red man as the Noble Savage of an earlier day and Uncle Tom as an Abolitionist projection were far behind them, and the rediscovery of the Negro opened fresh challenges to the imagination. They embraced him with an impulsiveness and fervor that must have proved embarrassing to the Negro at times. Another turning of the tables seems to have endowed the whites with the gift for imitation traditionally attributed to the blacks and made the latter the object of the most abject cultural imitation of modern times. Whites assiduously cultivated Negro slang, Negro music, Negro dance, Negro postures, Negro attitudes—or at least the slang, music, dance postures, and attitudes they fondly attributed to the Negro.

Jazz and Gospel songs penetrated the concert halls and jive talk became the language of the avant-garde. You were either hip or you were not with it. The White Negro was a literary creation of the times, and one of the most incredible performances in that role was a London beat holding forth at Oxford in what he doubtless believed to be the true idiom of 125th Street. It was acculturation in reverse. It was Harlem replacing the pre–Civil War plantation as a school for white savages manqués. What's more it was dead serious, at least to the true believers. In their eyes the Negro was the spiritual salvation for a bankrupt white civilization that had lost its vital juices and was destined for the dump heap of history. To question the postulate was the surest mark of a square.

The scholarly community was more reserved and less impulsive in its responses, but it did not remain unmoved. Its contributions were usually hedged with qualifications and cautious exceptions that were ignored by popularizers and propagandists. The historian was often shocked to read of the lessons his book allegedly taught, and desperately sought to disavow them. But the disavowals rarely caught up with the lessons. Such hypotheses as the one that "innately Negroes *are,* after all, only white men with black skins, nothing more, nothing less" quickly acquired uses beyond the author's control. The chicken-and-egg argument over slave status and race prejudice—which came first and which caused which—took on a polemical urgency far beyond the power of existing evidence to satisfy. To meet the needs of the Negro revolution, evidence was tortured to yield support for a heroic legend of slave revolt, and the image of the Abolitionist was burnished to a new brightness.

### History Garbled in Transmission

Comparisons of Anglo-American with Latin-American slavery and race relations have legitimately raised questions about the relative benevolence of the homegrown institution. But the lesson-teachers and the moral-drawers, with a hot commodity for the guilt-and-contrition white market, were not content with suggestive hypotheses or willing to wait for scholarly tests. One of them came forward confidently with the conclusion that "American slavery was profoundly different from, and in its lasting effects on individuals and their children, indescribably worse than, any recorded servitude, ancient or modern." Which took in a good deal of unexplored territory. And a sociologist thought the only remaining question was, "Why was American slavery the most awful the world has ever seen?"

Historians responded to the long-evident need for the revision of musty Reconstruction history with a copious flow of monographs, but the lessons the Second Reconstruction taught the historians of the First, and the lessons the First allegedly had for activists of the Second, were sometimes garbled in transmission. One historian suggested that the full-blown system of legally enforced segregation was not an immediate sequel of Appomattox, only to find himself cited as authority for the doctrine that Jim Crow was superficially rooted and easily eradicated. And when he called attention to the union of Negroes and whites in Southern Populism, he was interpreted as prophesying millennial developments in politics. It is no news to teachers, of course, that the lessons taught are not always the lessons learned.

How Negro Americans have withstood with such poise and humor as they have the crises they have recently weathered is one of the greatest marvels of the whole period. When one takes into account the constant barrage of publicity—front-page headlines for a decade or more—plus the attention, flattery, and imitation of the faddists, plus the adulation and eagerness of the activists, it would seem enough to have turned the head of the whole race. Perhaps it was because all this was more than neutralized by the indifference, hatred, and brutality of the other whites. Or because of what Ralph Ellison has called the Negro's "tragicomic attitude toward the universe." At any rate, it is clear that among the great majority of the leaders and the followers of the Negro movement, the racial reserve of patience and sanity and responsibility has never failed.

This cannot be said of a minority in whom the "tragicomic attitude" seems to have been in short supply. They have attracted an amount of attention disproportionate to their numbers because of a talent for making themselves conspicuous. Among them are the unfortunate few who have attempted to live up—or rather down—to the white myth of the Noble Savage, super-rhythm, super-lubricity, and all. A smaller number have solemnly shouldered the new black man's burden—another white invention—of playing redeemer to a doomed white civilization.

More prominent but still few in numbers are those who have elected to withdraw into some sort of racial exclusiveness, rejecting white allies and white society. Withdrawal takes several organized forms, including a cult of negritude, one that rallies to the cry of Black Power, and black nationalists of the Muslim and other varieties, all glorifying race and exalting racial identity. "A mystique must be created," reads a recent pronouncement of SNCC members which declares that, "If we are to proceed toward true liberation, we must cut ourselves off from white people. We must form our own institutions, credit unions, co-ops, political parties, write our own histories." Like the pronouncements of other separatist groups, this has the unmistakable quality of fantasy and a tenuous contact with reality. That all but a very few of the Negro leaders of national prominence have publicly repudiated this philosophy, along with any strategies of violence and racial exclusiveness and demagoguery, is one of a few reassuring signs of the time.

Any realistic appraisal of the prospects of the movement for Negro rights in 1967 and a Third Reconstruction to come would take full account of the ominous signs of reaction mentioned earlier. This would include the numerous white defections from the commitment to racial justice, the sudden silence in many quarters recently vocal with protest, the mounting appeal to bigotry, and the scurry of retreat in Congress. From past experience, it would be the part of realism to expect things to get worse before they get better.

It would not be the part of realism, however, to omit from the appraisal such assets as remain. Foremost among these surely is a corps of Negro leaders that has not been surpassed in dedication, astuteness, and moral force by the leadership of any other great social movement of this century. Their power is still great, and many of them have already enlisted for the Third Reconstruction. Although a smaller percentage of the Negroes now vote than voted in the First Reconstruction, their votes are more strategically located and more powerfully felt. While there may be further defections among the whites, a younger generation of blacks and whites that shares a powerful sense of identity with this movement and has made it peculiarly its own is coming on strong. It will be heard from further. Until its force is spent there is no realism in accepting the current reaction as irreversible and no rationality in despair.

# TURNED ON AND SUPER-SINCERE IN CALIFORNIA

## (JANUARY 1967)

## *Richard Todd*

*At 3.30 p.m. he said: "I feel terribly strange." Tom handed him a small toy animal he had played with as an infant.*

*Charley cuddled the toy, kissed it, and said: "There's something very reassuring about this." . . . Charley lay with a peaceful look on his face, cuddling the toy animal.*

*Tom lay down outside on a deck adjoining the bedroom and his face, too, filled with peacefulness.*

—San Francisco Chronicle, *May 30, 1966*

CHARLEY, THE THIRTY-SIX-YEAR-OLD man cuddling the toy, has taken LSD. He is acting strangely, but his trip will end in a few hours and with luck he will be back to normal. He arouses only your casual interest as you leaf through the *Chronicle,* in which LSD is as much a staple as recipes and rape. But you might listen more carefully to Tom, his observer and "guide," who has not had any acid and is speaking in his own voice:

> It was a wonderful few moments for me. I felt very much at one with Charley and I knew he was living for a while as a five-year-old child. . . . The guide grows in this experience of giving. What a privilege it is to be with another person in this way! No words can describe it.

These few lines represent with splendid typicality a way of talking that is not at all unusual at the moment here in California. The new idiom is characterized by self-revelation and utter seriousness. It places highest value on private emotions and "interpersonal relations," and considers restraint in talking about these intimate matters a signal of hypocrisy. The remarks of the LSD guide are faithful to these assumptions, and include some lesser, but important notions: for example, that childhood and simplicity are ideal states of being.

If the LSD milieu is particularly conducive to such innocence, the phenomenon is by no means confined to the drug set. Californians of many sorts are in its grip. Bulletins from the soul fill the air; all manner of private data is yours without asking. Telephone-talk-show callers crowd the switchboards for a chance to talk about their personal commitments; young marrieds eagerly discuss the state of their relationship; everyone will share with you the latest information on his "growth." Are you curious about anything? That fourteen-year-old playmate in bell-bottomed hip-huggers lolling down Sunset on the arm of a Beatlesque Older Man—do you wonder what her parents think? She will let you in on her hang-ups with them. Do you find it odd that the strapping Santa Cruz surfer has peroxided his hair into golden fleece? Talk to him; he will at least let you know that he uses Lady Clairol. The Berkeley girl will tell you that she smokes nickel cigars, lived with her boyfriend first semester, works hard, and that "I feel this growing . . . I guess I'm building my own truth."

Even where you would look for exceptions, you discover that the California language of soul holds sway: The academic community and its intellectual suburbs practice the new idiom without a blush. To a surprising degree, California intellectuals, particularly young ones, have forsaken traditional ironic speech, with its insistence on a certain distance between the speaker and his inner self. As a result, self-deprecation, wit, insouciance—all the cherished intellectual habits—are out of fashion here. If anything, they are taken as a badge of hated phoniness.

A listener unaccustomed to this attitude can experience some discomfort. You go to a party at the house of a young Stanford couple; he is a Ph.D. candidate and teacher. You don't know them well; as you arrive you note that since you saw them last his hair, once a shaggy pompadour, is now combed *à la mode,* draping forehead, ears, and neck. The party is distinctly academic: The air, which smells of beer and wine, is full of obscenities, "indeeds," and the music of Bobby Dylan, who is taunting some hapless middle-class lady for not being turned on: "Something is happening and you don't know what it is, do you, Mrs. Jones?" Talking over this din, you find yourself in an unexpectedly serious conversation with your host. He has taken LSD lately and, though you are not pressing him, he is anxious to tell you about it. The first time was up on the mountain, just after a rain. They went walking and . . . "The dripping leaves," he repeats, "the dripping leaves. It was so beautiful and it was sufficient . . . the forest seemed vast." But words are running out; the expression on his face suggests that it was an experience for which no words were necessary at the time and few are available now. He explains that they have taken LSD many times since, but always indoors. They sit on the sofa and talk. "It lasts for about twelve hours, and we talk the whole time. It has brought us much closer together than we have ever been before. We've been able to say things about our relationship that I wouldn't have thought possible. It's deepened our love . . ."

There is no adequate response for this kind of speech, delivered in a conversational way by a casual acquaintance, nothing, perhaps, except a similar disclosure. Yet you realize that if there is embarrassment in the silence that follows, it is entirely your own, and you suspect yourself of undue squeamishness. After all, what's wrong with saying what you feel?

For some, to be sure, openness in speech is more than an occasional matter, even more than a habit: It is a code. The code not only prohibits indirection but frowns on the use of the conventional language of social deceit. A successful California dinner party may suddenly swerve into failure with the conventional closing lines: "It was nice to see you." Suddenly everyone is on edge, a social blunder has occurred: The offender was speaking artificially, not of the self.

## THE GAME OF TRUTH

SOMETIMES A BELIEVER will explain the code in clear and vehement terms. You are on the top floor of a San Francisco apartment house on the edge of the Haight-Ashbury district—the West Coast, if not the worldwide center for psychedelic experiences. Cigarette smoke, only lightly laced with pot, thickens the air. Through the lone window at the end of the room, you can see the orange lights of the Golden Gate Bridge. Across the table from you is an authentic Haight-Ashbury denizen, a bearded Dane, swathed in corduroy, his head a torrent of hair. His wife is next to him, a Roger Vadim girl, with pouting insolent lips. When the Dane speaks, his English is immaculate, so perfect that his accent seems an affectation. But the Dane does not speak often. Indeed, he has sat, silent, sullen, but intense, for most of the evening. Suddenly, despite the late hour and the general grogginess, he whirls upon you. You have made an error, filling in a silence with an empty remark about the hour, the distance home, the necessity of a departure. The Dane exclaims, "Stop playing games. We do not know each other. We could sit here saying these polite things for a century and we would not know each other. Why don't you tell me what you think of me? Of course, you dislike me. But suppose I did not wear my beard; then you would like me, would you not? Tell me your opinion of me, and I will be candid with you, and perhaps we can get to know one another, but no more of this game."

"The game of truth," his wife exclaims, "the game of truth. Let's play the game of truth."

Now the game of truth is not about to become a favorite parlor game, and people like the Dane are easy enough to dismiss. At best they are trying to substitute a new and clumsy set of manners for the ones that have served fairly well to protect people from one another for centuries. At worst, they are "going through a phase." Taken alone, they are simply a curiosity. And yet they are not an isolated example; if there are few people who would express the code with equal vehemence, there are many who believe in it. They are impatient not just with "polite" language, but with all the old forms of literate speech, which they see as a barrier to feeling.

Could this be a hopeful development? Might the emergence of youthful minds willing to speak with directness suggest the bright prospect of mental energies not wasted on self-defense?

One popular observer (*Look* magazine) thinks so. For *Look*, the "turned-on Californian" is playing "a new game" whose rules include a "surprising openness in personal relations, a new intensity of personal commitment, a radical shift in the morally admissible, an expanded definition of education . . ." As these futurists get more adept at their game, *Look* says, "Relations between people will gain a new depth and subtlety."

You think of the B.'s and you wonder. They are not native Californians, but unequivocal Californians: "When we came here, we threw away our clocks. We eat when we want to, sleep when we want to, write when we want to, make love when we want to. It's wonderful." Martin B. is jack-of-all-sophisticated-trades. He has earned exotic degrees in technological fields, has held postdoctoral fellowships and rich jobs in California industry, but has turned, with equal success, to art: won creative writing fellowships, written a novel, is now rumored to be working on a play of outrageous political satire. Debby B. bakes more than two hundred kinds of bread. The B.'s are always talking about making love, and once said they practice the act each night. You sense that their preoccupation is an emblem of a larger concern: their contemporaneity, their freedom. The B.'s rid themselves of property each two years in a "potlatch." They have disposed of all books except reference matter, though they make voracious use of the public library. Their house, free of photographs or mementos, furnished entirely in beige and teak, is a monument to the present.

For the B.'s, whom you see from time to time, you suspect that you are a curiosity, and this is what they are to you. You listen to their exuberant conversation, which has a theme with limitless variations. On a night in June you hear them speak of the musicology of the Beatles, the intrauterine device, their friends ("we like anyone who's open . . . people who can share"), the Nike X, the Grand Tetons ("a wonderful place to make love"), model trains, childbirth, and plant chromosomes. Nothing out of the ordinary here.

You are caught off guard, however, when, on the porch as you are leaving, Martin remarks with no lapse in his ebullience, "We feel so close to you people!"

Outside in the air, you discover that you have a distinctly uncomfortable feeling, as if you had been kissed against your will. What Martin said is certainly not true. You do not feel close to the B.'s, it seems preposterous that they could feel close to you; you are somewhat annoyed by the imposition of the remark, which demands a response it is impossible to give. If there is a naïveté to their behavior, it is an insidious sort of naïveté, because it encumbers you, however briefly, in its untidy emotions.

This odd quality of contrived innocence is not limited to private lives; in California it is institutionalized. Experiments in human behavior abound: family therapy, group therapy, "movement therapy" (no one says a word), industrial "think-tanks," Joan Baez's Institute for the Study of Non-Violence.

The Esalen Institute flourishes at Big Sur—a handsome, well-endowed cluster of buildings overlooking the sea, which swirls about the rocks in beautiful subtleties of blue, white, and green. The Institute is dedicated to the "potentialities of human existence." It believes "People can change. Their institutions can change. All can change for the better, not just superficially, but deep down." Here you can come and participate in enterprises of self-improvement led by psychiatrists and therapists, for a cost of $67 (for a weekend) or $170 (for five days). Recent seminars included "Psychodrama and the Body" and "Bio-Energetic Analysis," also an arts-and-crafts event called "Down Home with Staff Members." (One of the staff is described as "potter, printmaker, and sometime breakfast cook," and of another it is said, "In addition to his jewelry and sculpture, he is well-known on the West Coast as a sandalmaker.")

There is that sound again: What is there about it that can simultaneously amuse and annoy? We all know that sandalmakers are respectable, and there is no real reason to suspect that "Bio-Energetic Analysis" is not on the up-and-up. And yet somehow these phrases seem inadequate to the exploration of "human potentialities." Perhaps it is the easy assurance, that certain chumminess ("sometime breakfast cook") with the confident implication that all within earshot are believers, that everyone agrees that we can push back the frontiers of human experience this weekend.

### "No Complicated Emotions"

IT IS THE same happy assumption that accompanies the activity that has inspired so many contemporary idioms—drugs. The use of drugs, it should be repeated, does not account for the phenomenon in question; not all the "turned-on" Californians are turned on in the literal way. Yet it is true that drugs are widely used in California, that they are never far from intellectual circles, and that they define the hip personality, the man who has, as Timothy Leary prescribes, dropped out to turn on. And while drugs are more a symptom than a cause, the function they appear to serve may offer a clue to the way minds are working here. From pot to LSD, all are used for the same ostensible reason: They "expand the mind."

"The music."

"Wo-ow."

"The levels, so many levels."

"I'm up here."

"Don't talk about it; you'll bring it down."

"Did you hear that? 'You'll bring it down.' Oh fantastic."

This conversation—as the joint (of marijuana) is passed around—is not so much an intimation of perceptions as an attempt to keep aloft the mystical communion. The most important effect of pot is evident less in the words that are spoken than in the looks on the faces of the smokers, who are most likely to assume a gentle, abstracted, beneficent, open expression; to let down their guard. The mind is expanded, to be sure; it is made large enough to hold in harmony elements of one's life that are in conflict when the high ends. Pot, like bourbon or nutmeg, is used to simplify, not to complicate, experience. That the experience can become very complicated indeed when stronger drugs are used does not mean that the goal is different. The air is full of tales of bad trips, the flesh melting away, etc. (One peyote-mescaline-LSD veteran recalled his first experience: "I thought I was all right until I saw a gorilla at the urinal.") The significant point is that the possibility of a good trip, a voyage to simplicity, a glorious regression to the imagination's childhood, is considered worth the risks. One of the *Chronicle*'s LSD subjects said of his experience, "I never get insanity or hallucinations anymore—just peace—and I feel love for everybody who is here." Another put the matter precisely, "I found I was young, about fifteen, walking down the streets of Rome. I was an Italian boy with no complicated emotions."

"No complicated emotions" says it well. After the drug scene has died out, been confined to the laboratory or legalized into dullness, the item of enduring interest will be that—for a short time anyway— simplicity of feeling was elevated to the level of a heroic ideal. It is what everyone, not just the acid head, seems to be striving for. You hope, half the time you believe (if you are a participant in this euphoric sensibility), that emotional prosperity is just around the cor- ner. In the meantime, though, you must prime the pump with LSD. Or—the more frequent alternative—you must rely on the symbol instead of the sensation, on the easy, "open" speech that marks you as a man of feeling.

When a society wears its heart on its sleeve, something curious is likely to happen. Berkeley is as good a place as any to search for these consequences. It is, of course, a magnificent place: After Berkeley nearly every other campus feels like Slippery Rock. There is turmoil, controversy, intellectual energy, a fervid unleashing of the mind. There is local color. It is no doubt true that Berkeley suffers from a tendency to appreciate the defiant act in any form, but these are usually harm- less. (No one seriously worries about the activities, say, of the East Bay Sexual Freedom League—including a nude wade-in in San Francisco last year.) Berkeley's present danger is probably not extremism but . . . contentment.

Contentment is a paradoxical word for the university that support- ed the Free Speech Movement. Any day of the week rows of tables dis- play the trophies and causes of the moment, advertise open-air speakers and a hundred diversions, including the "Cinema Psychedel- ica." But if you linger around the Plaza, you are likely to discover the peculiar kind of joy that is the result of self-absorption. The happiness of those who roam about the campus, sit dangling their feet in the fountain, or even harangue each other is the solid pleasure of the craftsman content in his work. You stroll through Sather Gate and take the pamphlet that is modestly proffered. It addresses itself to whether or not God is dead, and ends with the assurance, "We welcome any questions about life."

This is a nice complacency, which says not so much that we will answer your questions, but simply that we are *here,* and you are out there, and you don't dare laugh at us. This sense of rightness perhaps explains the familiar hip gesture of making non-jokes. You are sitting, to give an example, in the kitchen of an apartment on Grove Street. Its old tongue-in-groove boards were painted pink long ago and are now peeling to reveal green. There is almost nothing in the place: a few cans of garbanzo beans on the shelves, some milk and Vichy water in the icebox. You are having breakfast, Cheerios, with Walter, who lives there. The stairs to the apartment above lead through Walter's kitchen and the two tenants from upstairs appear: Blossom and Manny. Manny eyes the Cheerios box on the table, chuckles, and points, "Look." Blossom looks, shakes her head, and murmurs, "Fantastic." Manny chuckles, "Cheerios," and shakes his head. Exit. This routine is easily done with any object, the more ordinary the better: a radio, a toy (a plastic Jesus would be excessively obvious). You just stare at the thing in apparent wonder, as if you could see the absurdity of the whole civilization contained within it. You remain wordless, or utter a "fantastic," that word that hippies reserve almost entirely for the banal.

This air of sureness about the world has a kind of charm on the antic level, but it presents certain difficulties when the discourse moves to a higher plane. Think of all those fresh-faced girls who repeat the new categorical imperative with such artless confidence, "I believe anything's moral as long as it doesn't hurt someone else." The ease with which that remark dismisses tradition's offer of advice and asserts its faith in one's ability to weigh the implications of every act— these qualities can find their way beneath the skin. And when this kind of mind turns to matters of life and death, unnatural results can be expected.

A recent issue of the weekly Berkeley *Barb* contained a front-page elegy for a nineteen-year-old boy who died while on an LSD trip. The piece, entitled "Vernon P. Cox: an Elegy—HE DIDN'T QUITE MAKE IT," described the author's relationship with the boy (friends, fellow poets), appraised his talent (real, prolific, sometimes seventy poems a day), and, of course, lamented his death.

It reads in part:

> His name is Vernon P. Cox, and he didn't quite make it. A very decent human being, came from a good family of Stillwater, Oklahoma. (What a fitting name, what a still place. Cattle grazing, oil wells, fraternities. Devoid of original thought. Plain, every day Stillwater.) . . .
>
> So they come to Berkeley. Shaggy Dog adopted Sanders, who shared their two mattresses for a couple of nights. English from N.Y. and two-three girls were also guests there. Pot, nutmeg, always near, a refrigerator with some peanut butter—and nothing else—pregnant fifteen-year-olds, the beat scene. That's where he lived and wrote, and, a shame to say, didn't quite make it . . .
>
> He has his first LSD trip in company: Shaggy Dog as usual lay down, softly singing to himself. Their two other companions were busy and happy in themselves. Vernon free and exulted beyond belief suddenly realized that the trip to Europe he desired, but was afraid of, is a must. Packed his things to start then and there. His companions argued with, restrained him, and for a while he was quiet. Then knowing that for him nothing is impossible, that physical laws don't bind him, not bothering to use the door he walked through the window-pane. No one there was quick enough to block his way. He fell three stories. . . . It wasn't suicide; he only started for Europe and didn't quite make it.

The truth about this elegy is that it is comic. It is horrible, unconscious comedy, slapstick, a Charlie Chaplin movie rendered in earnest prose. It manages, through the tandem devices of undoubted sincerity and total mindlessness, to make an already senseless death almost irredeemably absurd.

And yet, it is not likely that the *Barb*'s elegy—whatever wretchedness it might have caused the boy's Stillwater, Oklahoma, family—disturbed many Berkeley readers. It asserts, after all, unassailable notions that youth, sensitivity, poetry, love, and freedom are good things. It only disregards the necessity for a double vision; it makes no attempt to imagine this tragedy as it might look to another time, another town, a parent, to the author himself a few years (months?) later. It only fails to throw a sop to a world in which walking through a window to one's death, with the illusion of going on a European tour, qualifies as a bizarre act. It speaks with absolute assurance, an assurance that is oddly justified by the complacence of its audience.

## LIKE SPILT MILK

THE "ELEGY," OF course, is a grotesque, a heightened version of unreality—but, like other grotesques, it has its instructive value. In one sense it can be taken as the careless remarks of a young writer, but in another sense it is the product of a culture as well; if ordinary restraints were operating the elegy would not likely have been written; certainly it would not be received with equanimity. In its painful assumptions that you need only feel, be straight, put down hypocrisy, say what you mean, it is utterly faithful to the unchallenged ideas of the intelligent people whose voice rules this coast.

If this intellectual style is not explicable, it at least is somewhat appropriate to the state whose residents—from hippies to systems men—share, if they share anything, a devotion to the moment. What California seems to need is what it clearly wants least: a past. It is possible to grow obsessed with this prescription, perhaps because everything looks like spilt milk. The land is always wrenchingly visible; from the heart of Berkeley, from the midsts of the most hysterical freeway, you can always see the brown hills, their contours too subtle to accept a building gracefully, waiting to be defiled by another onslaught of tract houses.

If your mood is right, of course, you can be bemused, even exhilarated, by the hodgepodge, as you can by its intellectual concomitants. But your mood can change, as quickly as the passing of the sun can transform the landscape itself—surely no place is as ugly as California on a cloudy day—and you are pushed toward visions of a distinctly hideous future for this state.

Whatever is to become of the place, it is no hopeful sign that so many bright voices are celebrating the self and the now and that much of the state is on a sentimental trip; high, indeed out of its mind—not on LSD but on language: oldest, strongest drug of them all.

# GEORGE WALLACE: A GROSS AND SIMPLE HEART

(APRIL 1967)

## Tom Wicker

*Had but the federal judiciary been as well read on their American and Southern history as on the peculiar sociological theories of the left; had but they perused, even superficially, Mr. Kipling's comment on the specific infusion of Scot fighting clan blood into the English strain of the South; had they but studied, from their lofty tower of impregnable authority, the demise of one Edward I whose authority was even loftier, until he bullied a Scottish clan called Wallace; then perhaps they would have busied themselves with quieter and less hazardous pursuits than encroachments on freedom guarded over by a little country judge. But they didn't . . . and his name is Wallace . . . and therein lies the tale. We cannot tell the ending to it; that will be written in the days that are with us now.*

—Official Inaugural Program
State of Alabama, January 14, 1963

MORE THAN FOUR years later, we still "cannot tell the ending" to the story of George Corley Wallace, Jr., but as in many another dark tale of the fighting clans of Scotland, the signs and portents cannot be ignored. As an Alabama backcountry ballad called "Little Stonewall Wallace" has it:

Dixie's lookin' fer a man, now listen to me well,
I kin hear it in the song of the whippoorwill,
I kin feel it in the sigh of the ol' pine trees—
Done got herself a man, you wait an' see.

Those not attuned to the Alabama omens need not go about listening to its whippoorwills and pine trees. The state's automobile license plates have borne for years the legend "Heart of Dixie." These days, on many a shiny new sedan or muddy farm pickup truck, another plate appears beside the official one. It bears pictures of George and Lurleen Wallace on a field of stars and bars, and the simple proclamation: "Wallace Country."

An Alabamian choosing to be more specific can adorn his bumper with a tin picture of George alone, superimposed on the battle cry of the Alabama Movement—"Stand Up for America—Wallace for President." For the restrained, there is a tastefully devout plate reading simply, "Wallace—My Governor," with no picture. Nor, in Alabama, is it necessary to speculate about the politics of those whose cars carry tags in support of "One Nation Under God," although these are daring enough to present the American rather than the Confederate flag.

Lurleen Wallace was elected to replace Little Stonewall as Governor last fall with the biggest majority in the state's history, not excluding his own in 1962. When the Gardendale, Alabama, city council dismissed one Earl W. Hall as city judge, Hall said it was because he was a Republican in a one-party system "that stamps out any competition."

One of the most eminent attorneys in the state confided recently that it was not now a good thing in his profession to become known as an anti-Wallace man "if you have to try cases before a jury." Newspapers that have opposed Little Stonewall have been known to lose state-controlled liquor advertising. Patronage, of which there is a great deal in Alabama, is pointedly administered. ("Was that fellow for us?" Wallace will inquire to someone calling to advocate an appointment. "I hate not to but if folks wasn't for you, it's hard as the devil to appoint 'em.")

State Senator Robert Gilchrist, a leading opponent of Mrs. Wallace in the Democratic primary last spring, failed even to carry his home county against her. ("My little wife, a girl who used to work in a dime store, beat this big state senator in his own home town," Wallace says.) So Gilchrist "got the word from the primary," as a Wallace man put it, and led the fight for the Governor in enacting a state law that attempted to nullify the federal school desegregation guidelines.

George Wallace has assembled in the "Heart of Dixie" a political empire to which the shrewdest Alabama political observers now see no practical limit. He has not been able to do so just because, in the eminently practical politics of this place, a Governor can call up the head of an asphalt plant who sells his product to the state and get a $25,000 campaign contribution in two minutes, under the unspoken threat of taking the state's ample asphalt business elsewhere. The reason is rather that so many Alabamians believe wholeheartedly that Little Stonewall has single-handedly "stood up for us" and "put the spotlight on Alabama" as the spearhead of a "movement" that is sweeping the nation and that promises to relieve the South of the burden of civil-rights pressures and federal "dictation."

Wallace is where he is today because he is a demagogue of unique sincerity, a profound student of human nature in its earthiest order who accords to that nature his highest respect, and thus a politician who more than any in his time has touched and played upon the deepest chords of belief among his people—chords that ring as truly in him as in them. He is an artist of defeat who, from a string of unbroken reverses, has made of himself a Southern Messiah. Whether or not this is an exercise in mass delusion or the shrewdest political buildup in recent history, his wife spoke nothing but the plain truth when she said of him, "He speaks out for [the people of Alabama]. He says what they think. When he's on *Meet the Press* they can listen to him and think, 'That's what I would say if I were up there.'"

There are about three and a half million people in Alabama. Despite their peculiar Southern heritage, they are not totally different from people elsewhere. George Wallace, in the 1964 Democratic Presidential preferential primaries in Indiana, Wisconsin, and Maryland, won from 25 to 43 percent of the vote. These and other evidences suggest that George Wallace may speak for some large, unknown number of Americans—five million, ten million, more?— not necessarily racist, not necessarily reactionary, not necessarily stupid or vicious or ignorant, but human, concerned, determined.

## A FEELING FOR THE FOLKS

HIS FIRST DAY back in his dark, paneled office in the Alabama state Capitol last winter, after the time taken out following Lurleen Wallace's smashing victory in the November election, was clear, cold, windy. Above the sparkling white building on Goat Hill, the Confederate flag snapped in the wind; the Alabama flag crackled with equal authority on the same staff; but there was no sign of the Stars and Stripes. On the columned gallery, which affords a decent view over Montgomery, a small medallion inset in the floor marks the exact spot where Jefferson Davis stood when he was sworn in as President of the Confederate States of America. Beyond enormous doors in a chilly rotunda, where beautifully designed staircases sweep upward without visible support, effusive Southern ladies distribute state maps, pamphlets, and honeyed words. A visitor from Washington is informed with insistent laughter that he must have brought the chilly weather with him. Intimidated suddenly by his own Southern background, the unquestionable primacy of ladies, and the priority on agreement, charm, affability, he agrees that indeed he must have. Alabama could not be responsible, even for its weather; it could only be an imposition.

The Governor's quarters are cramped into a new wing of the Capitol—new since Jefferson Davis, anyway. Audrey Henderson, Wallace's secretary, confined with her electric typewriter in a windowless cell, confides that someone once told her, "Honey, this used to be the janitor's closet." But that, she says proudly, was when "the Governor used to be a pretty quiet affair in Alabama"—which he is not now.

Reuben King, who heads the state's welfare program and occasionally fills in for George Wallace's administrative assistant, Cecil Jackson, points out, "In the last four years, every member of the Cabinet has been in the hospital. I've been in twice and I'm only thirty-seven years old. I tell you, when a man works as hard as the Governor does, with all that energy, you just don't feel right unless you do the same. He's down here until seven, eight at night. It just makes you feel kind of like you got to keep up with him." He sighs. "Miz Wallace, she's gonna be just the same. She's just like him, got a real feeling for the folks."

Wallace himself fidgets behind a big desk, and dashes out to his reception room periodically to shake a few hands and bandy words. (To a man from Tallassee: "Lots of good folks over there, ain't they? I made a speech over there and told 'em: You got more instinct than the *New York Times*. You knew Castro was a Communist all along, and the *New York Times,* they still don't believe it.") He receives particularly important visitors in the inner sanctum (to two well-regarded ladies who wanted his autograph on their copies of an admiring biography, *The Wallace Story* by Bill Jones, he confesses, "I ain't read that book yet myself"), and often answers his own phone. He dismisses the hectic atmosphere in which he works with a wave of the hand: "That's just life nowadays. Sometimes there's seventy-five people out there wantin' to see me."

Physically unimpressive, his cufflinks a bit too large, his hair too neatly waved, George Wallace still is one of those men who dominate a room by their mere presence. He is nervous, aggressive in the way of small men, assertive to a point just short of arrogance, with too much fire in him to permit wit, ease, or even backslapping. (He puts in a quick call to one of his backers, apparently for no reason except to instruct him to "tell 'em all hello for us. You tell all our friends hello, hear?" He plays with a gavel, smacking its head in his palm, gouging himself with its handle; there is a cigar constantly in his hand or mouth (a box of Hav-A-Tampa Fancys Extra is within reach) and he stabs at its stub repeatedly with a variety of desk lighters, chews it, removes it to spit in the wastebasket.

"I got people finding out which office in this building Jefferson

Davis worked in," he says. "I just might move in there when Lurleen moves in here."

Audrey announces another visitor. "I'm goin' to see that sonovabitch for just a minute"; he dashes out, returns, flops in the swivel chair behind the desk with its $100 State of Alabama note under the glass, its family photos, its Air Force plane model, its Confederate cannon model, its white leather Holy Bible, its six pens in their stands ("No use to fill them," Audrey confides. "The Governor doesn't believe they'll write unless you dip 'em each time"), its three phones, beige, red, and a green one with six buttons.

Everywhere he looks, there is tribute to his world and position—the long conference table beyond his desk, the dark leather chairs surrounding it, the color photograph behind him of two decrepit Confederate veterans saluting the Stars and Bars in eternal, dreamlike sunshine, the handsome green marble mantel around the fireplace, the ornate crystal chandelier suspended above the conference table, the magnificent portrait of Winthrop Sargent (Governor of the Mississippi Territory, including Alabama, 1798–1800) above the mantel, and just beneath the portrait the glorified bust of himself with the inscription: "George C. Wallace, Governor of Alabama. He Stood for the People of Alabama." There is a plaque that certifies him an honorary colonel in the Gold Run Gulch Horse Guards, a Civil War cannonball, "Presented to George C. Wallace by the Voters of Louisiana, 6-17-64."

An ancient television set perches on an ancient filing cabinet at one end of the room and, in sharp contrast, at the other, past rows of cracked black-leather-bottom chairs, is both a modern dictating machine and a 1920s glass lamp. Here, amid the Southern courthouse smells of tobacco, politics, earth, men, defeat, and age, George Wallace in his dark conservative suit, faintly pinstriped, his blue shirt with its pinched collar, his red, silver, blue striped tie, his gold watchband, gold cufflinks, and gold ring, cocks back in his chair and talks with the amazing frankness of conviction.

"If one of these national parties don't recognize that people are fed up with crime in the streets," he says, "and I mean people of all races are fed up with courts and politicians coddling these criminals; if they don't realize we're tired of handing out foreign aid while nobody helps us out in Vietnam, and we're tired of helping France when they won't help us, and we're tired of folks raising money and blood for them Vietcong under academic freedom and freedom of speech while our boys get shot at—we've got to differentiate between what's dissent and academic freedom and what's treason—if the two parties continue along this liberal path, attackin' private property rights and free enterprise, a lot of people will be out of a choice and I'll give them one."

He snatches a desk lighter, snaps it three times, rejects it, grabs a match, lights the cigar stub. "Course I ain't one of these ultras who's against everything. A fellow like that couldn't get elected to office here in Alabama. I couldn't get elected on a hate-Niggras platform. Down here, we made the government the issue, not the Niggra. And it ain't just here in Alabama and the South. People everywhere are tired of the government telling them when to get up and when to go to bed. The people need to be enlightened about this and we're going to do that."

### "Intellectual Morons"

SOMEBODY CALLS TO tell Wallace that his name is being used to solicit advertising in a magazine. He cradles the phone between shoulder and ear, grabs a lighter, jabs it against the inch-long Hav-A-Tampa Fancys Extra: "Well, I tell you, it's just as hard as the devil; I mean there ain't no way to keep people from invoking your name and I just don't know how to do it. Tell 'em all hello up there for us." He hangs up, whirls, dictates a memo to someone to investigate the advertising project.

"The real problem ain't race," he continues, as if in unbroken conversation. "The real problem is these intellectual liberals who take power and oppress people. Insist they got to vote, even illiterates, and then won't let them run their own affairs when they do. Like they insist the people of Alabama don't have the morality and integrity to run their own affairs, and so they got to be run for them, these guidelines and all. Why, there's more feelings against the Niggra in Chicago and New York than in Alabama. All this talk about the Klan, for instance. The only Klansman I know is — — and he hangs around the Capitol here and you can't help but know him. But at least a Klansman will fight for his country. He don't tear up his draft card. But the Klan, it's just innocuous in size and they're just concerned with segregation, not subversiveness."

He repeats—it is a favorite theme—that it is "the intellectual liberals, who come to power and think they know everything and what's good for everybody, who oppress the people. Intellectual morons, I call 'em. Sometimes theory just don't work. You got to be practical in dealing with human problems. Take Castro. Any man plowing a mule down here—and I don't mean a man plowing a mule didn't go to school—any man with a second-grade education knew Castro was bad just looking at his picture and reading what he said. Any cab driver in Montgomery—and I don't mean to throw off on them because I used to be one myself—knows more about why we're in Vietnam than a Yale professor sitting up there in his ivory tower. We got to get all this theory out of things."

But he is angered by the charge that he is just an unprincipled demagogue—for instance, that of a state senator who was quoted by Jack Nelson of the *Los Angeles Times* as saying that Wallace would be "the damnedest integrationist you ever saw if he thought that was what people wanted. He's got no sense of right or wrong about it."

A political leader, Wallace says, "sometimes has facts people can't get in everyday life. So he has to educate them; he can't just say, 'What will be popular today?' You're supposed to lead. If they think I'm just a demagogue what do they say about me and my wife? Nobody in this state but me thought she could get elected Governor. When I first got the idea I called up my friends and ever one of 'em said, 'I'm for Wallace but I ain't voting for no woman.' But we just kept right on, and that little girl that used to work in a dime store got 480,000 votes in the primary and eight other candidates only got 403,000 and then she got 550,000 in the general. And if I had just listened to what people said, she never would have run.

"Anyway, the people have the facts on this encroachment on the rights of the states. They know the score on that and they're tired of it. I don't think I've changed anybody's mind. If I wasn't in tune with the people of Alabama they wouldn't have elected me Governor. Besides, they ain't no integrationists in this country if you get right down to it, except a few long-haired gals and some bearded fellows and a few college professors and preachers and even they aren't when it gets right down to their children intermarrying. But I don't talk about that stuff."

He has never, Wallace insists, "made a racist speech in my life, not unless you count being for segregation as racist. I mean I never talked against Niggras as people. I got nothing against Niggras. Southern folks had the most practical approach ever devised for this race business. So what if we had paternalism as long as we had peace and folks were satisfied? What good are equal rights if it gets folks killed and ruins everything? Why, you're safer in the worst part of Montgomery than on the New York City subway. We got less integration but more mingling and more law and order. And what most folks of all races want is law and order." Then he adds slyly, "Of course, some folks just *like* to get out and throw rocks."

At lunchtime, Wallace trots down an interior stairway to a long basement corridor leading to the Capitol cafeteria. He speaks to everyone along the way, calling the girls "honey," the men by their names.

From the cafeteria steam table he chooses chopped steak, rutabagas, canned peaches, sliced tomatoes, a pack of Fig Newtons. As he takes his seat with the office workers, a waitress rushes up with a small dish.

"I saved the Governor some okra," she confides to his guest. "It's his favorite."

"You said it, honey," Wallace says, eating a Fig Newton.

Grover Hall, the witty former editor of the *Montgomery Advertiser,* now the editor of the *Richmond News-Leader,* a close personal friend but not always a political supporter of Wallace's, joins the luncheon party. He joshes the Governor about his table manners; Wallace obviously enjoys it. "One time I was going up to Richmond to make a speech and ol' Grover told me I had to polish myself up because it would be a real cultured audience," he says. "Well, I went up there to the John Marshall Hotel and it was the most cultured, polite, well-dressed crowd I ever saw in my life and I gave 'em a real cultured talk until I started getting warmed up and then I forgot and called the

Supreme Court a 'sorry, lousy, no-count outfit,' and you ought to have heard that cultured crowd stand up and cheer. People are about the same everywhere but ol' Grover here keeps trying to polish me up."

He douses the chopped steak in ketchup. "Course I talk like we all do down South," he continues. "You know—ain't got no, he don't, and all that—I know better but it's just comfortable. So I went up and was on television with Martin Luther King and I talked like I always do, and there he was with that grammar and those big words. And they quoted me in the paper the next day to make it look like I don't know anything, and then they quote a fellow like that that don't even know the origins of the English language."

Wallace rises to speak to an eager voter hovering over the table, and Hall offers an opinion: "That fellow can read your insides quicker than any man I ever saw. He's had a hard life, dealt with a lot of juries later on. He just *knows* people. Then, too, he's dauntless. He never gives up. He's just got more persistence than anybody else."

After three years, Wallace still is noncommittal about what he and President Kennedy said to each other when they met in Alabama during the Birmingham civil-rights crisis of 1963. He is willing, however, to talk about Kennedy, whom he met at the 1956 Democratic National Convention during the exciting race for the Vice Presidential nomination.

"Everybody from the South was against Kefauver," Wallace recalls, "and for Kennedy. Alabama was caucusing at 10:00 P.M. and he had to make a speech to some other delegation at the same time, so he asked me if I would take his sister to speak for him at our delegation. So I met them on the mezzanine of the Conrad Hilton Hotel and took her to the caucus, and she spoke right well. I don't remember which sister that was, but I sure hope it wasn't the one that kissed Sammy Davis, Jr."

### THE COPS' CANDIDATE?

ON THE WAY back to his office, Wallace is stopped by an elderly, intense party named William Wood, who has driven from Chicago to Atlanta to see Senator Richard Russell of Georgia and has stopped by Montgomery on his way home. He chats with Wallace about "your

Presidential candidacy in 1968" and predicts that "anybody" can beat President Johnson because his mainstays—"the Communists and the Negroes"—have turned against him.

Wallace is not impressed. "I don't see a Communist under every bed," he says, when he is back in his office. "Some of them may be behind all these riots. But I don't believe all this talk about poor folks turning Communist. It's the damn rich who turn Communist. You ever see a poor Communist? Like them Rosenberg folks and all. They were moneyed people."

He and Hall have been talking with indignation about the Selma marchers who congregated, thousands strong, before Wallace's Capitol building in 1965. "Now up in Chicago," Wallace points out, "when they started marching, they resisted 'em. And you know what happened? The federal courts restrained the marchers to only 500 people in a city of 5 million. We didn't put up a bit of resistance in Montgomery, and they just let 35,000 people march all over a city of 100,000. But the point is, now we can break up the next march down here after what happened in the North. We can call out the guardsmen and the police and go lay a billy club on their heads. If you're violent, they listen; if you're for law and order, they push you around."

Law and order concern everyone, he says again, and most of all the working class. "We run best in the industrial states," he says. "We got our biggest vote in '64 from organized labor. They're all concerned about crime and property rights. You take a working man: If he lives in a section where law and order breaks down, he can't just up and move like rich folks can. The police, too. I went out to the Governors' Conference in Los Angeles last summer, and the patrolman in charge of the police assigned to the conference came and got me to speak to the ones that was off-duty. I told them we believed in law and order in Alabama and we prosecuted criminals on Monday morning, not policemen. I told them, 'I wish you could run this country for about two years. You could straighten it out.' When I finished, the patrolman in charge told me, 'You're our Presidential candidate.'

"And when I went up to New York and they came down from Harlem and picketed me, the police drew this line in the street and they told them the first one to cross it would get his head split. And one of the police whispered to me, 'We drew that line pretty close to 'em, Governor.' The police are for me everywhere. I was at another Governors' Conference in Miami when Johnson was Vice President and spoke on civil rights, and the Governor sitting next to me said, 'I'm tired of this. There's two sides to that question in my state now.' That's a state would shock you if I told you the name of it."

It is midafternoon, quiet in the dark office; the phone has ceased to ring and visitors are being channeled to Reuben King. Wallace chews his cigar reflectively, gets up from his chair, leans against his desk. He gazes out of the window, across the lawns and the wide street where the Selma marchers heard Martin Luther King tell his dream, where Southerners in another, brighter time stood to see Jeff Davis take his oath. Wallace speaks quietly, rapidly, warming up now, as he did before the cultured audience in the John Marshall Hotel in Richmond.

"Of course, if I did what I'd like to do I'd pick up something and smash one of these federal judges in the head and then burn the courthouse down. But I'm too genteel. What we need in this country is some Governors that used to work up here at Birmingham in the steel mills with about a tenth-grade education. A Governor like that wouldn't be so genteel. He'd put out his orders and he'd say, 'The first man who throws a brick is a dead man. The first man who loots something what doesn't belong to him is a dead man. My orders are to shoot to kill.'"

Wallace sits down again, his black eyes snapping. "That's the way to keep law and order. If you'd killed about three that way at Watts the other forty wouldn't be dead today. But most Governors are like me. They got too much education. They're too genteel."

### THE POLITICS OF WELFARE
GEORGE WALLACE GOT his start in Alabama politics when he was thirteen by knocking on doors in his hometown of Clio on behalf of a candidate for Secretary of State. The candidate lost the race but carried Clio, and Wallace has been turning public defeat into personal triumph ever since.

Vaguely recalling those days, the ideas that drove him into politics, he says that he "used to think about junior colleges and things like that." And there is little doubt that he is one of those Populist-tinged Southerners (like Lyndon Johnson) who see politics basically in terms of "something for the folks."

It is a matter of record—if little-known outside the state—that in his four years in office, for $40 million, he has built fourteen new junior colleges and fifteen new trade schools (legally desegregated but so located that some are virtually all for Negroes), launched a $100 million public-school building program, provided free textbooks for all Alabama schoolchildren, set out on the biggest road-building plan in the state's history, and borrowed $300 million for various projects. As a young state legislator, he was the author of the Wallace Industrial Development Act, one of those devices through which Southern communities are authorized to build virtually tax-free buildings and lease them to industries that will relocate, and this once-backward state is blooming economically, at least in part as a result. Wallace is proud of the diversification with which this is being achieved and cites Opelika as a city profiting from a big industry where the people are "still rural and own their own homes."

"I don't think God meant people to be all jammed up in cities," Wallace says. "No courtesy, no time, no room—that's all you get in cities. But industry don't locate in mud and dust."

He is indeed not one of those "ultras who is against everything," and if the federal government is his favorite target he is still an eager recipient of its largess. Reuben King says that there are 388 Alabamians in every 1,000 of the state's population participating in welfare programs; only Louisiana has more. Eighty-five million of Alabama's $110 million welfare budget stems from Washington, and 80 percent of its $350 million state budget derives from federal grants of one kind or another.

Between 1963 and 1966, expenditures on all Alabama school systems were doubled. There is a liberal nursing-home plan, a plan under which communities build self-liquidating medical clinics for private operation, a water-pollution act to preserve one of a river-laced state's greatest natural resources, and such ambitious projects as one that would link the Tennessee and Tombigbee rivers by a canal and thus establish an unbroken waterway route from the Great Lakes states and the Ohio River through Alabama to the Gulf of Mexico.

Given the vast Wallace political power, Mrs. Wallace's four years in office ought to be as successful as her husband's. The Wallaces will have at their disposal, as all Alabama Governors have had, what amounts to a legal $600,000 political slush fund. The state provides its own insurance on rural schoolhouses that have no adequate fire and police protection. To make this "fair" to and competitive with commercial insurance companies, the legislature appropriates $600,000 yearly to pay "commissions" on the insurance Alabama sells itself. The commissions may be paid to anyone with an insurance salesman's license, which is easy to obtain in Alabama, so easy that many are held by legislators. The Governor, of course, distributes the commissions.

Even so, Lurleen Wallace must face some problems that have been building during her husband's administration. He pushed through a two-cents-a-can beer tax, raised the sales tax from three to four cents, doubled the cost of drivers' licenses, from $2.25 to $4.50. This heavy new taxation limits Mrs. Wallace's freedom to find new revenue.

Yet junior-college operating costs alone, it is estimated, will absorb the beer-tax revenues. The ambitious Wallace highway program demands a $25 million annual payroll, and another $15 million yearly for maintenance of existing roads. A seven-cents-per-gallon gasoline tax for highways brings in only about $30 million, so bond issues are necessary not just to build new routes but to operate and maintain the old ones. To keep paying for the bond issues, Mrs. Wallace may have to seek a higher gasoline tax, or push up the cost of the "Heart of Dixie" auto tags.

## HOW STRONG IS THE "MOVEMENT"?

THESE ARE MINOR annoyances, and no one—at least openly—predicts a decline in the Wallace popularity and power. In any case, despite his protestation that "there's no reason why somebody from

Alabama wouldn't make just as good a President as somebody from New York or maybe even Texas," it is not because of his liberal achievements as Governor or his state's prosperity that George Wallace is likely to be found in the Presidential race in 1968. Welfare politics, in which his record is creditable, is not what makes him such a formidable force in Alabama, the South, perhaps elsewhere. His willingness to spend money, build schools, construct highways, is not what endears him to the right wing in America, or to the "working class" in Gary, Indiana, and Baltimore, or to the police in Los Angeles and New York.

Nor is Wallace a national political figure because he is a blatant racist—as, for instance, Theodore Bilbo was. He seems to have the traditional Southern attitude toward Negroes—a mixture of contempt, distaste, amusement, affection, and appreciation for a valuable servant. And surely he did not win his share of the vote in those Northern primaries in 1964 because of any outstanding success in coping with the civil-rights movement in Alabama.

In fact, George Wallace's reputation as the man who "stood up for Alabama"—or for the South, or for America—although it is one of two major ingredients of his political fortune, has been built almost exclusively on defeat. It has been his genius—like that of the mysterious Big Brother of *1984,* who turned War into Peace—to make Defeat mean Triumph, Retreat mean Advance.

He "stood in the schoolhouse door," but the University of Alabama was integrated four hours later. In 1963, he used state troopers to block the desegregation of public schools, but Negro pupils ultimately enrolled. He once used state militiamen to stop federal marshals from serving a court order on him; the next day, he accepted the order. He resisted the federal government's school desegregation "guidelines" and caused his legislature to nullify them in Alabama; but even he does not expect the federal courts to allow this state action to stand.

From these dubious materials—from sheer defiance—Governor Wallace has built his "stand-up" reputation. He is, as Grover Hall suggested, "dauntless"—defying the federal government at every turn, without actually having stopped it. The psychological value of this exercise

*111*

in defeat has been enormous. "I guess George has showed 'em," a Montgomery man said. "He don't take nothing lying down, does he?"

Thus has the notion spread through Alabama that George Wallace has started a national "movement" that will reverse the twentieth-century course of federal government and restore to the South—and other states—the right to follow their old way of life.

The Governor and those around him share this view. They take credit for setting the example that led to Ronald Reagan's election in California, the defeat of the Police Review Board in New York, the demise of the 1966 civil-rights bill in Congress. Wallace believes that George P. Mahoney, the "white-backlash" candidate for Governor of Maryland, could have won if in the last days of his campaign he had not sought to dissociate himself from George Wallace.

Thus, the Wallace Presidential plans for 1968 are well advanced. He is planning a platform which will bear down heavily on "Constitutional government" and "law and order" but which also will have a farm plank, an attack on foreign aid, strong support for the war in Vietnam, and programs for assisting the sick, the old, and the needy.

He says he is "thinking more in terms of a third party" but also talks of entering some Democratic preferential primaries—notably California, where he believes the "movement" is strong. He will be in the race to win, he declares, but some of those who have long acquaintance with him are not sure he is all that mesmerized by the "movement."

They point out that if he can pick up some non-Southern delegates to go with those from Alabama, Mississippi, and a scattering from other Southern states, and that if he maintains his threat of a third-party candidacy, he could go to the 1968 Democratic National Convention in a powerful position to bargain about the platform and the party ticket.

Considering his showing in the three primaries in 1964, Wallace would scarcely have to argue that his third party might win just enough votes in some of the major states to change the outcome. ("Besides," he likes to say, "a man don't have to carry a state, he only needs a plurality in a three-man race to win the electoral votes.")

Still others think George Wallace's next move will not be for the Presidency at all but for the veteran Lister Hill's seat in the United States Senate in 1968. There are even those who believe he will hold back and run for the Governorship again in 1970, when he will be constitutionally eligible.

### SURVIVAL OF THE FITTEST

PART OF THE reasoning of those who think he will not really run for President is that the *prospect* of doing so is so much more valuable to him than the *fact* might be. The one thing George Wallace cannot afford, they reason, is to have the "movement" exposed as not so powerful after all, not so promising; if it were put to the test nationally and failed, then what would happen to Wallace's reputation as the man who is turning the tide because he "stood up for Alabama"?

Yet that reputation is not Little Stonewall's only political strength. As Grover Hall also pointed out, he "can read your insides quicker than any man I *ever saw.*" What he has really "stood up" for is the age-old streak of "practicality" and earthy common sense in mankind. *We got to get all this theory out of things.* Why should intellectual morons come into the God-fearing South and destroy its practical racial arrangements because they think they know more than ordinary folks? *What good are equal rights if it gets folks killed and ruins everything?* In Chicago, they resisted violently and got away with it. In Montgomery, they held back and were overrun. Violence and resistance, obviously, are practical, and it is only common sense that if policemen are to keep order they have to be violent. Even genteel George Wallace would really like to *smash one of these federal judges in the head and then burn the courthouse down.*

Thus, it is not so blatant a thing as racism, or even violence, but the old basic natural instincts of self-preservation, survival of the fittest, kill or be killed, that George Corley Wallace, Jr., appeals to in practical men, and he can be the ultimate demagogue not just because he is a spellbinding orator or a shrewd politician or a dauntless fighter but because he has recognized within himself, the prison of every man, the

truth that William Faulkner points to on the walls of the old city jail
in *Requiem for a Nun:*

> If you would peruse in unbroken—ay, overlapping—continuity the history of
> a community, look not in church registers and the courthouse records but
> beneath the successive layers of calcimine and creosote and whitewash on the walls
> of the jail, since only in that forcible carceration does man find the idleness in
> which to compose, in the gross and simple terms of his gross and simple lusts and
> yearnings, the gross and simple recapitulations of his gross and simple heart . . .

# RETURN TO VIETNAM

## (DECEMBER 1967)

## David Halberstam

*The reporter who won the Pulitzer Prize in 1964 for his brilliant dispatches tells why this bewildering war will not be won.*

ONE OF THE great exports of South Vietnam has always been American optimism, but this time I thought when I returned that it would be at least tempered; there would be an end of illusion, a knowledge perhaps of just how dark the tunnel really is. But we flew into Tan Son Nhut and the scenes were familiar: the jetliner waiting too long on the tarmac, its air conditioning off, then the waiting room with the American AID men come out to welcome their new arrivals and steer them past all the waiting Vietnamese at immigration. Finally I got through customs and Mert Perry, an old friend, five years here and one of the very best reporters in town, met me and assured me I was wrong: the illusions still exist. When you pay $30 billion a year you buy at least a fair share of illusions.

We drove downtown and checked into the American press office. Perry introduced me to Barry Zorthian, the chief press officer. While we were talking, Perry asked Zorthian: "Say, Barry, what's all this crap Komer [the chief of pacification, rank of Ambassador, six photos of Lyndon Johnson on his office wall] is putting out about the war being over in six months?"

Zorthian is a real pro, a very tough operator, and I think he has many changes of speed for different reporters. For people like Perry and me he didn't want that kind of optimism, he wanted it more controlled, an optimism that recognizes all the problems but triumphs anyway. "I don't think Bob said that . . . ," he began.

"No, goddamnit," Perry said. "He's told it to a couple friends of mine. Different friends. Six months."

Zorthian began again: "Well, what I think Bob meant is that the conventional war phase would be over in six months, you know. They've got one good campaign in them."

That night a group of us, experienced reporters here, went out to a restaurant in Cholon. The subject of the Komer-Zorthian quotes came up. Everyone boggled, and reminisced about the last campaign and its lineal antecedents: the *dernier quart d'heure* [for the French] . . . the corner being turned . . . home by Christmas 1965. Then one of the group picked up the inevitable box of toothpicks always in the Vietnamese restaurants and spilled them all over the table. "Each toothpick," he said, "represents one French or American spokesman who over the last twenty-one years has said they have one last campaign in them."

I have never been a dove or a hawk—few reporters who have spent any length of time here are. When I was here in 1962 and 1963 I belonged to a group of reporters who thought the war was worth winning but who doubted the effectiveness of the fight against the enemy and sensed the seed of failure in our own efforts. That group was roundly attacked by American officialdom for being too pessimistic, but in retrospect I think the great sin was that we were not pessimistic enough.

More than three years later, I still think the enemy is a real one. I think the evidence is more complete than ever that Hanoi has controlled this war since 1957, but now I doubt our capacity to win. The important things in talking about Vietnam now are: Can the war be won? Do we have the resources to win, and can we really afford these resources? People here now are talking about reorganizing the Vietnamese Army, just as they did six years ago. But it is very late here, the fabric is strained at home now, and what guarantee is there that the Vietnamese Army can be reorganized, or that it will make any difference? Can you have a fine young army in a rotting society?

The morality of this war has always been mutually ugly. We are waging a very tough war, and the enemy has waged a tough war on its own people since 1945, when Vo Nguyen Giap systematically murdered hundreds of non-Communist nationalists so that the choice for the Vietnamese would be the Vietminh or the French. So the questions have become more pragmatic than moral. "The only difference between Richard Russell and me," Senator Fulbright is reported to have said recently, "is that he thinks the war can be won." Or as Senator Symington said of both Fulbright and Russell, "They went into the woods separately and came out holding hands."

So is the war being won?

The answer is yes it is, and no it isn't. On those occasions when we can use our massive power, those rare instances when our main force units find their main force units, our power is decisive, and there is more often than not a victory.*

SIMILARLY IN THOSE areas which we choose to saturate with American troops, the Vietcong must move back, and in that specially protected, hothouse atmosphere a kind of pacification takes place. But the sense one finally gets is of the fragility of the situation rather than the permanence. It may be that to a particular American general, five months into his twelve months' tour, the progress of the war in his zone is a final and concrete entity, but to an experienced Indochina hand there is more hesitance. Progress at a given moment is a fleeting experience unless it is brought about by the deep-rooted desire of the

*The exception to this would be the area near the Demilitarized Zone, where we have repeated French mistakes and placed Marines in static outposts within artillery range of the North Vietnamese. There the Marines are taking a terrible pounding and quite heavy casualties from the enemy with very little hope of the situation changing. In effect we are giving away one of our greatest advantages—our mobility—and permitting them one they usually lack—artillery—in a sad repeat of history. Worse, the U.S. seems paralyzed by its own mistakes. Recently Westmoreland told Time magazine Con Thien was a "Dienbienphu in reverse."

Vietnamese peasants themselves. That is why I am so pessimistic, for the other war, the nation building, helping the Vietnamese to help themselves, has not changed.

There is no doubt that the arrival of half a million Americans here has brought considerable military progress to Vietnam. In 1965, ARVN (the Army of the Republic of South Vietnam) had been defeated and the country was the Vietcong's to take. The Americans instead came and have fought well. Even General Westmoreland's critics—and their number is increasing—praise him for the way he imposed a growing American commitment on a very weak base, maneuvered his troops, and staved off defeat.

Nor is there any doubt of the massive power we have accumulated here. The mind boggles at the firepower an infantry company possesses. If anything we may have too much firepower, and with it there may be too much of a tendency not to come to grips with the more subtle problems of the war. The Vietcong and the regular North Vietnamese units have been hurt, and at times hurt badly, although it would be a great mistake to underestimate, as Westerners traditionally have, the enemy's resilience and durability, his ability to recover from his wounds, and his *passion* to keep coming.

The Americans here talk a good deal about rooting out the Vietcong infrastructure, the invisible shadow government which is the Communist key to local success. Yet it is frankly admitted that the infrastructure has barely been touched. Thus while the enemy has lost bodies, it has not lost its apparatus, which is a very important distinction. Hence the real power of the Vietcong has not been affected.

The escalation of the war has escalated the pressure the Vietcong are putting on the population. They no longer have the luxury of working side by side with the peasants in the field, nor do they have the Ngo Dinh Diem government to help them with their own recruiting as in the old days. The VC are inflicting higher taxes on the population, recruiting boys at younger and younger ages. A friend of mine who has always been a dissenter from official optimism feels that the most striking change in the last two years has been the weakening of the Vietcong. "In 1963 and 1964 they controlled 50 percent of the population, and they did it while being liked," he said, "and now they are down to about twenty-five. The important thing, of course, is that the South Vietnamese government has not been able to move into the vacuum, there's been no real government pickup. But there's no doubt of the problems the VC face—a couple of years ago if I were a young Vietnamese boy I'd have gone with the VC, but now it's different. They're putting a lot of pressure on the population too. They've lost some of their mystique."

(It should be noted that this has been done at a very high price to the Vietnamese peasants. In the Delta, for instance, the Vietcong has been hurt, but not by an aggressive Vietnamese Army searching out and waiting at night for VC units, but rather by constant bombing and shelling of those villages not controlled by the government, so that finally life becomes unbearable. The people either drift out of the villages toward government-controlled areas, or sleep at night, not in their huts, but in the paddies themselves to escape the shelling. Thus they no longer welcome the Vietcong into their villages, and when they come into the government areas, they say, yes, we understand why you are shelling us, yes, we know it's the Vietcong's fault; but I have my doubts about what they really feel and what the final political outcome of this will be. In the past, methods such as this have come back to haunt us.)

Yet for that reason our task seems immense. If the mythmakers with the fine speeches—a Vietnamese war which can finally only be won by Vietnamese—are right, and I think they are, then anyone with a serious knowledge of this country must be more pessimistic than ever. For the easy way of building a nation is to rally behind a popular national figure. There was one rare chance when Diem fell and Duong Van Minh, the one truly popular figure in the South, took over. That missed chance is a landmark. Now if anything effective is going to be done, it will be the hard way.

The society is rotten, tired, and numb. It no longer cares. Twenty-one years of the war, of first the French and then Diem, have weakened the Vietnamese deeply. The sons are more corrupt than the fathers. The few patriots increasingly withdraw from the society and the struggle. The fine young men do not want to die in the U Minh forest; they want to drive their Hondas, get their draft deferments, and sit in the cafés. We are not building a nation.

BEFORE I CAME back I was assured again and again by people who had been in Vietnam more recently that I would never recognize it, that it was not the same country. The American presence was so great. And yes, there is Cam Ranh Bay, and the endless Long Binh military complex outside Saigon, trucks, generators, barracks, helicopters as far as the eye can see. There is American television, and one sees American troops still in combat gear watching *Combat,* and a blonde weather girl pointing at the map of the U.S. and saying "Los Angeles is clear and sunny . . . ," and most Vietnamese seem to have Batman T-shirts for their kids. And there is a strip of bars in Bien Hoa so long that one American there calls it Tijuana East, with sign after sign offering CAR WASH. (The Vietnamese are ingenious that way. One friend of mine has a song which goes, "Baby, won't you wash my car.") All these are signs of Americanization, but what finally struck me was how little had really changed here.

For it is the essential problems of this society that have not changed. They are the same problems, virtually insoluble, caused by the same terrible historical truths. The government of Vietnam is largely meaningless to its citizens. The rare good province chief or district chief is talked about avidly in the American Mission. (Perhaps Romney was sent to see him.) Yet it is a fact of life that most province and district chiefs are corrupt and incompetent. There is talk of improvement in the Vietnamese Army, yet it is widely known that ARVN is still poorly led and barely motivated. Its officers represent a microcosm of existing privilege in Vietnam. It does not change, per-haps because it cannot change and let in new blood—but unless it does it is dooming itself to its own defeat.

The pacification program, known periodically as The Other War, heir apparent to a long line of programs tried, programs vaunted, pro-grams praised, programs failed—*agrovilles,* strategic hamlets, spreading oil slicks, national priority areas—is a study in the past. At very best there is creeping pacification. Pacification, of course, is always difficult. The social and political problems which the Americans can avoid when they simply are fighting the war and killing VC suddenly reappear when we try to create something here.

There are Americans here who have become over the past five or six years good but bitter diagnosticians. They know the reasons the programs have failed in the past, and the best of them fear the same failures rising again out of the same causes. They are angry but powerless. The ones in the field are angry at the Americans in Saigon; Saigon does not get them any leverage. Perhaps Saigon is angry at the top Vietnamese, and privately shares the frustration of the field.

Yet the pressure from Washington is greater than ever, pressure which produces the optimism, coonskins, yes, coonskins, to be hunted and tacked to walls, and the sooner the better. Progress is reported here as certain as the tide, and the tide comes in each day at the exact hour of the daily press briefing.

The third day I was here I went to a briefing by a high pacification official. He began by saying that Quang Ngai province was going to be the success story of 1967, and to mark his words: *Quang Ngai.* Even as he was talking the Vietcong were walking into Quang Ngai and freeing twelve hundred prisoners from the jail there. He was saying *this* pacification program, his pacification program, was different from the other pacification programs, because this time we had the *resources.*

I thought to myself, My God, man, didn't they tell you about the strategic hamlet program, how the province chiefs used to choke to death on resources, how they were afraid to stand out on the little airstrips for fear of being buried alive by resources tumbling out of the sky: barbed wire, bricks, pigs, rat killers, pig fatteners, mosquito killers, snow plows? In those days I talked with one British expert on Malaya, and he said there was one thing which bothered him about this war: too much in the way of resources, too many material goods. He had never seen so much gear in his life, stuff going to rust and rot, being black-marketed, creating all the wrong attitudes in the Vietnamese.

The day after the briefing I was with one of the rural pacification workers, a competent American professional who had spent four years here. He recounted his past year: more of the same Vietnamese apathy, American indifference to his pleas, faking of provincial operations, increased corruption by his Vietnamese counterpart, resources not reaching their destination, his counterpart's interest in his own building business.

The American had documented it all, handed in his report, and for a brief time the job of his Vietnamese counterpart was in the balance, and then he was given it back. "I'm going to stay in this country until I see that son of a bitch in jail," the American said. "Pacification," he said, "what the hell is pacification? You find it." Then he added: "We are losing. We are going to lose. We deserve to lose."

THERE IS A reason for all these problems. It is not simple happenstance, although some Americans here think it is. One knowledgeable American colonel thinks it is just bad luck catching up with the Americans: we had fine commanders and leaders in World War II and Korea, and now we have fallen short in *American* leadership. If only Wesh or Taylor or Lodge had been a real leader, had really put the blowtorch to old Ky, made him get with our program and stay with it, things would be different.

There is much subsurface criticism of Westmoreland here, particularly among experienced Americans, because they feel in large part he has abdicated his responsibilities with the Vietnamese. The job was just too tough, and so he preferred to work with the Americans, which was natural enough. Push an American button and an American jumps; push a Vietnamese button and then push it again. And then again.

Certainly Westmoreland accepts too much at face value what the Vietnamese say they are doing, and he is too eager to impress on reporters his own debatable view of the quality of Vietnamese troops. But at this late hour he cannot make the Vietnamese do what they really don't want to do. And so because the Americans were easier to work with and because the problems were so immediate—imminent defeat—he worked with the Americans, and the situation of the Vietnamese military remained unchanged.

But the frustrations go so very deep. They are the product of the colonial era and the divisions brought about by the French-Indochina war, and to a much lesser degree the Diem era, both of which saw the destruction of anti-Communist nationalism. We are prisoners of that time now, more than we know. All of our failings, I think, are traced back to then. The enemy has had a revolution, and we, failing to have one, have tried to compensate for it piecemeal. But we have never really changed the order of the society. Rather, our presence, despite our words and our good intentions, has tended to confirm and strengthen the existing order.

The French-Indochina war divided this country in a more important way than the separation at the seventeenth parallel. In the process of driving the French out of Vietnam, the Vietminh—Communist-led and Communist-dominated—captured the nationalism of the country. They drove the white man out and they appealed to the highest aspirations of the best young Vietnamese of a whole generation. There was no choice; it was French or Vietminh. If later some of these same Vietnamese became disillusioned because of the dominance of the Communists, the apparatus and the system survived.

The Communists had not only driven out the French, and developed a new and cunning type of warfare, but had also brought the best men in their ranks to the fore. They offered hopes to the peasants, they released something latent and very powerful in the country, and they broke down petty divisions until finally that which united them was stronger than that which divided them.

One of the most telling stories from the first Indochina war is recounted in Jean Lartéguy's *The Centurions*. A French officer by the name of Glatigny, just overrun and defeated at Dienbienphu, sees his enemy counterpart for the first time:

NO CANVAS SHOES on his feet and his toes wriggled voluptuously in the warm mud of the shelter. Glatigny's reaction was that of a regular officer. He could not believe that this *nha que* squatting on his haunches and smoking foul tobacco was, like him, a battalion commander with the same rank and the same responsibilities as his own.

This was one of the officers of the 308th Division, the best unit in the People's Army. It was this peasant from the paddy fields who had beaten him, Glatigny, the descendant of one of the great military dynasties of the West, for whom war was a profession and the only purpose in life . . .

THE OTHER DAY I interviewed a Vietnamese lieutenant colonel who had recently defected. He came from a stock slightly above that of peasant. His father had been something of a low-level medicine man. Although he had been a Vietminh since 1945, he had spoken with a slightly different accent and dressed a little better than some of the others at first, and though he excelled in combat he was sure that his lack of true peasant origin had been held a little against him—perhaps if he had been a pure peasant, he said, he would be a general now . . .

Equally important in these years was what happened on our side. Our Vietnamese, by and large, had fought under the French. The enemy had revolutionaries; we had functionaries with functionary mentalities. Our high officers were former French corporals.

Things which divided men below the seventeenth parallel were far more powerful than the things which united them. The nearest enemy was the real one; the Communists were an enemy, but they were distant, and there were the French and then the Americans to hold them off.

Under Diem and for a long time afterwards no book could be published here which told at all about any Vietnamese struggle against the French. To this day, despite the talk of revolution, a Vietnamese who collaborated with the French can get a job with the Americans or his own government much more easily than anyone who had fought against the French but had become disillusioned. The Americans push hard for a Chieu Hoi center for defectors, but they admit privately it is almost impossible to integrate any ranking defector into the open society here on anything above a cab-driver level. The Army in the South, rather than having any national purpose, is riddled with intrigues and divisions.

I talked with another high-level defector, a major, and asked what he could do if given an ARVN battalion. "I could command a division in North Vietnam," he answered. "I have the ability to do that. But a platoon here, even a squad, I could not do that. What can you do? They have no purpose."

But if the troubles go back to the French, we can no longer blame them. When I was here in 1962 there was a tendency to blame everything on the French legacy of training, of tactics, of civil service. Now, however, we have been here long enough on our own. The French are a vanishing scapegoat.

Near Danang not too long ago one of the foremost figures of American television was talking to a tough little French female photographer. He started talking about an area where he saw some improvement since his last visit. No, she quickly disabused him, it was not good in that area, it was getting worse. So he discussed another area. Again she disabused him. Finally he raised his eyes to the sky and said, "Well, I guess the only answer then is to give the whole country back to the French." "No, no, monsieur," she said. "You sleep in your own shit."

One of the smartest Americans in the Embassy, spelling out the progress the Americans had made here since 1965—the dead VC, the improved security in certain areas—told me, "The VC are hurting and they're licking their wounds, real hurts and real wounds this time. This time we're really getting to them. The trouble is that every single thing that's taking place here is directly attributable to the presence of half a million Americans."

Was there anything local that was viable? I asked him.

"No," he said, "I don't think so. We can go into an area and improve the security. Pacify if you want to call it that. But then pull the American boots out of the area and it would go Red in a week."

RECENTLY THE AMERICAN Mission, realizing that among the longest suffering people in this country were the ARVN veterans, decided to do something to improve their morale and at the same time perhaps improve the society. The Mission decided to offer 120 four-year scholarships to colleges in the United States for deserving veterans, with a full English-language course thrown in. It was a widely praised idea in Mission circles, and no one really minded that it came from the Americans and not the Vietnamese. And the Vietnamese were enthusiastic.

The idea was taken to the Ministry of Education, which shortly presented the Americans with a list of 120 deserving veterans. Just by chance someone at the Mission checked out the list—Americans are learning to do that these days—and found that any relationship between those nominated and veterans was purely coincidental. All 120 were simply brothers, cousins, friends, creditors, debtors of people in the ministry.

Then the Americans went to veterans' groups themselves and advertised in the newspapers. Eventually the deserving recipients were found and chosen, and off they went to America. The Mission congratulated itself, both on the idea and on catching the fake list, and it was not until several weeks later that someone found out that each veteran had been forced to pay a bribe of 40,000 piastres (six months' pay at the very least) in order to get his passport so he could leave.

This corruption works from the top down, from the corps commander selling everything in his area, the corruption of venality, to the poor schoolteacher making only 1,400 piastres a month, selling questions and answers to exams to all of her students, making an additional 8,000 piastres a month—all to offset the terrible inflation, the corruption of survival. It is very bad and getting worse. Each day in the Vietnamese government and the Vietnamese Army it is a little more likely that if a position is any good it must be bought.

We have created a new class here, at a time when men are supposed to go out and die for their country. We are rewarding all the wrong values, the grafters, the black marketeers, the 20 percenters. There are some in the American Mission who believe that worrying about Asian corruption is naïve, that it is traditional, but I do not think this is true. One of the reasons for the success of the other side has been its relative lack of corruption. The corruption here has long since* passed the marginal phase and now dominates and indeed paralyzes the society. Unless it is checked and checked quickly and ruthlessly it is impossible to win this war.

Thieu and Ky are reportedly not corrupt, but they are propped up by men who are rank with corruption. They can fire one or two generals or province chiefs for corruption (usually men not of their cliques—who have been a little too blatant, or no longer useful), but although they talk articulately to the American Ambassador about what a serious problem it is, they have shown neither the capacity nor the desire to stop it or punish it. Perhaps this is because it goes beyond individuals into the system.

Cao Van Vien, chief of staff of the Vietnamese armed forces, a favorite of the Americans, and his wife, Madame Vien, are deeply involved in the system. In the resort city of Vung Tau, Madame Vien has exploited government land holdings and developed buildings which she rents to Americans at a total profit of 400,000 piastres, roughly $3,000, a month. In addition she has considerable property in Saigon, and manipulates government land on the Bien Hoa highway.

Recently a young American, a Vietnamese language officer, was with her and some local officials in Vung Tau. She was giving orders on how the distributorship for San Miguel beer would be handled. "What was so amazing," he said later, "was not the extent of her financial interest, which was very considerable, but the *flagrancy* of it—the absolute indifference to what we thought. She knew I spoke Vietnamese and she simply did not give a damn." (One high Mission official, when asked about her, said, "Well, she has been quite forceful and successful in her real-estate dealings.")

The province chief of Bien Hoa province, a former airborne officer, is a protégé of Vien's. Bien Hoa is one of the most profitable provinces

---

*Corruption has always been a problem here, as has American indifference to it. In 1963, when Marine Major General Victor Krulak was assigned by President Kennedy to find out whether or not the war was being won, he sent the American military command here a questionnaire with about sixty questions. One was: "Is there government corruption?" The answer: "To our knowledge there is not."

in the country for graft because the Americans at the Long Binh base use it for relaxation. The Americans there have tried to get the province chief on graft charges several times, but Vien has intervened for him. The Americans are now convinced that Madame Vien is sharing in the Bien Hoa profits.

BUT VIEN IS one of the better ones. The corps commanders are the worst, particularly in Two, Three, and Four Corps (there is too much fighting these days in the first corps area, near the Demilitarized Zone, for very much profiteering). They have become the new warlords of Vietnam, holding a certain balance of power which in the past has supported, or not supported, the government in Saigon. They buy and sell almost everything conceivable and a few things which are inconceivable.

They sell the province and district chiefs' jobs: up to 3 million piastres for a province chief's job; 1 million or more for a district chief's job, plus of course a monthly kickback, varying from 10,000 piastres a month to 10 percent of the chief's budget. A division commander's job may cost as much as 5 million piastres.

The profits vary. Smaller fry make money off what are known here as ghost soldiers, the 30 percent of a unit roll which does not exist— dead or never existed—but for which the commander still draws money. But the bigger men make the real money off the new construction wave. Everything that is built has its take, an immense percentage. Nothing can be done without bribery, and the bribes go to the highest officials in the region.

Then there are the vast amounts of material brought in by the Americans. The docks become a gold mine, as do the bars which the Americans frequent. One corps commander is the opium king. In the Delta there is massive taxation on the rice harvest, which slips out illegally to Cambodia while Vietnam imports most of its rice. Along the Cambodian border there is a thriving two-way illicit traffic—rice and beer going out, food, fish, and clothes coming in.

A division commander like Nguyen Van Minh in the 21st Division (lower Delta) will make an agreement at rice harvest time to share the profits on collected taxes with absentee landlords and thereupon launch operations for that purpose. He will share also in the profits of outgoing charcoal and of trucking beer and supplies into the area. Minh is the prototype of the new Vietnamese officer. He is very popular with the Americans, speaks good English, knows American staff styles, and is on the surface quite cooperative. In Saigon among the Americans his division is considered a good one. But in the area, provincial advisers who are not directly in his chain of command feel that he is vastly overrated and that his division does not pursue the Vietcong all that actively.

The province chiefs make theirs in construction (faked sealed bids, with Americans there to watch the surface honesty—one province chief even created his own proxy building company) and local smuggling. In Kien Phong and Chau Doc provinces, district chiefs along the border are so wealthy that they have to kick back at least 50,000 piastres a month to their superiors. The price for certifying that Cambodian fish is indigenous Vietnamese fish is 2 piastres a kilo, and since as much as 20,000 kilos may enter a day, the profits are very handsome indeed.

In Bien Hoa, typical of those provinces where there are large numbers of Americans, bars are big business: at Tet alone the province chief has made an estimated 10 million piastres from the bars. He gets an estimated kickback of 10,000 piastres a month from each bar and he periodically extorts more by threatening to open new ones. The Americans have documented his corruption, but so far he has managed to stay in power.

And this works down. The assistants to these men, assistant province chiefs and district chiefs, buy their jobs and then make the payoffs back by selling positions under them. The assistant district chief for security sells police jobs, and the police get their smaller payoffs at resource checkpoints or working the bars. Finally everyone is selling something: 5,000-piastre bribes to get a driver's license, 20,000 piastres to get a Honda out of the docks, 6,000 piastres to get a free place on a military aircraft, 50,000 piastres to get permission to have a job with the Americans.

Someone both honest and capable like General Nguyen Duc Thang, head of revolutionary development, is almost overwhelmed by this cynicism. He is trying to run an honest program, and corruption has become his favorite subject with visitors. An able Vietnamese friend of mine was offered a province in the Delta to run. He went there for a month and was told at the end of the month to kick in. He asked where he would find the money. That is your problem, the corps commander said. He immediately asked to be relieved. "It is very bad," he said. "If you are not one of them you become a threat to them and very dangerous." The handful of Americans who are fighting the massive corruption are numbed by the problem now. One of them told me, "You fight like hell to get someone removed, and most times you fail and you just make it worse than ever. And then on the occasions when you win, why hell, they give you someone just as bad who's a little more careful about it. I mean he's been warned about you, that you're a little smarter than the other long noses, and the guy you had relieved, why they promote *him.*"

There was for a time earlier this year an American Mission committee on corruption, but it met three times and has not met in six months. The problem is so delicate that it can only be handled by the very highest Americans, and indeed it is so delicate even there that it may not be discussed in the blunt and strong terms which it demands. A real attack on it, and real punishment, have yet to come, and there lingers among fair-minded Americans here a good deal of doubt that the government has either the desire or the capacity to take strong steps.

Right now there is some talk about a military reorganization which would strip the corps commanders of their power, and make the province chiefs responsible to the central government. If so, it would be a significant step. But as with many other things that are being talked of here, this reform has not come. The Ky government in the past has been more notable for words than deeds.

I have described this at length not just because the corruption is so serious and so corroding, but also because there is a new and growing Mission view of the war, a view which I think is the product of frustration in pacification and other nation-building programs. It says, in effect: military power will not win the war alone, and though the government is weak and indeed frequently venal, and ARVN is a myth, we Americans are doing so many things, so much gear is going into so many places, that relentlessly, almost in spite of ourselves, we are producing results.

"We are smothering them into victory," one very high official said. The failure of the past, this official added, was not just weak people and a weak policy, although that is now acknowledged. It was a lack of resources: 15,000 Americans and a half billion dollars a year simply weren't enough.

This is a philosophy that is at times quite well argued here, and it has the advantage of admitting the weakness of our Vietnamese. But I am not so sure: the failures of the past were deeply tied not so much to lack of resources—we always had more helicopters than the enemy—but to lack of leadership, motivation, unity. I am not sure but that the more resources we feed into this country, the more we weaken the fiber and the more we corrode our own Vietnamese.

WE FLEW OVER the southern part of Long An province. My guide, an experienced American here, pointed down to the strange scene: deserted pathways leading nowhere, mud paths leading up to shacks which barely existed, a few deserted huts still left. "You know what that is?" he asked. I shook my head.

"Strategic hamlets," he said. "All that's left. You can see the outlines of where they used to be, where they built up the mud for paths. Part of the scenic beauty of Long An. Vacant since November 3, 1963, the first day the new government said they could all go; they left. I'm not even sure they waited that long. Those that we controlled, that is, and that was damn few enough. Mass desertion. Funny people, they preferred their ancestors' ashes to our barbed wire."

I looked down and he was right, there they were. One could still see the traces of the paths, neatly laid out, neatly eroding, and it all came back to me, the visits to Long An, and the other provinces, the hamlet program, the *key* to success, making the population turn on the enemy, all those fine charts showing that we were way ahead of schedule, only X hamlets programmed and 3X completed.

In 1963, when Washington's confidence about the hamlets mounted and doubts mounted in the field, a young American civilian named Earl Young came down to take over Long An as province representative. Long An was allegedly almost completely government controlled; Young was appalled and quickly told Saigon that 80 percent of Long An was VC controlled and the war was virtually over in it. It was a report which jarred Saigon's sensitivities, and as a reward for this Paul Reveremanship a two-star American general tried to have Young fired.

Long An is not exactly typical; its problems are more serious, but they are not much more serious than in other areas. If we cannot make real progress in Long An, then we cannot win this country. The area touches on the Plain of Reeds on the west, a traditional VC bastion, and it has a long history of VC influence and government stupidity. Part of the population, says one American, does not have a Vietcong infrastructure. It is actually a Vietcong society, more than three generations of it.

What is astounding about Long An is that it sits just south of Saigon, virtually a suburb—500,000 people in a very rich province. It sat there and always got its resources, through 1963, but never got any more than some very distant province. Ambassador Lodge, having saved Earl Young his job, was unsettled by the idea of the VC controlling what amounted to his backyard. He made Long An a priority area. The 25th ARVN Division was brought down from the coastal region, and two of its regiments placed there with much heralding and exclamation. (There is still much exclamation about the 25th, not only that it may be the worst division in the Army, but the worst in any army.) But resources did not arrive, local officials were lethargic and unsure of their standing, and the 1964 priority failed to succeed.

Later in 1964 and 1965 Long An became a *hop tac* area, the spreading of oil slicks out from Saigon, the gradual driving back of the enemy. One American who was there said, "We knew what we wanted to do, but we couldn't get them to do it. There would be agreement, this was a priority operation and this or that program would be done, and they would nod and say yes, and then nothing would happen. You ask me why, I don't know why. If I had known why, I'd have been able to do something. So you'd send the word up to Saigon, and the top Americans there would say, 'Yes, look, we just talked to the Vietnamese about that problem and they're taking care of it—it's all okay.' And of course not a damn thing would happen."

In 1965, still almost completely Vietcong controlled, still squeezing Saigon, Long An was dubbed a National Priority Area. One American told me, "I don't know what happened to all the other national priority areas, but we couldn't cut it there. It was the same old goddamn story. You could tell the story of this country from Long An, like a dying man seeing his whole life flash before him. Their battalion commanders, peasants from the area who had everything to gain and nothing to lose if the VC won, had a rainbow waiting in this war. And up against them our little ARVN officers all from the upper or middle class, holding those damn baccalaureates, hating Long An a hell of a lot more than I ever did, with nothing to gain if there was a victory and a damn lot to lose down here, not wanting a bit to get wounded. So they tore us up when we went out. Most of the time the division advisers would be reporting how many operations they were on and all these things they were doing, and the troops wouldn't be doing anything at all, just sitting around and letting the VC have it free."

The National Priority Area never got off the ground there; Long An remained a particularly ugly sore. By late 1966 it remained as bad as ever (no American troops set foot there until September 1966) until by American estimates the VC controlled the entire rural province at night and all but 5 percent during the daytime. Bridges were out, ferries were out, yet another try was made.

American troops were sent into the area and Colonel Sam Wilson, then Lodge's Mission coordinator, left his high Saigon post to try and oversee all operations there. He was somewhat appalled by what he found: "The province chief and the district chiefs do things for the people as if it were some form of largess. If a district chief wants to build a marketplace it doesn't really matter whether the village wants it or needs it—that's what it gets." But the Wilson experiment, started with the best of intentions, floundered too. There was always some doubt over just how much control he had over the American military; and the Vietnamese military was always divided between the province chief's wishes and the division commander's whims. Finally neither high nor low goals were reached.

Now, in late 1967, Long An is somewhat better. There is what one American who knows the past failures calls "marginal improvement or even better under difficult conditions." A brigade and a half of American troops, in addition to two Vietnamese regiments, are operating there. The Americans, working the difficult terrain, are paying a high price but have hurt the tough Vietcong battalions in the area. Latest intelligence is that these battalions are at about 60 percent strength, which means that they are still quite effective fighting forces. Security is somewhat better and some areas have been opened up.

But the local officials are no better, the ARVN forces are as bad as ever, and knowledgeable Americans speak of progress in muted tones, knowing it can vanish the next day. In addition, the Americans here— as elsewhere in the Delta—are wary of areas where they think local forces have reached an accommodation with the enemy. One Vietnamese described it to me in Long An: "They sit there and make their gentlemen's agreements. The VC let our people know when they want to move and not too much happens. If the boss comes down from Tan An, the local commander lets the VC know and the province chief arrives. So everyone walks around freely and the chief tells the local man what a fine commander he is."

Long An is at least without illusions.

ONE OF THE smaller wars in Vietnam these days is the one taking place between the American military command and the American reporters over that most time-honored subject, the quality of the Vietnamese Army. To the military, they are constantly improving. To the reporters, nothing has changed. There is the same vast discrepancy between their statistics and their actual performances.

The other day an American officer from Three Corps, the area right above Saigon, was brought in to brief reporters on the ARVN units in his area. The briefing was standard: the officer patiently and politely went through his line about better leadership, better motivation, better morale. But the area is close to Saigon and most reporters have friends there; they listened in obvious disbelief. After the officer finished his briefing and was moving toward the door, one veteran reporter caught him and asked what could really be done to shape ARVN up. "Fire all three goddamn division commanders and two-thirds of the regimental commanders," he said, and walked out the door.

Yet there are some here who claim that we have one last chance in Vietnam. The history of Vietnam in recent years has been littered with last chances. One follows another faithfully. But, say men whose judgment I have respected in the past, this is another: we have all the material and we have just had an election, and perhaps now all the mistakes can be corrected. President Thieu will have the power he lacked before and we can get him to do these things which all his predecessors have failed to do. Thieu can use power; he can crush the little warlords.

Perhaps so, but one senses in Thieu a clever operator who will play it close to his vest. His ability to perform these late miracles is questionable. Give him six months, one very high American says. But what is it going to be at the end of it? Something dramatic—or just more statistics and briefings?

There are a few good things happening, friends of mine in our Mission say. At this writing, the National Assembly elections are stirring feelings never stirred here before. They are touching basic regional and factional feelings in this pluralistic society—and for the first time giving people a sense of representation in the government. These developments are certainly to be encouraged, for they might be the one thing which could save us in a political showdown with the Communists. But otherwise they amount to a very small plus in a very tired country.

They say also that there are changes within the Mission; the real dissenters are getting a better hearing in Mission councils than ever before. Yet there is little in what the Mission says, or thinks, to support this hope. I fear for the dissenters in the months ahead as the pressure for results intensifies; for that kind of pressure does not want to hear dissent or complicated answers. It wants reams of prepared statistical documents, and it most surely will get them.

AND THE ALTERNATIVE solutions?

Putting American and Vietnamese troops together into joint units, thereby improving the morale of the Vietnamese—where tried so far in this country it has worked . . . Giving the Americans complete command of Vietnamese forces, and giving them good American leadership . . . Forgetting about the Vietnamese and bringing out 1 million more American troops and do the job right.

But instead I have a sense that we are once again coming to a dead end in Indochina. We have in the past narrowly staved off defeat several times in the South. In 1954 at Geneva, in 1956 with Diem, in 1961 with the Taylor report and the beginning of the American buildup, in 1965 with the commitment of American combat troops. Each time we have averted defeat and grabbed victory out of the hands of Hanoi, but in doing it, we have always been forced to up the price of the game, we have increased the stakes, so that now we stand with the present frustrating situation, neither victory nor defeat, a half-million troops, a heavy bombing program, with the military wanting more troops and more bombing. Yet meanwhile we are more aware than ever of the frustrations of that particular war and of the strains that a commitment of half a million men places on our own society at home.

Or perhaps all the very best critics, such as the late Bernard Fall, will be proven wrong: you *can* gain a military victory without any decent political basis. You can simply grind out a terribly punishing war, year after year, using that immense American firepower, crushing the enemy and a good deal of the population, until finally there has been so much death and destruction that the enemy will stumble out of the forest, are stunned and numb as the rest of the Vietnamese people.

What would become of the country in this case I do not know. It could happen, but I doubt it. For though the highest Americans here have talked in terms of victory through a war of punishment and attrition, I have my doubts that we can win in a war of attrition. Attrition, after all, is not just a physical thing, it is a psychological state as well, and I wonder if they will fold first. Rather, the war is to them an immediate thing; it is their highest priority, their most important commitment, like the Israelis viewing the Arabs; they see it in terms of *survival*, while we are far away. We have our other fronts, other commitments, other priorities. We talk about this as a war of our national security, but we treat it as a war of luxury. Nothing shows this more than the casual way the war has been reported from Saigon to Washington, the willingness to pass on gentle fallacies instead of hard and cold truths. The general who tried to have Earl Young removed would, I am sure, give a very accurate report to Washington if the Vietcong were moving north from San Diego.

Perhaps. Perhaps. I do not think we are winning, and the reasons seem to me to be so basic that while I would like to believe my friends that there is a last chance opening up again in Vietnam, it seems to me a frail hope indeed. I do not think we are winning in any true sense, nor do I see any signs we are about to win. That is why this is such a sad story to write, for I share that special affection for the Vietnamese, and I would like to write that though the price is heavy it is worth it. I do not think our Vietnamese can win their half of the war, nor do I think we can win it for them. I think finally we will end up lowering our sights, encouraging our Vietnamese to talk to their Vietnamese, hoping somehow they can settle what we cannot. That is what this country longs for right now, and it may well be that even if we stay here another five years, it is all we will end up with anyway.

# Performing Arts
## FILMS: THE BIGGER THEY COME
### (JANUARY 1968)

## *Robert Kotlowitz*

STANLEY KRAMER'S *Guess Who's Coming to Dinner* is another of his Euclidean problems in human geometry, worked relentlessly through step-by-step to the last tear and the neat solution, both of which are designed to provide full satisfaction. The problem this time involves a liberal newspaper publisher and his wife—Spencer Tracy and Katharine Hepburn, lord and lady of all they survey in San Francisco—who have their liberal faith tested when their daughter brings home a Negro fiancé. The liberalism quickly weathers the test. The Negro, it turns out, is a world-famous expert on international hygiene problems and in terms of character he is a near-perfect mixture of Albert Schweitzer, Louis Pasteur, and Ralph Bunche, while looking like Sidney Poitier, who plays the role. Who could resist that? Only the fathers of the young Negro and his girl, it seems, both of whom recoil momentarily at the realistic projection of the troubles the couple will have to face.

The mothers have other ideas, however. One believes that sex should carry the day, although the young couple have so little physical contact—they barely touch throughout the film—that it is hard to believe in the passion everyone talks so much about. The other is romantically sure that her daughter's happiness will be her own. In the end, they carry the day. Only the Negro's father is left dubious and down-at-the-mouth, uncomfortably isolated from the crowd's opinion. His wife, in the meantime, has piously insinuated to everyone present, including a Monsignor of the Church, that her husband is, besides intransigent, something less than a man these days.

Working against all this, to put it mildly, is a credibility gap between what is happening in gorgeous Technicolor on the screen and what the audience knows is happening in pain and real blood in life. If miscegenation is a problem in our national life (and the movie sees it as a kind of summation of the entire racial situation), it is almost totally a middle-class problem. No doubt brilliant, gentle, and handsome Negro doctors will marry pretty, educated, and middle-class white girls in increasing numbers; and their parents will probably face the fears of Matt and Christina Drayton in settings just as expensive and fastidious. But one indication of the film's unreality is the curious possibility that it will have trouble being shown in both the South and in the Northern ghettos. In the South, where habit has bred a near-pathology on the subject, it will surface those ancient sexual anxieties about mixing the races; in the ghettos, where extremity has bred another kind of pathology, it can only insult its audience. I would not want to watch *Guess Who's Coming to Dinner* in a Watts or Harlem movie house, where it may well be stoned by young Negroes who know better about miscegenation.

The film is the last that Spencer Tracy made before he died, and his forthrightness and spunky conviction almost made me believe at moments in the Draytons' agony. He and Miss Hepburn glisten with style. They are crusty, tough, intelligent, and sentimental, the essence of Yankeeness. Without even holding hands, they manage to suggest that they have had a bracing physical life together. Their intimacy crackles on the screen, and it is their exchanges—snapping and barking and laughing at each other—that give the film its only reality.

Miss Hepburn's niece, Katharine Houghton, plays the Drayton daughter and makes her a ninny with shining eyes. Sidney Poitier seems slightly embarrassed by his role. The film's "plot" hinges on the necessity for him to announce to Spencer Tracy and Katharine

Hepburn that he will not marry their daughter without their unqualified approval. Without that ultimatum, of course, there is no suspense. Still, Poitier manages an emotional wallop in a rather cruel scene in which he reads his father off and puts him, once and for all, in his lower-middle-class place as a retired postman.

Everyone, in fact, has his set piece in *Guess Who's Coming to Dinner*, explosive speeches of varying lengths, pithy as the screenwriter, William Rose, could make them. The Draytons' cook makes an "uppity-nigger" speech to Sidney Poitier. Poitier's father complains about the 75,000 miles he walked on his mail beat in order to raise money for his son's education. His wife talks about his old-time sexual prowess and Katharine Hepburn speaks on maternal identification with children. In the end, Spencer Tracy, standing in the middle of his living room, ticks off everybody's position on the problem, then provides the solution. Everyone embraces: curtain.

It's a climax as static as the rest of the film, which has been set and directed in the boxed-in theater style of the Thirties. The action almost never moves out of the confines of the Drayton home, where someone is always remembering that he is wanted in the kitchen (or library or terrace) so that two other characters can be left alone to play out a scene. Everything in *Guess Who's Coming to Dinner* suggests the Thirties, when we liked our drama cut like crystal, with no edges left unhoned to disturb us. We must have believed then that we could cure the world by making it tidy.

# VIETNAM NOTEBOOK

## (APRIL 1968)

## *Ward S. Just*

ONCE EVERY TWO or three months General Westmoreland would summon the press corps regulars to his conference room at MACV (American Military Headquarters) for a progress report on the war. This would be the official version of the state of the war, and everyone made an effort to attend. These sessions had a startling similarity, which I have realized only after consulting my notes on the half-dozen or so that I attended. The General gave the order of battle, ours and theirs, and then went on to a discussion of strategy and tactics. It was not a discussion of Vietnamese strategy and tactics, but American strategy and tactics; sometimes Westmoreland would refer to the Free World Forces, sometimes to the Allies. But he meant the Americans. There was always a monsoon offensive, either just beginning in the highlands or just ending in the North (or the reverse), an enemy effort to "cut the country in half" (spoiled by American offensive maneuvers), an estimate of two or three enemy divisions in, over, or under the Demilitarized Zone, an improvement in the security around Saigon, equilibrium in the Delta. Captured documents showed the enemy was hurting. The Americans were on the offensive, the North Vietnamese and the Vietcong were on the defensive. But there was no sign of a break. Are there any questions?

Haltingly and diffidently, a correspondent would observe that the pattern did not seem much changed from the last time the General had met with the press. Westmoreland would pull himself to his full height of six feet one inch, pat the blouse of his immaculately starched fatigues, gaze at the correspondent through clear blue eyes, imperceptibly raise and jut out his jaw, and rumble the statistics his colonels had assembled for the occasion: enemy KIA, weapons captured, rice seized, *chieu hoi* defectors, documents purporting to show a decline in enemy morale. Occasionally a document would admit failure of this or that objective, and that too would be cited as evidence of success. The correspondent listened to the statistics, and never followed up the question. He would nod glumly and the General would ask if he had answered fully and frankly and the correspondent would say, Yes, he had.

So he had. It was a great and winning performance, and contributed materially to the generally good relations between the correspondents and the senior officers at MACV. Westmoreland's relations with the Saigon press were excellent, and he was never caught in a gaffe. He never predicted when the war would end, nor would he forecast the end of the beginning or the beginning of the end, or when the corner would be turned or if, indeed, there was a corner. He would only say (accurately, by the statistics) that there was progress, and imply that the more men he had the more progress he would make. But he was very careful about that. At the end of the briefing, Westmoreland would leave the room first, the press corps rising as a mark of respect.

A four-star general is a king among princes, and if the four-star looks and behaves as Westmoreland looked and behaved, he is a king among kings. He is not a man with whom to argue or trifle. Barry Zorthian, the USIS director in Saigon, was greatly amused at the feckless performance of the American press when dealing with Westmoreland. Zorthian contended that the press alternately protected and pampered the General, persistently refusing to tax him with embarrassing questions. He regarded the General as the foremost practitioner of the art of public relations in Saigon: Zorthian insisted that sophisticated correspondents laughed in his face when he gave precisely the same answers, with precisely the same statistics, that were received gravely and seriously when they came from Westmoreland.

Of course Zorthian was right. General Westmoreland was protected (if that is the word) precisely for the reason that he was unable to dissemble; he was so transparently honest and dedicated that no one thought of holding him accountable for the ambiguities and curiosities of American policy. It was all right to ask a colonel why the South Vietnamese Army refused to fight, but the same question asked of Westmoreland was phrased delicately and with circumlocutions:

Do you think, Sir, that the performance of ARVN has improved?

Answer: Definitely.

The same question, asked informally of a colonel, was put this way:

The ARVN 25th Division has killed only four Vietcong since last Thanksgiving. The division commander is both corrupt and a coward. Why is he not relieved?

Westmoreland was admired, both as a man and as a general, and my suspicion is that the press knew that he would have to dodge the question on the theory that no useful purpose could be served by candor. He had enough troubles with Vietnamese without adding to them by indiscretions in the press. It was a curious fact that however much critics, newspapermen and others, thought that Vietnam strategy was misguided or wrong, Westmoreland never took the blame for it. Neither did Ambassador Henry Cabot Lodge. The fault was found either at staff or at province, or most often in Washington. Administration critics inside the Embassy were dumbfounded that the Ambassador and the General were never called to account. I have never read a searching analysis of the Vietnam performance of either Westmoreland or Lodge, and I never expect to. It is not somehow writable, not now—and probably not even when all the returns are in. Until the future can be seen clearly, it is impossible to know whether the strategy inside the country (one specifically exempts the bombing of the North) was right or wrong. But even if that can be seen with any certainty, will it be possible to name the authors of the strategy? Were both the Ambassador and the General prisoners of events?

Was not everyone a prisoner of events, caught in a quagmire, watching the falling dominoes of increased commitment: money became aircraft, which in turn necessitated advisers who became battalions, then brigades, then divisions, then corps, until finally there were 500,000 men in the country with no one able to say how or why it happened? Inside the madhouse there was a logic, and the more time you spent in the field looking at dead men the more powerful the logic. And every time you talked to a general you were told that things were going very well—a reversal here and there, but generally going very well. They saw the valor, and from the valor victory.

One of the last great distinctions among men is between generals and everybody else. It is not a matter of money, for a full general's salary is still under $25,000 a year. There are certain perquisites, but these are insignificant compared with the expense accounts of successful corporation executives, to name the obvious parallel. Most of it has to do with command. Generals do not lead, they command; subordinates do not follow, they obey. Obedience is an unfamiliar word in the vocabulary of the 1960s, almost an anachronism in liberated America.

The typical general is white, Anglo-Saxon, Protestant, mid-fifties, Midwestern. Surprisingly, many are from the South, the only American region to retain a military tradition in families. His roots are middle-class; his politics, if any, conservative. His loyalties are no more complicated than those of most Americans with a similar background, save one important difference: a strong and emotional tie to the Armed Forces, and specifically to the unit to which he is attached (or commands). A lieutenant commands a platoon, a captain a company, a lieutenant colonel a battalion, a colonel a regiment or integrated brigade, a brigadier general an independent brigade, a major general a division, a lieutenant general a corps, and a full general an entire army. At any of these ranks, a man may be on another man's staff—but the objective is to secure one's own command. The distinction begins with the independent brigade. All military officers are subject to orders from above, but some are less subject than others. General officers, beginning with brigadiers, command independent units . . . which fight . . . other men.

There is no greater responsibility than a general's, and around it hovers a kind of mystique. There are a whole set of assumptions that go with being a general which are absent from politics, business, medicine, and corporate law. The first of these is that the general has gone through combat and is personally brave. Another is that he is smart enough and adroit enough to leave his fellows behind at that crucial point when a major is promoted to lieutenant colonel and, later, when the lieutenant colonel is promoted to full colonel. If there is a snag in the career chain, the wise officer opts out, and thus the second difference between the military profession and the others. The bright lawyer or motor company vice president, dissatisfied with company policies, resigns and goes to work for the opposition. In the American military, there is no opposition. Sam Rayburn, the late Speaker of the House of Representatives, had a maxim for incoming Congressmen: . . . To get along, go along. . . . It is equally true for the military services. Initiative can propel a man from captain to major, and sometimes from major to lieutenant colonel. But at that point caution commends itself. In the American military services, expressions of conventional wisdom are raised to the level of an art form.

The military staff system, short on initiative and long on efficiency, was devised for the management of a conventional war, where too much individual initiative was self-destructive. There, it was a matter of making certain that orders were executed fully and promptly with no slip-up, in a coordinated attack which might involve 40,000 men. In Vietnam, strategy and tactics were often improvised—with general officers sometimes overseeing (literally, from a helicopter 1,500 feet above the battle) the operations of a battalion or one or two companies. But even with the improvisations, many officers found it difficult to break the traditional molds of conventional warfare.

They were some of the most attractive men in Vietnam, from the old-shoe, rumpled, unshaven manner of Major General William R. Peers (commander of the 4th Infantry Division, and a practiced guerrilla fighter from World War II days in Burma) to central casting's spit-and-polish image of a modern major general, Jack Norton (commander of the 1st Cavalry Division, Airmobile). Westmoreland's father had been a small-town businessman; Norton's a colonel; and the father of the dour, aggressive, and feisty commander of the 1st Infantry Division, Major General William DePuy, a banker in North

Dakota. There was an open-shirted masculinity about dinner in a general's tent in An Khe that made it somehow preferable to the mixed tables in Saigon. Norton's general mess had a white cloth on the table and polite waiters passed large, dry martinis; there was camaraderie and storytelling, and Norton would always ask his guests to make short speeches. They were heckled, and one was reminded of a fraternity at college; except these were men who were fighting a war.

The generals talked of military tactics in their off-hours in precisely the manner of dedicated insurance executives arguing about premiums. But unlike the insurance man, the military man is ill at ease with outsiders, which is to say civilians. His attitude is either defensive or condescending, as if he had a special wisdom withheld from civilians; but all of it somehow understandable within the context of "the military." The perfect battle does not exist, and postmortems invariably reveal egregious errors. The wise journalist may laugh about his cloudy crystal ball, for he knows that nothing is written on stone tablets and no permanent harm done. But when a military operation is fouled, men die. When the logistics supply line clogs, it costs the taxpayer millions. It is difficult for military men to point out that error is inherent in any battle: They can say it among themselves, but not to outsiders. Such an admission requires a sense of irony and fatalism, and it is precisely these characteristics which are bred out of successful generals.

## AIR, ARTY, AND THE CIVILIANS

IN MAY OF 1966 battalions of the 1st Infantry Division were operating on the fringes of the sprawling Michelin rubber plantations, about fifty miles northwest of Saigon. It was in Binh Duong province. This was before the huge multidivision operations were assembled in War Zone C and the area called the Iron Triangle. These first operations were probes around the edges, to test enemy strength and to get a feel for the terrain. The plantation and the area around it was a bad place to work, first because it was saturated with Vietcong and second because it was filled with civilians, most of whom were sympathetic to the revolution. There were villages everywhere, and in the villages were children, women, old men—and guerrillas. The rules of engagement were less precise than they are now, but the general procedure was that if you were fired on, you could fire back. This was not a problem with small arms. Where the dilemma came was in deciding whether or not to use artillery and air strikes—air and arty, in the vernacular—when, how much, and where. The matter was often argued among the men on off-duty hours: You approach a village and receive rifle fire. You take casualties. You know that air and arty can wipe out the village. You also know there are women and children in the village. What do you do?

There was no solid answer, and no rule in the book to go by. Most infantry officers, if asked about it, would reply that their first duty was the safety of the men under their command. To ensure that safety most officers would take the village under artillery fire. When the village was flattened, the men could move through it in relative safety. The safety was still only relative because certainly some snipers would be left. The Vietcong knew the problems, and often deliberately fired at troops from villages, or fired at planes which flew too low over villages. The air or artillery barrage that followed usually killed enough civilians to embitter the community permanently against the Americans. Some officers knew this, and knew also that the disaffection of an entire community was not worth the handful of Vietcong that would be killed in a retaliation. So the argument was joined.

This was precisely the choice faced by a young battalion commander of the 1st Division one day that May. In the morning, two companies from the battalion were lifted by helicopter to a point just south of Thanh An village. The day before, the Vietnamese district chief asked that the village not be pre-struck with either air or artillery. The village was under the control of the Vietcong, but the district chief assured the Americans that there were friendly people inside.

This was before there was any trouble. The young battalion commander landed with the two companies and immediately ordered them to move out along a line of rubber trees toward the village. The first contact came when the point man of the lead squad spotted five Vietcong preparing a booby trap. Shots were exchanged and the five men fled into the bush toward Thanh An village.

From another position to the north, still some distance from the village, the commander of the second company saw the flash of a mortar. He moved his lead squads to the fringes of the village, received machine-gun fire, and withdrew. There were several wounded. "We didn't get too far," the battalion commander said later. "We stopped and returned the fire."

All of this sounds precise and a little sterile, as if the action were taking place on a parade ground or in a city park. In fact the geography of the villages near the Michelin plantation made them very difficult to fight in. There were clearings surrounded by rain forests, and thick cover was everywhere. The village was not a neat entity, like a city block, but a scattered collection of wooden and straw huts, which meandered out from a common center. The land was flat and filled with brush, so progress was slow and uncertain. It was difficult to know exactly where you were. In the case of the battalion commander, whose name was Hathaway, there was great difficulty in locating the lead squads. The mortars and arty could reach into the village with impunity. But for men to move in and occupy the village was a tricky and intricate business; it was dangerous. The terrain favored the enemy, and so did the position of the village. From time to time the infantrymen saw women and children hurrying on the footpaths that laced the area; it was obvious that when they returned to Thanh An they would give the guerrillas a detailed explanation of the American positions.

And there was the heat. Each man carried three hundred rounds of ammunition, food, three filled canteens, a pack, his six-pound rifle, usually two or three hand grenades, and other amenities meant to make life in the jungle tolerable. But the heat reached 120 degrees in that jungle. The infantryman would begin to sweat in a steady stream and then, without warning, dry up. When he stopped sweating, he dropped from heat exhaustion, retching, brain burning up, semi-conscious. When it was hottest, large red soldier ants would drop off the trees and onto the neck and shoulders, where they would chew the flesh. It is an impossible way to fight, and commanders learned that a battalion could not be kept in the field more than four or five days at a time. Too many men would be lost to the heat.

Hathaway was faced with the question of bringing artillery to bear. If the village was a typical Vietcong village, there would be reinforced bunkers made of concrete and wood under most of the houses. These were so carefully constructed that they could withstand anything but a direct hit. If the guerrillas followed true to form, they would withdraw at the first sign of an artillery barrage. If the artillery pattern were well laid, there was a fair chance of killing a few as they withdrew. If an air strike were brought in, the chances were better than fair. There was no question that the village was controlled and dominated by the Vietcong. It was not a matter of bombing peasants who had pledged themselves to the Saigon government, or the Americans. Hathaway knew that peasants in that part of Vietnam, particularly the women and children and elderly men, rarely undertook conscious political commitment. To his conscience they were civilians. Hathaway thought about the artillery and then decided against it. The cost of life would be too great. He decided to meet the Vietcong on its own terms.

His men advanced in the early morning, keeping low and moving steadily as they had been taught at the camps in the United States. They moved from house to hut down the narrow paths. They were hit from entrenched positions, as the guerrillas evacuated out the rear of the village, retreating before the Americans coming in the front. Vietcong leaflets were scattered everywhere, slogans in English painted on the walls:

Don't be a tool of the Wall Street warmongers.
American Yankee imperialists go home.

The advancing Americans found a tailor shop for manufacturing enemy uniforms, and a cache of sixty-eight weapons. Hathaway's troops moved slowly and carefully through the village, firing as they went, the VC retreating just ahead of them. As the Americans passed the houses, women and children emerged from the tunnels beneath. There was a tunnel beneath each house. At midafternoon the village was cleared in a final skirmish. A dozen armed men were seen to move through the high grass near a stream, mingle with civilians, then disappear. Hathaway lost fifteen men to gunshot wounds. There were no civilian casualties. More important, from the viewpoint of the division general staff, there were no Vietcong casualties. None. Not a single body was found. There was no evidence the guerrillas suffered a single wound.

The Americans were cut down as they advanced through the village. As they fell, medics applied morphine and helped them to the rear. Then medical evacuation helicopters flew them off to the field hospital. By dusk, the Americans had occupied the town of Thanh An.

It was just dusk when the assistant commander of the division, Brigadier General James H. Hollingsworth, arrived in his helicopter. Hollingsworth had heard of the fifteen wounded men and went immediately to Hathaway's command post. He was angry, and as he came out of the helicopter he had his helmet tucked under his arm and moved quickly and powerfully, swinging his arms like a college halfback. Captain Gerald Griffin, a veteran company commander, and now the operations officer of Hathaway's battalion, stood nearby, nervous and looking straight ahead. Hathaway and one of his staff majors watched Hollingsworth approach across the clearing.

There were a few pleasantries and then Hollingsworth asked how many men had been hit.

"The report isn't in, sir," Hathaway said.

"I heard on the radio that it was fifteen, and maybe more," Hollingsworth said.

"Well, they weren't KIA. They were wounded," Hathaway said.

"It was about fifteen wounded. We're getting the complete count now," said Griffin.

"That's a lot of wounded. Any KIA at all?"

"No KIA."

The general asked the lieutenant colonel what had happened, and Hathaway told him the story. "I didn't fire the artillery into the town. There were hundreds of them in there. We counted more than two hundred women and children, and fifty elderly men. I guess there were about a squad of VC. Twenty, maybe thirty of the bastards."

Hollingsworth nodded and said nothing. He still had the steel helmet tucked under his arm, football-style. He was looking at the ground, the toe of his boot describing a small circle in the dust.

"It was my decision to make," Hathaway told him, "and I elected not to do it."

"Well, you took some wounded," Hollingsworth said.

"Yes, sir," Hathaway said.

"And didn't get any VC."

"No, sir. Maybe if I had it to do over again, I'd do it differently." Hathaway was a tall, handsome career Army officer from somewhere in Virginia. Before he had come to Vietnam he had been in charge of assignments. He once remarked that if he didn't want to be in Vietnam, he wouldn't have been. Now he was nervous and standing ramrod straight before Hollingsworth.

The General patted Hathaway on the shoulder and made as if to go. He asked him if he had enough C rations and water for the night, and if ammunition was plentiful. The men in the clearing were digging in. The two officers stood for a minute saying nothing, looking out over the field and to the rain forest beyond. It was dark now and the battalion headquarters was battening down for the night. Hollingsworth grunted and said Jesus, he didn't know what he would have done in that situation. He thought that probably he would have brought in the arty, and the hell with the civilians. A military officer is responsible for his men in a war, and goddamnit it was a war. But it was a hell of a war. The General turned to Hathaway and patted him on the shoulder again and said he thought it was a decision no man should be forced to make. *No man should be forced to make that kind of choice.* What kind of enemy was it that hid behind women and children?

## MEATBALL, A GOOK DOG

WILLIAM TUOHY OF the *Los Angeles Times* and I came down to Danang from Dong Ha after covering the Marine assault into the Demilitarized Zone in May 1967. Danang, called Tourane by the French, was the nerve center of the I Corps military establishment, a seaport of narrow streets, indifferent buildings, and hostile population. Dong Ha was the forward Marine command post, the locus of seven full American battalions, a gray and uninviting collection of wooden barracks and canvas tents erected on an airstrip and radar station about fifteen miles south of the Ben Hai River, the muddy stream that separated North from South Vietnam. About five miles north of the camp was the celebrated "barrier," which looked from the air like a superhighway and was supposed to prevent infiltration south from the DMZ. It was surrounded with barbed wire seven miles inland from the sea, and guarded by Marines from bunkers along its edge.

The camp at Dong Ha had been built from practically nothing in mid-1966 to provide the base from which to attack North Vietnamese then entering in strength through the DMZ. The only relic of the old days, when Dong Ha was a radar station, was an Air Force officers' club, which served good Scotch and had sixteen Japanese slot machines. Dong Ha was the end of the world in South Vietnam, in summer hot and dusty and in winter cold and rainy. The scenes there, as the Marines dug in for the heaviest fighting of the war, were reminiscent of the trenches at Verdun or Passchendaele. When it was cold you could stand shivering at the end of the rutted and bumpy airstrip and look toward the North Vietnamese mountains, and west toward the mountains bordering Laos. Peasants continued to work the rice fields around the airstrip, and tiny three-wheeled Lambrettas bussed passengers from Hue, fifty miles to the south, to Gio Linh just below the zone. Gio Linh became important when the Marines decided to emplace .175 mm. guns to reach twenty miles into North Vietnam; then the North Vietnamese emplaced their own guns to reach to Gio Linh and Dong Ha, and there were artillery duels. It was a gray command, gray mud, houses, vehicles, weapons, aircraft, and men. It was a place to stay away from in the best of times, which spring and summer of 1967 were not.

Tuohy and I had been in Dong Ha to report on the battles near the zone, and had by luck been there when the Marines made their first ground assault into it. We arrived after the shooting was over, but there would be three bloody battles in two days, and it looked as if the campaign would continue. We were anxious to return to Saigon to write and file the stories. There was difficulty in getting a military flight to Tan Son Nhut, so on a hunch we went to Air Vietnam, the Vietnamese civilian airline which ran regular schedules between Danang and Saigon. At the end of the huge airfield there was a filthy terminal and we learned there would be a flight that afternoon. So we bought tickets and went into the bar and ordered a drink and sat back to wait the two hours.

It was hot in Danang and the heat brought out the flies, which collected on the sticky beer-stained table. The sun beat through the open windows in full shafts of light, making the room seem even dirtier than it was. There were Vietnamese civilians waiting, and they were seated at places around the windows, guarding children and small bundles and talking quietly. Four ceiling fans whirred and moved the air and the smell was of asphalt and oil and airplane fuel. Across the tarmac were the silver-colored unmarked aircraft of the CIA, ancient C-46s, C-47s, and DC-3s. Some of these same planes had seen duty in China in the 1930s, in Burma and Indochina during World War II, in Korea six years later, and now in Vietnam, Laos, and Thailand. They were the symbols of American involvement in Asia, and perhaps significantly, perhaps not, the Far East headquarters of Air America, the cover corporation which owned the aircraft, was said to be located in Taiwan. In one country the planes ferried troops, in another food, in a third money, in a fourth drugs. They dropped bulgar wheat and rice to the Montagnards in Vietnam, agents in the North, money in Laos, and weapons in Thailand. Many of the pilots had been in the Far East since the war, collecting danger pay and outrageous stories.

We were drinking beer and watching the planes on the tarmac when two young Marines, an infantryman and an MP, joined us and said they wanted to talk; both were drinking Seagram's whiskey and Coca-Cola and looked as though they had been sitting and drinking most of the afternoon. They were both about nineteen and, in their baggy fatigues, looked pudgy and out of shape.

The private asked us where we had been and when we said Dong Ha he brightened and said that was where he spent most of his time. He had been posted at Dong Ha and now he was going home to California. The private indicated his friend and said that he only had

155

three months to go, and that his job was guarding the two slow transports that took corpses from Danang to Saigon. The planes were loaded at night and he worked an eight-hour shift watching the bodies placed aboard the planes. The MP said nothing, sat slouched in his chair, and pulled quietly at the Seagram's and Coke.

The private talked a bit about Dong Ha and his six months there. He said a lot of men had died in and around the zone and the newspapers weren't reporting it. He himself would be twice dead were it not for his dog, Meatball. It had got so in Dong Ha that he would go nowhere without the dog; the entire country was controlled by the Communists (he said this in the same way that zealots speak of the "Red Menace" in America) and his only protection was the dog.

The problem was in getting the dog back to the United States. The Marines would not permit him to take the dog back because it was a Vietnamese dog, "a gook dog." The private had written to the Mayor of Los Angeles, where he lived, and the Governor of California, and the two California Senators, but had not received replies. Perhaps it was because he did not know the names of these officials. He had addressed the letter to the Governor simply:

Mr. Governor
California
USA
APO San Francisco 96243

since he figured the Governor, like everybody else, had an APO number to which letters were sent. Now he was drafting a letter to the President of the United States to secure a release for the dog; the story was so unusual that the President could not fail to respond. There was nothing very special in the breeding, the private said. It was just a mongrel Vietnamese dog.

This was all being said in a low, quiet way, between sips of Seagram's and Coke. The private was being very helpful in supplying specifics, and Tuohy was jotting notes; he thought there might be a story in it for the readers of the *Los Angeles Times:* "HOLLYWOOD GI BIDS HELP FOR HERO DOG."

The private was from Hollywood. The part about the hero dog

would come later. He gave Tuohy his street address, which sounded suburban and somehow typical of Southern California. It was a name like Wistful Vista or Twenty-Nine Palms. He said his father was a corporation executive in Los Angeles. The private went on to talk about the difficulty of writing letters to politicians who did not understand the war in Vietnam anyway. It was a disgrace. The trouble with the war was the politicians who ran it.

"We ought to go in there and end it," he said. "End the goddamned war with bombs."

"You know what?" the MP said. "The commandant of the Marine Corps doesn't give a damn what you think."

"It's all right," the private said. "I can have my own opinions."

The friend snorted. "And it doesn't make any difference."

"Well, at least they ought to take care of the dog."

"Tell us about the dog," Tuohy said.

The private was twisting a matchbook in his hand, and put it down and picked up his drink. Meatball was no ordinary gook dog, he said. For one thing, it was a dog that hated Vietnamese and loved Americans. "That dog loved us Marines and hated the gooks," the private said. "He hated the gooks and would do anything to get them; all he had to do was see a gook, and he would begin to growl; I had to restrain him, go around with him on a leash or he would attack." The dog knew about the Vietnamese because it was Vietnamese. "It takes one to know one," the private said.

The dog, in fact, was a hero of sorts. Twice he saved patrols from ambush. The first time, Meatball braved enemy fire to scurry back to the command post to bring forward bandoliers of ammunition; the second time he barked and disclosed the position of a sniper. For that he had been wounded. "Meatball can smell gooks a mile away," said the private. "When he smells them, he barks."

Tuohy wanted to hear more about the bandoliers and the wounding. The private ordered a Seagram's and Coke for himself and the MP, and two beers for Tuohy and me.

"We were pinned down under fire at night," the private said. "And I ran out of ammunition, and the dog went all the way back to the CP and got the bandoliers and brought them back. We had cleared out the gooks by then but Meatball was great. He got hit by some sort of fragment in the leg. He did a lot of crawling on his belly." The private had been staring across the room and I followed his eye. He was looking at a Vietnamese man who had an enormous growth on the back of his head. It was as big as a grapefruit. "Meatball is in the hospital now," the private went on, "with some sort of growth. It looks sort of like that gook over there." He pointed across the room.

He wanted to take the dog back to the United States but the authorities were forbidding it. He wanted to do it legally, no matter how many forms there were to fill out, or how many letters there were to write; you got used to red tape in the Marine Corps—"the right way, the wrong way, and the Marine Corps way," the private said. But if he could not, he would do it illegally. He would not leave Vietnam without the dog. You wouldn't either, if you knew how terrible life in Dong Ha was; the dog was what made it bearable. He began to talk after a while of life in Dong Ha, and what it was like on the patrols that moved out from camp at dusk and did not return until dawn.

You never knew where you were and you never knew where the enemy was. There was only the darkness and the rain forest, and the heat of the rice fields. The country looked the same from one field to another. He had patrolled the same fields, sometimes at night and sometimes during the day. It was dangerous either way. A booby trap would go off or a sniper kill or wound a man and the platoon would re-form into a careful unit. In the afternoon you would be listening to the Tijuana Brass on a transistor radio, and in the evening be scared to death in the middle of a rice field, watching the tree line and hoping nobody was there. In the morning you would be back with the Tijuana Brass. It was worse when the Vietnamese went along on the patrol, as scouts or in the combined action platoons. You never knew what was going to happen, or when. You never knew if the Vietnamese were going to desert, run back to their own lines, or perhaps work with the Vietcong. Maybe they were the Vietcong. None of the American troops spoke Vietnamese so you could never be sure what they were saying.

All of this was endurable with Meatball, the gook dog. Meatball, being a gook, knew all about gooks, could smell them and smoke them out wherever they were. When a patrol went out with gooks, Meatball went along as insurance.

"How did he get the name Meatball?"

"It's just a name," the private said, "like any name."

While the private talked, I watched the tarmac and now saw an ancient Dakota transport with Air Vietnam markings easing into a berth in front of the terminal. I walked outside and verified it was the plane for Saigon. It was brutally hot on the asphalt runway, and I paused under the wing to look over the field and its burden of jet fighters, four-engine transports, and at the far end a Pan American jet loading Marines bound for Rest and Recreation in Okinawa or home. One of the unmarked planes was being loaded with a mysterious cargo by its civilian crew. I was standing in the heat and looking at the planes when I felt a tap on my shoulder. It was the MP.

"You know I'm taking him to Saigon," the MP said, motioning to the terminal where the private was still talking with Tuohy.

I nodded and asked what the trouble was.

"Maybe you noticed that I am carrying a weapon, and he isn't."

I hadn't noticed, but it was true. The MP was carrying a .45 pistol without the clip. The private had no weapon. The MP smiled and said almost apologetically that the private was a loony, and had gotten loose in Danang and had gone to Dong Ha. He had disappeared for six weeks. No one knew what he had done in Dong Ha, how he had gotten there, and how he managed to evade the MPs. But he was found, arrested, and taken into custody. The private was a loony, the MP went on, a troublemaker. There was no dog named Meatball, and no letters to the Mayor of Los Angeles, the Governor of California, or the President of the United States.

"You better tell your friend this, before he writes it up for his newspaper," the MP said.

I said I was glad to know it, and thanked him.

"You don't have to worry about him or anything," he said. "He's not violent. He won't cause no trouble."

We went inside and the private was still talking about the dog and the difficulty of getting it to Los Angeles. He was telling the whole story over again. Tuohy was no longer taking notes, just sitting and listening to the private.

"You know something?" the MP said.

"No," the private said.

"The commandant doesn't give a damn about your dog, either."

"I know that," the private said.

"Well, why do you keep talking about it?"

The private shrugged and the MP said they were going. Everyone shook hands all around and wished luck. The two walked out of the airport bar very slowly, the MP behind and slightly to the rear of the private.

# ON AIDING AND ABETTING

## THE ANGUISH OF DRAFT COUNSELING
### (SEPTEMBER 1968)

## *Stephen Minot*

*Any person who . . . knowingly counsels, aids, or abets another
to refuse . . . service in the armed forces . . . shall be punished
by imprisonment for not more than five years or a fine of not
more than $10,000 or by both . . .*
—Universal Military Training and Service Act, Sec. 12

"I DON'T KNOW about that Supreme Being bit. I mean, like I haven't
seen my parish priest since I was about thirteen. He wasn't the type
you could sit down and talk with. Besides, I don't think anyone takes
all that straight anymore—not even my parents. But of course they
wouldn't say so. It's not something you could discuss with them. You
know, God's off bounds like sex and the drug scene. I remember once
during my senior year in high school Mother asked me why I hadn't
been to Mass for a year and I told her . . ."

The boy is talking too fast. It's his first session with me. He's sitting
between me and the afternoon sun, which comes in through dirty
windows. I am an assistant professor of English and am listening to
this kid tell me about his version of God and his parish priest and his
mother and I'm wondering, What the hell is a professor of English
doing with all this personal information? What kind of crazy system is

it that makes a student rehearse all this with me and then go on to testify before the five old men of his draft board and then be judged for sincerity and piety and sentenced to life or death? I'm wondering, What in hell is going on here?

"But I pray," he's telling me. "My parents don't know about that. They wouldn't understand. I mean, prayer to them is a social act. You know, a woman's got to have her best hat on, a man has to be in a suit and tie."

"What or whom do you pray *to*?" I ask, getting him back from the social commentary to the concern of the draft board. The question has to do with Series II on his Selective Service Form 150. He must answer the question, "Do you believe in a Supreme Being?" If he checks "No," he will be sent into the Army; if he checks "Yes" and defends his position to five old men, he may be allowed to serve two years in civilian work.

The boy is a pockmarked, crew-cut, nail-bitten specimen of manhood. He is the third counselee this afternoon and there are two more to come. It occurs to me that I have spent more time draft counseling today than I have teaching. I have spent more time listening to students today than I have to colleagues. I squirm in my seat and long for a cup of coffee in the faculty lounge and for casual conversation with some assistant professor about such major questions as the makeup of the curriculum committee or the identity of this year's commencement speaker. The lounge is well insulated against the sounds of the real world.

As the boy talks, he bends a paper clip back and forth and I wonder how long it will be before he breaks it. I am suddenly aware that he is quoting St. Thomas Aquinas. Good God, how many members of his board will have read Aquinas?

My mind wanders back to a Jewish student of mine who built an elaborate case for pacifism on the words of Spinoza. I would have given an A for the brief he presented to his board. It had sincerity and it had style and it was documented. I was six months younger then and I thought his statement was beautiful. But I should have known what would happen. The old men wouldn't even let him finish reading it. "Never mind all that," they told him in the middle of his oral presentation. "And who's this atheist professor of yours, this Spinoza?"

My student of the hour sits between me and the afternoon sun talking about Aquinas and I'm wondering if I should tell him about what another board did with Spinoza. Once again I'm walking that fence between optimism and realism.

"Can we say," I ask, "that your concern for moral values stems from your early religious training?"

"That's sort of a lie, isn't it?" He looks me in the eye and his pockmarked face is that of a contemporary. I have tried to move him too fast. I have given the hated parish priest of his childhood too good a rating. I wonder if I'm pushing the interview because I have two more students this afternoon, because I have a wife and two young boys waiting at home, because I'm thinking about a double Scotch on the rocks and some talk about the really important things in life like extending the lawn another fifty feet back into what is now woods to make room for baseball practice, and encouraging my wife to enter her paintings in a local art show.

"Is it really a lie?" I ask. "I mean, would you be here talking with me this afternoon if you hadn't been exposed to moral concerns at an early age?"

"I've got moral concern *in spite* of Father O'Brien."

"I think maybe there's a connection," I say—more for my own integrity than from any hope of convincing him. "How about the next question: Does your belief in a Supreme Being involve duties which are superior to those arising from any human relation?"

SO ONCE AGAIN I have failed to convince a student of what to me is an obvious cause-and-effect relation: The students who strike back hard against their parents or church are usually the ones who were convinced early in life that ethics are worth taking seriously. It will take, perhaps, two more sessions before this boy can see that his hawkish priest and militant parents were the ones from whom he, in the words of Form 150, "received the training and acquired the beliefs" that he now holds.

But we're on to his duty to the Supreme Being.

". . . so maybe I really don't understand their question," he's telling me. "I mean, like to me the Supreme Being is in all of us so it isn't a matter of duty to *Him* or *it* being above those arising from human relations, it's one and the same thing. I mean, that's the trouble with their theology."

*Their* theology? What an incredible thought. I sit up straight and look at this kid with new interest. The Selective Service has been defining a State Religion? Of course! All these medieval questions contain implied "right" or "wrong" responses in inquisitorial fashion. Put all the "right" responses together and you have what the state demands as minimal religious convictions. And the punishment for wrong convictions is ordeal by fire.

"I mean, to *their* way of thinking, God is up there and we're down here and in between . . ."

Disappointed, I realize he didn't mean the theology of the draft board. That was *my* theory. Once again I chastise myself for inventing sophomoric theories when I should be listening to him, for Chrissake. I'm as theory-prone as some of my too-intellectual students.

Last week (or was it last month?) a math major sitting in that same chair was telling me how filling out the SS 150 would in effect involve him in complicity since the SS (odd echo from *my* war) wanted above all else to keep things moving smoothly. Anything he did to conform with the law would aid them in their general purpose. They had already reclassified him I-A for failing to re-register as a student in the fall.

I'd heard the argument before, of course, but I hadn't *confronted* it. It was the difference between reading about "police action" and hearing an ash club strike a boy's skull.

He was long-haired, that one, a regular Prince Valiant; and in three years of college he'd earned all A's except for one B in, I think, economics.

His theory was tight and complex. Like chess. I've never mastered the game, but I can follow it.

"So you have two alternatives," I said to him.

"Three," he said to me. He was already two moves ahead of me. He had written off jail because "They'd probably kill me and then where would I be?" An interesting question, that. I begged him not to pursue it on my time.

"Second option is Canada," I reminded him.

"Can't do," he said simply. "I couldn't live abroad. This is my country. Know what I mean? Like I'm American. This is where I'm at."

I made a note to tell the American Legion that the next time they asked me to address the national convention.

"I'm taking the third option," he told me. "Taking it on the lam."

Being an English professor, I naturally wanted to play with *lam* and sacrificial *lambs,* and the pedant within me clawed to be let loose. But then I thought of this honors student grubbing it for the next five or ten years.

"Like a killer," I said. "On the run."

"Yeh, man, like a killer."


HE'S DROPPED OUT of sight now with his record of A's and one B and no degree and no address, and I recall his face now hesitantly, the way you resurrect friends who are dead.

But that was all weeks ago—perhaps months. I glance uneasily at the clock and realize that we are running twenty minutes behind. With two more conferences to go, I'll be late for supper. Another warmed-over meal. More apologies to the family. I try to steal a look at my engagement pad to see which ones are coming in—some take longer than others—but the kid has his eyes on my every move. I can't even yawn. There he is, still sitting there between me and the afternoon sun.

"Perhaps we can come back to that one," I say, and the seat of the chair suddenly feels hard at the prospect. "Let's tackle Number Five."

*Tackle?* Wrong verb. Number Five of Series II asks under what circumstances, if any, the applicants would use force. I listen to him begin with a tortured definition of force. I have heard several such that day and more than several that week. They always start abstract. I figure that if *I* can't make sense of them, what of the board?

They are not evil men, these board members, but they are busy with other things. They have not read recent court cases relating to classification appeals, and some of them are not even familiar with the draft laws themselves. A student of mine was told that he would have to be either a Quaker or a Seventh Day Adventist to apply as a conscientious objector, a limitation which didn't apply even twenty years ago. It is an awkward thing for a student to explain to his elders about the court cases which will affect his life. He must inform without appearing to lecture. He must make certain, for example, that they understand the Seeger case. That was in 1965 and the ruling held that "belief in a Supreme Being" is acceptable under the law if it "occupies a place . . . parallel to that filled by the orthodox belief in God of one who clearly qualifies for the exemption."

Whenever I review these cases my mind wanders in an undisciplined fashion, speculating on Roman courts which must have tangled with legal definitions of religious faith, and to Spanish courts centuries later.

Yet, oddly, it is not the medievalism which is the major threat facing this boy sitting here; it is the arbitrariness of the judgment which will be made of him. Here he is telling me about his view of the Supreme Being—or are we onto the use of force now?—and yet I know that his board will make its decision mainly on non-philosophical grounds: on what their quota is that month, on whether the newspaper that morning reported another draft-card burning, on whether the previous applicant was surly or polite. Dare I tell this boy that much of their judgment will also be based on what he looks like and how he sounds? He has, of course, won points by being white, short-haired, and having an accent which is still more city than college; but he will lose points if he doesn't put on a tie and a clean shirt. As a general rule, cleanliness is more meaningful to them than Aquinas or Spinoza.

When I'm tired, I brood about these men and their power. It is easy to think the worst of them. I have to remind myself that they are unpaid, that they are busy, and they are old. I remember one board which had to resign *en masse* when it was ruled that members couldn't serve after age seventy-five. Many were originally selected during *my* war—over twenty-five years ago now. Often they confuse the two wars or place all wars in a single category. It is difficult for many of them to understand why these young men can't respond unquestioningly, as most of us did when faced with the threat of Nazi Germany.

"So it seems to me," he's saying, "that one could practice *constraint* or *restraint* against those who are about to use *force* or *violence,* but the case of *coercion* is a more difficult one."

I AM ONLY half-listening to this parade of synonyms, but obviously I must hear him out. I have to remind myself that he is not just describing someone else's philosophy, he is constructing his own in my presence. He is trying to define himself. It occurs to me that some adults manage to get through a lifetime without being forced to tangle with the issues he is facing this afternoon.

Like this boy's parents, perhaps. Still, I don't know them and it would be unfair to prejudge them. Unfair and all too easy. Like the fraternity boy whose father was an Army career officer with thirty-one years of service behind him. I suffered preconfrontation pains with that boy for weeks—and with good cause—but of course it was not the pattern we had imagined. It was the mother in that case who went hysterical and used the ultimate weapon—charged her son with homosexuality. Shrieked it, in fact. This jolted the father into compassion, and the two men had a heart-to-heart with each other for the first time in their lives. How astounded they both must have been! And later the father wrote a letter to his boy's board. He didn't defend pacifism, of course, but he resoundingly defended his son in terms which sounded almost military—courage, honor, self-respect. The boy is now teaching in a ghetto school.

And will this one sitting before me now have the same opportunity? All I know is that I cannot predict. My gaze passes beyond this student and through the dirty, mullioned windows to the lawn outside where a group of three seniors spin a Frisbee in the spring air. The flying disk moves slowly, an easy target, I'm thinking, like a helicopter. The one nearest me, in a torn, dirty T-shirt and bare feet, makes a leap for the Frisbee and misses, falls, turning gracefully with a comic exaggeration like a stuntman on *Combat.* Somehow he makes one complete revolution forward before he lands on the grass and goes limp, sprawled out, arms and legs pointing in all directions. His classmates laugh.

"I don't really know what to say about force," my student is saying. "How can I tell? I mean, I've never been in a situation where I even had to hit a person. A shove, maybe." He tries a grin, perhaps wondering if counseling sessions can afford such luxuries.

"Never murdered a roommate?" I ask, wide-eyed.

But enough of that. The time has come for a shift of pace. I sit up in my seat and look at him hard. I feel my head clear.

"I'm going to ask you some specific questions," I say. The smile is miles behind us now. "I don't want long, philosophical answers. Not now. Tell me, what if Australia were attacked by China tomorrow morning? Would you fight?"

"Well, I guess not. I mean . . ."

"Why not?"

"I haven't seen a war solve anything. I guess that's why not. I mean, like we had to fight World War I and now we're fighting the Civil War over and . . ."

"Chinese troops land in San Francisco. Would you fight?"

"Why Chinese? Do you really think . . . ?"

"But *if*. Would you?"

"No." This comes out sharp. He's getting sore.

"Okay, now let's say you're married, happily married. And you have two kids." He stiffens. He understands that I have become the prosecutor. I'm playing dirty but he's not sure how to call foul. I'm fully awake as I always am at this phase of the interview. "You're in an isolated house in the country and three enemy soldiers break down your front door . . ."

"Oh, come on now . . ."

"You have a loaded revolver in your hand."

He opens his mouth in protest but closes it again. He looks up at the ceiling, trying to escape, and then back at me. "I'm not talking about *your* life," I remind him. "I'm asking you about this wife and these two children. The soldiers are moving in on you. What do you do? Don't

*168*

give me arguments—tell me what you'd *do*. You have to decide, you know. Even no action is a decision. So decide. Come on now."

"Damn it," he says like a pistol shot. "I'd do the wrong thing, that's what I'd do. I'd shoot. Hell yes, but don't you understand, *it would be the wrong thing.*"

I lean back in my seat, nodding, rubbing my aching eyes with both hands. You'll make it, I'm thinking, you'll make it. CO or Canada or jail or wherever, you'll make it.

"Enough for today," I say. I stand up and for some reason I'm grinning and he's standing and smiling back at me. There is, of course, nothing whatever to laugh about. That's the joke we share.

# CASTRO'S CUBA

## DRUMS, GUNS, AND THE NEW MAN

### (APRIL 1969)

## *John Corry*

*"It is no good," this report finds, "trying to romanticize the
revolution—one of the great crosses being thrust upon it by
young American radicals—but it is no good trying to dehumanize it either." For the revolution is remote from the fantasies of both its friends and foes abroad.*

THE FIRST THING about the Cuban revolution is Fidel Castro, who is
the Maximum Leader, Big Daddy, and the Old Spellbinder, and the
curious thing about him is not what he says or does but his style,
which means that he can get right in there, mix it up with his constituents, and hit them right where they live with rousers like, "No
fewer than 2,760 hectares of onions and 308 hectares of garlic will be
planted in Havana Province this year." This is a great heap of onions
and garlic, a hectare being 2.47 acres, but it does not seem enough to
awaken an audience, which is exactly what it did do, unless you realize
that in Cuba the punch lines are all different and that if you are truly
with the revolution, as they say, 308 hectares of nearly anything are a
big deal indeed. Consequently, to the bourgeoisie Fidel can sound stu-
pefyingly dull, and when he rose in Havana on January 2 to speak on
the tenth anniversary of what is always called "the triumph of the rev-

olution" he was full of snappy one-liners about sugarcane, tractors, and the nitrogen content of fertilizer. One government official said there were one million people in the Plaza of the Revolution to hear him that day, and one said there were 800,000, and some resident correspondents decided that 600,000 might be about right; no matter, it was a gigantic collection of Cubans, and they were there not because they were forced to, which is the conventional wisdom outside Cuba, but because Fidel, I think, with his onions, garlic, and one-liners, is their sign that the revolution is making it.

The Plaza is a big, open space, and at one end there is a statue of José Martí, Cuba's national hero, atop a sort of upside-down concrete bowl with steps and bleacher seats. It is one of the world's great places for a mass rally, and when Fidel speaks he stands with the statue looking over his left shoulder and dominates all those Cubans out there in front of him. From the side and slightly below, he is framed against the sky, looking the way Hubert Humphrey's ad agency must have wanted *him* to look in the last Presidential campaign, and it is impressive, especially if your peripheral vision is good enough to take in Fidel and his constituents at the same time. The constituents face Fidel, and at their backs, ringing the Plaza, are three big office buildings, their whole walls given over to giant revolutionary murals. There is Che in one, with his famous dictum, "To create two, three, many Vietnams," which, when you think of it, is in consummate bad taste, and there are Fidel and Che in another, looking heroic and determined and revolutionary. What saves the murals is that they are pastels, and they are gay, and it is pleasant to see a couple of guerrilla leaders done up in pansy colors. There is a lot of this kind of thing in Cuba, wherein bongo drums or something always seem to be getting mixed in with the tommy guns, and it makes the revolutionary zeal and revolutionary ardor easier to take.

The crowd in the Plaza that day had begun collecting itself before dawn, the first arrivals being the rural people who are Fidel's truest and best constituents, and it stood in a great, patient mass, not making much noise and not doing much of anything except communing on itself and waiting. The first distinguished guest to arrive was the

Chinese Ambassador, who wore a floppy fedora and looked inscrutable, and the second, beaten by about three minutes, was the Soviet Ambassador, who was also looking inscrutable, and who did not speak to the Chinese Ambassador. Meanwhile, some young New Yorkers, members of what is loosely called the New Left, were raising a homemade banner, "North Americans with Cuba," which neatly blotted out the view of the foreign military attachés who were sitting behind them. Suddenly, there was applause, some shouts, and all the constituents began to wave their flags and placards. Fidel, materializing from out of nowhere, was making his way through the distinguished guests to the lectern. ("Actually," a wiseacre said, "they're applauding because he showed up on time.") Somewhere, artillery charges were being set off, and the noise was echoing and reverberating through the Plaza, and the national anthem was being played over the loudspeakers, and Cubans everywhere were sucking in their paunches and standing at attention.

When Fidel spoke he got into it right away, stowing his gunbelt in the lectern and not wasting much time acknowledging the cheers. The effect, then, was of great urgency, and he got his first applause when he said there would be no military parade on this anniversary because a parade would waste motor fuel and keep people away from work longer than was good for them. An instant later he got his first laughs when he said that this marked the beginning of a year that would be eighteen months long. "Have you ever heard of anything so screwy?" a diplomat remarked the next day, and the hell of it was that Fidel was absolutely serious, and the people knew it, and there they were applauding anyway. "This year we have to complete the 1969 harvest and carry out part of the 1970 one," he said. (Applause.) "Thus, we have to work in two harvests. Next year, the traditional year, that is, next December, and quite probably next January second, it is quite possible that we will not be able to gather here in this Plaza since a great many of us in this country will be out in the fields cutting sugarcane." (Applause.) "Thus, the next New Year will probably be celebrated on July first, while the next Christmas will be celebrated between the first and twenty-sixth of July." (Applause.)

The diplomat was right; it was absolutely screwy, and there was no way of telling if all that the constituents were really thinking was, "Dear God, this guy is nuts," or whether, in fact, they thought it was a smashing idea. I do not think the Old Spellbinder knew either, but he acted as if he did, and acting as if you know something is 90 percent of the battle when you run a revolution. Therefore Fidel went on, unrolling his statistics, sometimes waggling the fingers of his left hand in and out of his beard, and occasionally, very occasionally, ranting. From New York, or Washington, or Waterloo, Iowa, Fidel looks like the last of the great ranters. Mostly, I think, this has something to do with that scraggly beard, and the army fatigues, and his being naturally windy. Up close he sounds better. When he ranted on January 2, jerking his body, tossing his head, it was over things that mattered. "When 80 or 90 percent of a country's children don't drink milk, then fifty thousand cows suffice to provide for all the children who do drink milk," he said, ranting spectacularly about what things were supposed to be like in the old days, and also explaining why Cuba now needed a few million more cows. Fidel is hardly kindness itself, he is certainly graced with a monumental ego, and he is probably capable of great cruelty. Still, along with so much of what is Cuban and Communist, he robs himself of his own menace. While he was speaking some children were popping up in the visitors' section, just about under his nose, and when one threatened to wet himself a soldier with about a four-pound automatic on his hip hoisted him up and carried him off to the can. It is no good trying to romanticize the revolution—one of the great crosses being thrust upon it by young American radicals—but it is no good trying to dehumanize it either. Children in Cuba threaten to wet themselves, even under Fidel's nose.

All the while Fidel was speaking, the sun kept moving in and out of the clouds, the edges of the crowd kept in constant motion, and people kept passing out in the Plaza. (It is nearly a Cuban commonplace to see someone being handed over the heads of a crowd to the stretcher-bearers.) Soon, Fidel was listening to the voice of the people, or acting as if he were, and then he and they were off together on one of the slightly mad roundelays that are supposed to be the true participatory democracy. "It is necessary for us to adopt measures of self-control this year, or to limit the consumption of sugar to a rational amount," he was saying, and as the thought got through some people started to clap. "If you agree, well, let's see: The best thing would be to set a rational limit this year that is still more than what the people need. Let's say a little more in the countryside, a little less in the cities, but a limit that amounts to what is really consumed, more even than is really consumed, to save those 200,000 tons of sugar."

That was the opener, and then came the question: "If you agree on six pounds, for example, in the capital . . ." Someone, at least, agreed and started to clap, and Fidel pressed on. "Is six pounds per capita per month enough?"

While it did not seem as if Fidel were winning much of a majority, there were shouts nonetheless. "Let's see, is six pounds enough here?" (*Let's hear it for six pounds, folks.*) More shouts, more clapping. "Do you agree that this will be enough?" (*Now this time let's really hear it for six pounds.*) A little more shouting, a little more clapping. "We could make it a little higher in the interior—in Las Villas, Camagüey, and Oriente. . . . If it's all right with you, this measure will go into effect beginning tomorrow." The next day the official transcript said the Old Spellbinder had carried the day then with SHOUTS AND PROLONGED APPLAUSE, which presumably meant a clear majority was in on it. It was not quite so, and there are infinitely more SHOUTS AND PROLONGED APPLAUSE when the favorite comes up two lengths to the good in nearly any race at Aqueduct. Still, I do not know if that matters much, and if you are with the revolution, as they say, it does not matter at all.

The world press was little represented at all this, and this was a pity because it was a fine show. There was no one from a major American daily, for instance, although there was a big clutch of photographers from nearly everywhere else. Indeed, when Fidel and his little band were trudging through the mountains and harassing Batista there must have been a great many photographers around because there are now a great many photographs of Fidel trudging through the mountains. Along with posters, the Cuban graphic arts being more or less spectacular, photographs of revolutionary leaders make up most of the interior and exterior decorations, and it is far easier to get a Communist to pose than to make a statement. About midway through his speech in the Plaza the first of a couple of Cuban photographers got near enough to Fidel for some in-close work, and then the man from *Life* magazine, and then one or two others, and then inexplicably it was decided to stop any more photographers who wanted to get there. In Cuba the people who stop you from getting places usually have sidearms, or maybe a Czech automatic rifle. This does not mean much, since weapons have a way of becoming nearly invisible when there are so many of them around, but they do show a certain earnestness on the part of the people who carry them. Nevertheless, there was a fine American blonde taking pictures that day, and the fine American blonde, who wore a miniskirt and carried a camera with a defective shutter, walked through the armed guards and began taking pictures about six inches from the Maximum Leader. This annoyed Raúl Castro, who is, among other things, the commander in chief of the army, and he passed the word that those guards had damn well better shape up. There is clearly a profitable lesson to be learned here about militarism, blondes, and the revolution, but the decent thing to do is to let it pass.

WHEN FIDEL IS not speaking to the people he is visiting them. He is, in fact, the constant visitor, swooping off to isolated cane fields in his helicopter, or jumping from his maroon Alfa Romeo, security men trailing behind, to talk to college students. Sartre, who was enchanted by it, once described a mawkish scene in which Fidel confronted a little girl who was selling orange juice. Why, Fidel asked, is the orange juice so warm? Because, the little girl said, the refrigerator is kaput. Tell your superiors to fix it, the great man said, or else they will hear from me. Fidel probably was conning Sartre, but that may be beside the point. The point is what the little girl thought, and she almost certainly thought it was just great. Life in Cuba is hard, hard, hard, and Fidel is the walking promise that things will be better, and when you make over a nation, which is what they are doing, you are dead unless you have big beliefs. Consequently, there is a lot of talk in Cuba about building a "new man," and while no one can build a new man save God, who is probably busy elsewhere, the point here is that some Cubans think they will.

"Our main hope is that youth follow the pattern set by Che," the Communist functionary said. This was a secretary of the Union of Young Communists, and the secretary, who looked like a teenybopper but was really twenty-one, said that "to be like Che" meant, of course, "to be like Che." And the new man? "It doesn't really need an explanation," she said (whereupon some Cuban hangers-on cheered), "but I will tell you. The new man will be like Che. He will overcome national barriers, be ready to do his duty at any time. He will be—like Che—an example of internationalism, wishing all for the people and nothing for himself." Then she smiled, and shrugged, and looked as if she knew a marvelous secret. This was at a place called Sandino, which was built after the revolution to house counterrevolutionaries. Its first occupants were families from the Escambray Mountains, who, the Cubans say, had been mobilized into counterrevolutionary guerrilla bands by the Central Intelligence Agency in 1959, before being put out of business by the new Cuban army in 1961. Subsequently, the leaders of the bands were executed, but their followers, poor peasants mostly, were taken to Havana, given some rudimentary training in reading, writing, and revolutionary consciousness, and then resettled in Sandino. They work the crops there, and since Sandino and its 756 houses looks pretty much like any other new Cuban town, utilitarian and slightly unfinished, the old counterrevolutionaries presumably live like other people, even though they cannot travel without special permission of the Ministry of the Interior. Cuba is more humane in treating its counterrevolutionaries than you might expect, and there is a feeling, even among Cubans who don't like him, that Fidel doesn't shoot people for saying bad things about him. Nonetheless, you can be shot for *doing* something bad, and *doing* something bad, as opposed to *saying* something bad, seems to be what separates counterrevolutionary from merely antisocial behavior. Last fall, for example, word leaked out from one of the provinces that a couple of men had been shot for burning down, or trying to burn down, a warehouse. This was at about the same time that Fidel, in a speech in Havana, which got prolonged applause, said that "before the revolution ceases to be, not one counterrevolutionary will remain with his head on his shoulders."

A GOVERNMENT MAN guessed that there might now be 200 political prisoners stuck away in jails, and a non-Communist source, who is supposed to be up on these things, said he guessed there were 15,000 to 20,000 persons in enclosed prisons, with perhaps 30,000 political prisoners working in farms or camps. He also said, however, that his figures might be out of date, and I suspect that they were far too high, just as the government man's were too low. It is generally accepted, even among the people who don't care for the government, that, except for a few of the real hard rocks, all political prisoners have been offered a chance at rehabilitation. This means a job on a farm or in a camp, with possibly a later passage to normal life. Not too long ago, however, it became known that Huber Matos, probably Cuba's most famous political prisoner, was alive and well in La Cabaña, the old fortress on Havana harbor. Matos was a major in Fidel's guerrilla forces, and in that first year of victory after Batista had fled he was accused of treason, arrested the same day, and packed off to prison. This was at a time when Cuba was full of rumors of plots and counterplots, and Matos, who was supposed to be wildly popular among the people, apparently had protested too loudly about the rising Communist influence. Now he sits in La Cabaña, one of about eighty incorrigibles, I was told, who swear everlasting enmity to Fidel, don't want to be rehabilitated, and brood together over the injustices of the revolution. The other thing I know about La Cabaña is that a lady who periodically visits there stops off at the foreign embassies and cadges magazines for the prisoners, and that now the only place in Havana to get a back issue of *Time,* say, or *Punch,* is in that jail.

Havana, though, is not where the revolution is. Havana is running down like a tired clock, and it is a little shabby, and the government doesn't seem to mind at all. The fruits of the revolution are in the country and the small towns. Havana always had it pretty good, even before the revolution, and now Fidel and his people show less interest in it than they do in other places. Pound for pound, there are more counterrevolutionaries, antisocial types, and people who are just not with the revolution in Havana than anywhere else, and the best information is that there have been four assassination attempts on Fidel's life, and that all were made in Havana. Still, while it is a convention to write about the city as being sad and shabby, and its people as being dull and dispirited, it is a little less than the truth. There are long queues there for virtually everything, for the little that is sold in the stores, for bus tickets, for reservations in a restaurant, and nothing in Havana works quite the way it should. The power fails, and the lights go off. The water pressure fails, and the toilet won't flush. It is not the same city in which John Payne romanced Alice Faye in *Weekend in Havana* (of course it never was) and it is certainly not the same city that attracted tired Americans to its fancy cathouses.

True, there is a bit of this left, but vice in Havana is now amateurish, with the old pros having been run off the streets and the slack being taken up by thin, reedy girls or short, dumpy girls who say they are actresses or dancers and who prefer just going to a better restaurant with foreigners than really trying to make money. Even the number of *posadas* in Havana has declined in the last year from twenty-five to twelve, and *posadas,* which are where couples go to make love, are one of the last places for conventional pleasures. They are hotels or motels, the price being $3.50 for the first three hours and 50 cents for each additional hour, and the government is supposed to give you a pair of paper slippers when you get in so you will feel at home. On Friday and Saturday nights there are queues outside the *posadas,* and some of them are managed by men who look the way night clerks look outside the Brooklyn Navy Yard. Nonetheless, there are queues, proving that flesh cannot be consistently mortified, even under Communism.

One night in old Havana, which still looks exactly the way Graham Greene said it did, except that now it has pictures of Fidel, the fine American blonde and I were invited into a house party. It was held in a dark, dismal courtyard, and there was only one sad bottle of rum, but it was a party, and the people at least looked as if they were having a good time. And one night when there was music from somewhere I joined a bunch of men who were dancing in the street, strutting and shuffling for no one other than themselves, and doing it with great style, and proving that, yes indeed, Cubans really do have a natural sense of rhythm. Private pleasures are still the best pleasures in Cuba, and when the government raises its big red star over them they can become something else. On New Year's Eve the government reopened the Tropicana, which is an old gambling hall, and the kind of big, open-air nightclub that would have driven Busby Berkeley crazy with desire. There are trees and bushes all over the Tropicana, and midway through dinner there was a fanfare from a band that was planted in the foliage. Then a light fell on the densest part of that jungle, and there, rising high into the night on a revolving platform, was a Negro in a sequin jacket, playing a polonaise on a baby grand. By the time he was nearly out of sight there were people popping out all over that forest, with the last two being a couple of comedians, one of whom hit the other with a bladder.

THIS, REMEMBER, WAS in an underdeveloped country where you win salvation by hard work, and where the beau ideals wear beards and are always shown staring off into the distance. Nothing at the Tropicana made a bit of sense, unless you understood that in Cuba the economic and political revolution is one thing but that the social and psychological revolution, which is what the Cubans talk about the most, is something else again. When Fidel defended the Soviet invasion of Czechoslovakia he did so partly by saying there was something cancerous in Prague, and that it was as elusive as subliminal advertising and as real as the pennants outside a used-car lot. Here we interrupt him midway:

"The imperialists are carrying out a campaign, not only in Czechoslovakia, but in all the countries of Eastern Europe, even in the Soviet Union. They are trying in every way to conduct a publicity campaign in favor of the way of life of developed industrial society, in favor of the tastes and the consumer habits of the developed bourgeois societies. . . . And they exploit—they do it everywhere—their kitchen equipment and appliances, their cars, their refrigerators, their laces and their luxury of all kinds."

And here, offering somewhat the same thought, is Dr. Osvaldo Dorticós Torrado, the President of Cuba, speaking before a congress of intellectuals in Havana:

"That is why, when we speak of culture and the masses, we understand it not in the sense in which it is understood by the capitalists—that is, as culture aimed at satisfying pseudoaesthetic, cheap, and ignoble appetites of the masses in a gregarious sense, a dehumanized sense . . ."

And so on.

Fidel and Dorticós were saying that bourgeois depravity is a threat to the revolution, and they were right; but there is a lot of it around, and it is far harder to lick than the CIA, or the blockade, or even some of Mr. Nixon's windier statements. When all other things have failed, it may in fact do in the revolution in the end. No one can hate the Cuban government and all its works like a Cuban émigré, and when an émigré sends a color photograph of himself and the wife and kids back to the folks in Cuba, he most always seems to have them posed on a nice long sofa, next to the big TV set, or else in front of the nearly new Chevy, right next to the carport. There is a small cruelty in this, but war is war, and the point is to win. Bourgeois taste dies hard, surviving in the most revolutionary of societies, and it can make you laugh fit to die, or maybe to cry, when young American and European revolutionaries confront the real thing in Cuba. It is like putting some nice ladies from a suburban Hadassah into a dusty kibbutz.

FOR THE TENTH anniversary there was a crowd of kids in from all over the Western world. They were *invitados,* invited guests, and the American delegation included members of Students for a Democratic Society, young Trotskyists, a contingent from the underground press, some Mexican-Americans (who may have been the most serious of all the *invitados*), a few young people who were unattached, and some who were members of groups that no one else had ever heard of. One night there was a special performance of the Ballet Folklórico for the *invitados* and all the other foreign visitors, and they filled the balcony of a rather lovely old theater. The *invitados,* in fact, took up most of the balcony, or seemed to, and they talked loudly, smoked the free cigars, dangled their feet in the aisle, and frayed my own middle-class sensibilities. (When the performance started, a dark brown boy with a paunch and a Malcolm X sweatshirt kept murmuring, "Out of sight, out of sight.") There was also in the audience, in a box seat, the Chinese Ambassador. I have seen him applaud "glorious Comrade Ho" with a face made entirely of stone, shake hands with Fidel and not twitch, and look like his own pallbearer when he met the champion antiaircraft gunner from North Vietnam. But that night he turned very slowly in his seat, looked at the *invitados,* and sneered. It is a small observation, but it is all my own.

The *invitados,* I think, were uptight. Nearly everyone who comes to Cuba for the first time does become uptight, and this is because deep down nearly everyone wants to believe in demons and angels, and the question is which side is Cuba on, and how can you tell? There is none of the old liberal baloney in Cuba, and this is unsettling, but it does help you know where you are. "No liberalism whatsoever! No softening whatsoever! A revolutionary people, a strong people—this is what is needed throughout these years." This is Fidel speaking, and he is kicking in the teeth all that a great many other men have died for. We are in America not much inclined to have great expectations any longer, but some Cubans do, and this is unsettling, too. The other thing about Cuba is that, just as some Cubans *believe,* others are not in the least bit sure about where they are going. (Others hate everything, of course, but this is another story.) "The reason we Cubans are so nice to one another," an official said, "is that if we are not we kill one another." This is more or less the same thought offered by a lady who once carried bombs to Fidel in the mountains. "In war," she said, "all you can lose is your life, but in peace you can lose your mind." Nevertheless, here is this sweaty country, ninety miles from Florida, fewer than eight million people, kissing off everything that Jack and Bobby and Gene told us to believe in. What is more extraordinary is that the country, like Havana, does not work very well itself, and it is fully capable of lousing up even the simplest things. It stores several million dollars' worth of pine seedlings in a tobacco warehouse, forgets about it, and then sprays the seedlings and kills them. It allows a United Nations man to come in and work for months on a new way to raise bananas, and then it allows a *comandante,* or someone with epaulets, to come by, decide they are likely-looking, and cut them down for lunch. It allows tons of butter to go rancid on a dock. It screws up constantly, and at its most earnest it allows high comedy, or low camp, to creep in. Inside the door of an old English bus I traveled on it said: "For good work we must conserve our equipment." Next to it was a picture of Mickey Mouse.

Moreover, there is something marvelous in the sanctification of Che. He is nearly always pictured in full Jesus beard, wearing a black beret with the single star of a major, his eyes cast upward, the whites in a semicircle under those dark, glittering orbs, looking like a Latin St. George warning off the next dragon. He seems incredibly romantic, and he probably was, and when a boy from the New Left made a meager joke about there being some sexual hanky-pank between Che and Fidel, the government told him to get on the next boat to Montreal. Che was an Argentine doctor who went to the mountains with Fidel, and then spent a good deal of time losing his way, losing his troops sometimes, and trying to get a Thompson submachine gun to work. After Batista fell he became the president of the national bank, signing the banknotes Che, and then minister of industries, this being a job in which he decided that Cuba should be an industrial nation. It should not, and under Che the sugarcane crop went all to hell. Eventually Che moved to Bolivia to start a revolution, and this was not a success either. He is, nonetheless, a folk hero, and to get the full effect of this you must stand in a hot crowd of Cubans, their flags and pennants all aflutter, and keep your eyes fastened on his picture while they play "Hymn of the Guerrilla" over a loudspeaker. It is not for nothing that "Che, we will follow you" is now graffiti.

THE OTHER SIDE of the bungling is that Cuba has accomplished some magnificent things, while the rest of Latin America seems to be sliding into a long decay, and it has accomplished them while getting nothing but grief from the United States. The revolution measures itself in statistics, great handfuls of statistics, and they show something reaching out and altering the lives of people. The statistics are always the government's, and so they may be suspect, not for political reasons but because the government may not have a talent for accurate statistics. Nonetheless, they show that there are more doctors, nurses, dentists, hospitals, and blood banks than there were ten years ago; that fewer people die from things like acute diarrheal disease, polio, typhoid fever, malaria, and gastroenteritis than ten years ago; that there are more students, schools, and teachers than there were ten years ago; that there are more cows, houses, and tractors than there were ten years ago; and even that there are more books being published than there were ten years ago. I do not know what the human cost of all these things has been, but it has been considerable, and I do not know if it has all been worth it, but I would like to think that it has. There is no good way of measuring the quality of life in Cuba, and the statistics show only a change in the quantity of things. Still, it is impressive, and if you remember that much of the middle class fled, along with many of the professionals, and that the country was underdeveloped to begin with, it is monumental. If you insist on trying to measure the quality of life, however, you look at people, and talk to them, and this is inconclusive too. Who could measure life in New York City through random conversations with citizens? Just like revolutionary zeal, quality and substance, whether good or bad, exist in the eye of the beholder. Cuba, for example, has the world's largest collection of cars that can barely move, and the collection dwindles a little every year as individual automobiles finally roll to a halt and just die. They are not interred in a junkyard then; they are stripped, taken apart, dismembered the way Edinburgh medical students dismembered the corpses they got from ghouls, and the parts are implanted among the survivors. These survivors make extraordinary sounds, clunking, thudding, and gurgling, and you may see in them (1) proof that things are bad in Cuba and that the blockade is working, which means that *our* side is winning, or (2) a testimony to Cuban initiative and ingenuity in the fact that the damn things run at all. In Santiago de Cuba, a young mathematics professor from the University of Oriente owns one of the two Austin-Healeys in town. It runs on parts of an old Russian motorcycle, and the young mathematics professor, who lives in a single room, is painfully teaching himself English. He does this by reading four old American paperbacks, three of which are pornographic and one of which is Sherlock Holmes. I found him and his Austin-Healey and his dirty books touching, but you are free to see in him proof that Fidel can't deliver car parts and learning aids to even his most devoted constituents.

So, how you feel about the revolution really depends on your own style, and this is true even if you are Cuban. "I am with the revolution intellectually," a prominent man said, "but I cannot be with it emotionally. When they applaud out there in the Plaza I am not really a part of it. I am over thirty-five, and when you are over thirty-five all that you were comes back to be a part of you, even the way your father told you to sit or to stand. I cannot feel the revolution the way the others do." This was an intellectual and a militant Communist, and while it is a convention to say that the middle class has been disenfranchised by the revolution, the intellectuals may have been disenfranchised even more. There is a good deal of mediocrity in Cuba, and they know it, and a dictatorship is not an ideal form of government, and they know that too. Being over thirty-five, or maybe even thirty, can also make you feel disenfranchised in a country where the Maximum Leader, ten years in power, is only forty-two, and where officials are forever turning up in their twenties. Even though nearly everyone still calls it the Isle of Pines, the splashiest, most publicized development in Cuba is on what the government calls the Isle of Youth. This is where Fidel proposes to build the first truly Communist region of Cuba, and where everyone is trying hard to build the "new man."

THE ISLAND, WHICH is about six hours away from the mainland by the only boat that stops there, had 7,800 people, twelve schools, and thirteen whorehouses in 1959. It also had an abortion mill that charged fancy ladies from New York $1,500, which included the price of their hotel. In 1966, after a hurricane ravaged the island, young people went there to help rebuild it, and the next year Fidel turned a romantic notion into an official doctrine when he said that henceforth it would be youth's own island and that here would be realized the deepest ideals of the revolution. There are now a little fewer than 50,000 people living there, and this includes perhaps 18,000 part-time workers, young people mostly, who will be there from forty-five days to twelve or eighteen months. There is, however, not much to see on the Isle of Pines except the young people and the work camps. It is undistinguished country, as so much of Cuba is, and parts of it look like Lowndes County, Alabama, and parts of it look like the foothills of the Catskill Mountains, even though the harbor, approached through a great reef, is lovely in the morning sunlight. There are citrus groves and cattle farms, one fair-sized city, and eight work camps. Some camps are more comfortable than others, but the general decor is functional-revolutionary, which is what it is throughout Cuba. Concrete floors, double-decker bunks, and a great many flies. A pretty Italian girl, who put in time at one of the work camps, said the thing that bothered her most was the absence of doors on the toilets. (Since she loved the revolution, this lapse into bourgeois decadence amused and slightly bothered her.) Nonetheless, it is here that a new man is being put together, and he will be, an official said, "a man with his feet on the ground." The official, who was the island secretary of the Committee for the Orientation of the Revolution, and was himself young and enthusiastic, went on: "We want a society with a different kind of man. We have a society with a low cultural level, and the man we create must have a high cultural level and high technical ability. He must know how to meet problems and have a high degree of political orientation. We must develop a man who does not live only to eat or to sleep, but a man who feels his highest occupation is to create spiritual and material things. We want a man to be essentially productive, who works because he feels it is necessary to do it, and you cannot develop this man in an abstract way, but only in a very concrete way." This, of course, sounds like so much revolutionary bushwa, except that the official was serious, and also sophisticated enough to say that many of the young people who joined the work camps did so to solve their own emotional problems, and not because of their revolutionary zeal.

There are also young people on the Isle of Pines who are there because the place they worked for on the mainland simply sent them, or because they had nothing else to do with themselves, and I am pretty sure that one girl I met was a hooker who was just trying to get right with the authorities. Nonetheless, there are young people there who are striking, and they are striking because they seem to feel good about themselves. There are no conventional rewards on the Isle of Pines, the days being filled with things like digging holes in the ground, the nights being filled with classes of one sort or another, but the most interesting of the young people there seemed to believe they were doing something important. There was, for example, a slender Negro girl who lived in a stone cottage with eleven other girls. Inside, it was a clutter of cardboard footlockers, steel cots, and old work shoes; outside, the revolution had dolled things up with gravel footpaths. The girl said she had been there twenty months, and that she wanted to stay a little longer. "After all the time I've been here," she said, "I want to see the results." Nonetheless, she said, she had decided to go on to a university, although she wasn't sure what she would do there. "I will study," she said, "whatever will be good for the revolution. I want to help my country. I was working in Havana making men's suits, and then I heard Fidel's speech about this place, and I decided to come here." What had she been doing all these twenty months? "I've been washing cows," she said.

It is easy to sentimentalize these things, and most foreigners do. It is especially easy to sentimentalize the young women, some of whom can look wonderfully feminine and enormously pleased with themselves while picking up a load of manure. Still, the road to a new man, or new woman, is long and tricky. The Moncada barracks in Oriente Province, the army stronghold against which Fidel led a disastrous attack in 1953, is now a school, and in its third grade the children jumped to attention when I walked in, and the class monitor said, "We will be like Che, comrade visitor. Can my class sit again?" In the fifth grade the children got up and the monitor said, "We will follow the lines of our hundred years of fighting for freedom. We will perform like all the heroes of our revolution. We will be like Che." Later, the director of the school, a gentle, coffee-colored lady who taught peasants in the Sierra Maestra when it was a rebel stronghold, and is now another true believer, answered questions: "How do you teach children to be like Che? How do you train the new man? You do it through the subjects somewhat, but mostly through the activities in which they participate. For example, they study in a collective way. They do things in a collective way. Then there are the examples we give them of the defense of the fatherland, of the heroes, and of the struggles in other countries that are exploited by the imperialists. It is a complex of living, a way to live, the total of all that they receive every day—that is how we teach them to be like Che." The lady was pleasant, and the teachers were friendly, but I felt discomfited, and it was not helped when I learned that the students went under military discipline when they reached junior high. Regimentation can be unattractive, and Cuba hopes that by 1975 all its schools will be boarding schools, which will allow for nearly unlimited regimentation. I was brooding on this when I left the Moncada school, and as I walked back to my car I came across some of the fifth-graders I had just heard swearing fidelity to Che. They tried to hustle me for cigarettes, and when I said no, they ignored me and kept hustling. It was, in a way, reassuring.

ONE DAY IN a town called Pinar del Rio, the foreign press was brought before a panel of provincial Cuban journalists for what was supposed to be a frank exchange of views. The panel asked us what we thought of Cuba, and no one knew what to say until a reporter from Stockholm said he liked it just fine. From then on the discussion went straight downhill, and when it finally became unbearable I slipped away. Outside in the plaza, "Thanks for the Memories" was being played over a loudspeaker, and I walked about, talked to Cubans, and decided again that anti-Americanism, on the part of the people, at least, simply wasn't there. When I returned to the discussion a nice little girl from the New Left was asking the middle-aged Cuban journalists what they thought of the underground press. The question had to go through a translator, who plainly didn't know what the underground press was, just as those provincial journalists didn't know either. The American girl tried again, and finally one of the Cubans said something about the underground press telling the real truth, while the capitalist press served only the interests. Everyone looked relieved, and the American girl beamed. Then, when the discussion ended, she walked up to the Cubans, all in suits and quiet ties, and showed them her underground paper. The Cubans were polite, and she was still beaming, and she opened to the centerfold, and there in the middle of the page was an ad that said, "Do you want some pussy?" Two of the Cubans didn't get it at all, one got it and hung his head, and one looked absolutely terrified.

It was all a question of style, really, and of who you are, and of what you are. "But you don't understand," a Cuban friend once told me. "The question of individual liberty is irrelevant in a revolution." We were discussing the need for freedom, and he said that the traditional freedoms were frivolous as long as there were workers being shot in Bolivia, or peasants starving in Colombia. I said I didn't think the question of freedom had anything to do with that, and I thought once again that I was a liberal American and he was a revolutionary, and as much as I wanted to go over to his side I couldn't. I admired him, and I admired his revolution, and it was my final sadness about Cuba. If we couldn't agree, then what chance had our governments? God help us both.

# THE SELLING OF THE
# PRESIDENT 1968

(AUGUST 1969)

## *Joe McGinniss*

*How do you "correct" a candidate's lack of warmth? When does he need "more memorable phrases"? How do you "create an image without saying anything"? These are just a few of the considerations that went into Nixon's campaign—at the heart of which was the adroit manipulation and use of television.*

HE WAS AFRAID of television. He knew his soul was hard to find. Beyond that, he considered it a gimmick; its use in politics offended him. It had not been part of the game when he had learned to play, he could see no reason to bring it in now. He half-suspected it was an Eastern liberal trick; one more way to make him look silly. It offended his sense of dignity, one of the truest senses he had.

So his decision to use it to become President in 1968 was not easy. So much of him argued against it. But in his Wall Street years, Richard Nixon had traveled to the darkest places inside himself and come back numbed. He was, as in the Graham Greene title, a burnt-out case. All feeling was behind him; the machine inside had proved his hardiest part. He would run for President again and if he would have to learn television to run well, then he would learn it.

Nixon gathered about himself a group of young men attuned to the political uses of television. They arrived at his side by different routes. One, William Gavin, was a thirty-one-year-old English teacher in a suburban high school outside Philadelphia in 1967 when he wrote Richard Nixon a letter urging him to run for President and base his campaign on TV. Gavin wrote the letter on stationery borrowed from the University of Pennsylvania because he thought Nixon would pay more attention if the letter seemed to be from a college professor.

> Dear Mr. Nixon:
> May I offer two suggestions concerning your plans for 1968?
> 1. Run. You can win. Nothing can happen to you, politically speaking, that is worse than what has happened to you. Ortega y Gasset in his *The Revolt of the Masses* says: "These ideas are the only genuine ideas; the ideas of the ship-wrecked. All the rest is rhetoric, posturing, farce. He who does not really feel himself lost, is lost without remission. . . ." You, in effect, are "lost"; that is why you are the only political figure with the vision to see things the way they are and not as Leftist or Rightist kooks would have them be. Run. You will win.
> 2. A tip for television: instead of those wooden performances beloved by politicians, instead of a glamor boy technique, instead of safety, be bold. Why not have live press conferences as your campaign on television? People will see you daring all, asking and answering questions from reporters, and not simply answering phony "questions" made up by your staff. This would be dynamic; it would be daring. Instead of the medium using you, you would be using the medium. . . . Television hurt you because you were not yourself; it didn't hurt the "real" Nixon. The real Nixon can revolutionize the use of television by dynamically going "live" and answering everything, the loaded and the unloaded question. Invite your opponents to this kind of debate.
> Good luck, and I know you can win if you see yourself for what you are; a man who has been beaten, humiliated, hated, but who can still see the truth.

A Nixon staff member had lunch with Gavin a couple of times after the letter was received and hired him. Gavin began churning out long, stream-of-consciousness memos which dealt mostly with the impor-tance of image, and ways in which Richard Nixon, through television, could acquire a good one: "Voters are basically lazy, basically uninter-ested in making an *effort* to understand what we're talking about," Gavin wrote. "Reason requires a high degree of discipline, of concentration; impression is easier. Reason pushes the viewer back, it assaults him. . . . The emotions are more easily roused, closer to the surface, more malleable . . ."

So, for the New Hampshire primary, Gavin recommended "saturation with a film, in which the candidate can be shown better than he can be shown in person because it can be edited, so only the best moments are shown. . . . [Nixon] has to come across as a person larger than life, the stuff of legend. People are stirred by legend, including the living legend, not by the man himself. It's the aura that surrounds the charismatic figure more than it is the figure itself that draws the followers. Our task is to build that aura . . ."

William Gavin was brought to the White House as a speechwriter in January of 1969.

Harry Treleaven, hired as creative director of advertising in the fall of 1967, immediately went to work on the more serious of Nixon's personality problems. One was his lack of humor: "Can be corrected to a degree," Treleaven wrote, "but let's not be too obvious about it. Romney's cornball attempts have hurt him. If we're going to be witty, let a pro write the words."

Treleaven also worried about Nixon's lack of warmth, but decided: "He can be helped greatly in this respect by how he is handled. . . . Give him words to say that will show his *emotional* involvement in the issues. . . . He should be presented in some kind of 'situation' rather than cold in a studio. The situation should look unstaged even if it's not."

Some of the most effective ideas belonged to Raymond K. Price, a former editorial writer for the New York *Herald Tribune,* who became Nixon's best and most prominent speechwriter in the campaign. Price later composed much of the Inaugural Address. In 1967, he concluded that rational arguments would "only be effective if we can get the people to make the *emotional* leap, or what theologians call 'leap of faith.' "

To do this, Price suggested attacking the "personal factors" rather than the "historical factors" which were the basis of the low opinion so many people had of Richard Nixon. "These tend to be more a gut reaction," he wrote, "unarticulated, nonanalytical, a product of the particular chemistry between the voter and the *image* of the candidate. *We have to be very clear on this point: that the response is to the image, not to the man . . .*"

So there would not have to be a "new Nixon." Simply a new approach to television.

This was how they went into it. Trying, with one hand, to build the illusion that Richard Nixon, in addition to his attributes of mind and heart, considered "communicating with the people . . . one of the great joys of seeking the Presidency," while with the other they shielded him, controlled him, and controlled the atmosphere around him. It was as if they were building not a President but an Astrodome, where the wind would never blow, the temperature never rise or fall, and the ball never bounce erratically on the artificial grass.

And it worked. As he moved serenely through his primary campaign, there was new cadence to Richard Nixon's speech and motion; new confidence in his heart. And a new image of him on the television screen, on live, but controlled, TV.

I FIRST MET Harry Treleaven on a rainy morning in June of 1968, in his New York office at Fuller and Smith and Ross, the advertising agency. Treleaven was small and thin. He had gray hair and the tight frowning mouth that you see on the assistant principal of a high school. He seemed to be in his middle forties. He looked like William Scranton. Treleaven, it turned out, did not work for Fuller and Smith and Ross. He worked for Richard Nixon. Fuller and Smith and Ross was only incidental to the campaign. An agency was needed to do the mechanics—buying the television time and the newspaper space—and this looked like a nice, quiet one that would not complain about not being permitted to do creative work. Treleaven had been born in Chicago and had gone to Duke University, where he was Phi Beta Kappa. After that, he moved to Los Angeles and worked on the Los Angeles *Times* and then wrote radio scripts. One night he and his wife were having dinner in a restaurant in Los Angeles with a couple he did not like. Halfway through the meal he turned to his wife.

"Do you like it here?"

"You mean the restaurant?"

"I mean Los Angeles."

"No, not especially."

"Then let's go."

And Harry Treleaven threw a twenty-dollar bill on the table and he and his wife walked out. He took a plane to New York that night and found a job with the J. Walter Thompson advertising agency. He stayed with Thompson eighteen years. When he left it was as a vice president. He did commercials for Pan American, RCA, Ford, and Lark cigarettes, among others.

Harry Treleaven was sitting on the beach at Amagansett one day in September of 1967, drinking a can of beer. A summer neighbor named Len Garment, who was a partner in the law firm where Richard Nixon worked, approached him. Harry Treleaven knew Garment from a meeting they had had earlier in the summer. Garment had vaguely mentioned something about Treleaven and the advertising needs of the Richard Nixon campaign. Now he was more specific. He offered Treleaven a job. Creative director of advertising. Treleaven would devise a theme for the campaign, create commercials to fit the theme, and see that they were produced with a maximum of skill.

Len Garment's office was on the third floor of Nixon headquarters, at Park Avenue and 57th Street. A man named Jim Howard, a public-relations man from Cleveland, was with him the day I came in. Jim Howard was talking to Wilt Chamberlain on the phone.

"Wilt, I *understand* your position but they just don't pay that kind of money."

Garment was a short, pudgy man, also in his middle forties, who once had played saxophone in a Woody Herman band. He had voted for John Kennedy in 1960. Then he met Nixon at the law firm. He was chief of litigation and he was making money but he hated the job. He found that Nixon was not so bad a guy and very smart. When Nixon asked him to work in the Presidential campaign, he said yes. He had been practically the first person to be hired and now he was chief recruiter.

Jim Howard had been trying to get Wilt Chamberlain to appear on the Mike Douglas show for free. The idea was for Chamberlain to explain why Richard Nixon should be President. Chamberlain was the only Negro celebrity they had and they were trying to get him around. The problem was, the Douglas show did not pay. And Chamberlain wanted money.

Len Garment started to explain the Nixon approach to advertising. Or the Garment-Treleaven approach to advertising Nixon. "The big thing is to stay away from gimmicks," he said.

"Right," Jim Howard said. "Never let the candidate wear a hat he does not feel comfortable wearing. You can't sell the candidate like a product," he said. "A product, all you want to do is get attention. You only need 2 percent additional buyers to make the campaign worthwhile. In politics you need a flat 51 percent of the market and you can't get that through gimmicks."

Two weeks later, I met Frank Shakespeare. Treleaven, Garment (who this June became special consultant to the President in the area of civil rights), and Shakespeare made up what was to be called the media and advertising group. But of the three equals, Shakespeare was quickly becoming more equal than the others. He had come from CBS. He, too, was in his forties, with blond hair and a soft, boyish face. When he was named director of the United States Information Agency, after Nixon's election, a *New York Times* profile reported that, although he had spent eighteen years at CBS, no one he worked with there could recall a single anecdote about him. He was working for free because his progress at CBS had been stalled when Jim Aubrey got fired. He had been one of Aubrey's boys. Now, it was said, he was trying to give his career some outside impetus. An association with the President of the U.S. could hardly hurt.

ON THE MORNING after the Russians invaded Czechoslovakia, Harry Treleaven got to his office early. He was in an exceptionally good mood. The invasion had proved Nixon was right all along. The Russians had not changed.

"Makes it kind of hard to be a dove, doesn't it?" he said, smiling.

Treleaven was leaving for Teletape, the film-editing studio, right away. The day before, he had cut Nixon's forty-five-minute acceptance speech to thirty minutes, and he wanted to see it.

Len Garment was at the studio when Treleaven got there. "What about this Czech thing?" he said. He looked really worried. Treleaven smiled. "Oh, I don't know, Len. Look at the positive side."

"Well, yes," Garment said. "I think it will bring a restoration of realism to American political discussion."

But Treleaven had been thinking of something else. "Unless we make some really colossal mistake," he said, "I don't see how we can lose."

Then Shakespeare came in. He was exuberant. "What a break!" he said. "This Czech thing is just perfect. It puts the soft-liners in a hell of a box!"

Harry Treleaven had used the CBS tape of the acceptance speech to make the commercial. "Better camera angles," he explained. "And besides, NBC has a peculiar form of editorializing. For instance, they'll cut to some young colored guy who's not applauding while Nixon talks of bridges to human dignity."

In the beginning of the acceptance speech, Richard Nixon had made a sweeping motion with his arm and shouted, "Let's win this one for Ike!" and all the Republicans cheered. Harry Treleaven had cut this line from the speech.

"Good," Shakespeare said, "very good, Harry. That's the one line Rose Mary Woods wanted out of there." Rose Mary Woods was Richard Nixon's secretary. Because she had stuck with him through all the bad years, she emerged in 1968 as an adviser, too.

Another thing he had cut was a reference to "the era of negotiation" with the Russians. Shakespeare was very happy this had gone. It would have been awful, he thought—they all thought—to have a reference to negotiations now that this invasion had occurred. This was the Cold War again, and adrenaline was flowing.

A big meeting was scheduled at Fuller and Smith and Ross for lunchtime. The agency had ordered ham sandwiches with a lot of lettuce and big pots of coffee. Everyone sat down and took little bites out of their sandwiches while Frank Shakespeare stood up and talked.

Already, there was bad feeling between the agency people and the Nixon group. In the beginning, the agency had believed it actually was going to create commercials. Then Harry Treleaven walked in. Without even saying good morning. Now the agency was making money but it was embarrassed. Treleaven would not tell them what he was doing. "No need to," he said. He said he had been thinking it over, and rather than rush something new into production he would prefer to continue the sixty-second excerpts from the acceptance speech that had been running as radio commercials.

Art Duram, the president of the agency, immediately lit his pipe. "But your exposure on that speech—" he said. "You're going to be horrendously overexposed."

"I'm not sure that's bad, Art," Treleaven said. "He's saying some awfully good things."

"But psychologically—"

"Well, the problem is we have nothing else to use and there's nothing else we could have ready that quickly unless it were a real emergency and I just don't think it is."

Duram shrugged.

Then a red-haired lady named Ruth Jones spoke up from the other side of the table. She had been hired by Shakespeare to supervise the buying of television and radio time for the commercials. "Nixon should go on the air tonight with a special broadcast about Czechoslovakia," she said.

Shakespeare shook his head. "He'd have to be too good. He couldn't get ready. He's better off not saying anything. He's been Mr. Cool and Mr. Calm through this whole thing."

Ruth Jones shrugged. "I still think he should do it," she said. "But let's move on to something else—we're going to get bold listings in the *Times* starting immediately."

"Bold listings?" Shakespeare asked.

"Yes, in the TV section. Listing our commercials in bold type in the schedule. They had been doing it for McCarthy and not for us. But I tossed a couple of hand grenades. At the networks and the *Times*. And I got immediate results."

Then a man walked into the room with a big colored poster under his arm. The poster was a closeup of Richard Nixon smiling. Beneath it were the words: THIS TIME VOTE LIKE YOUR WHOLE WORLD DEPENDED ON IT.

"This is the new slogan," he said. "And together with the picture, this will run in the center spread of *Life* magazine and on our billboards."

Frank Shakespeare was staring at the picture. "Do you like the photograph?" he said, turning toward Len Garment.

"I have a little bit of a problem with that tremendous smile, tied in with the serious line," Garment said.

The man with the poster was nodding. "We're still looking for the right picture," he said, "and it's difficult. But this expression is not a laugh to me. It's a youthful expression. It has vitality. To look at it inspires confidence. The picture has sensitivity, and one of the reasons we ran the line behind him—in back of his head—is so he wouldn't appear to be speaking it. See, it's there, but just as part of the image. The connection is not direct."

"Yes," Frank Shakespeare said. "All right."

"It will make a tremendous billboard," Treleaven said.

"There's character in the face," Shakespeare said.

"We've got the best-looking candidate, no doubt about it," Treleaven said.

"So it's a cheerful, grim, serious, and optimistic picture," Len Garment said, smiling.

"And youthful," Shakespeare added.

"Ah," said Ruth Jones, who still wanted him to speak on Czechoslovakia, "a man for all seasons."

Then they talked about fund-raising. "The first McCarthy telecast raised a hundred and twenty-five thousand dollars," Ruth Jones said.

"Who gave the pitch?" Shakespeare asked.

"Paul Newman."

"Oh, well, that made a difference."

"It was a personal-involvement pitch. Dick Goodwin wrote it for him."

"We'll use the same pitch," Shakespeare said, "but we don't have as strong a man."

"Who do we have?"

"Bud Wilkinson."

AT FOUR O'CLOCK, Treleaven walked to a West Side theater to look at a film that had been made with Spiro Agnew at Mission Bay, California, the week after the Republican convention.

"It could be a great help, particularly with Agnew, if it's any good," Treleaven said. Shakespeare and Garment already were at the theater. So was the man who had made the films—a TV documentary man whom Shakespeare had hired especially for this job. He was wearing sneakers and shifting nervously from foot to foot. There were two separate films, each containing an interview with one of the candidates. The Agnew film was shown first. It had been shot in color, with sailboats in the blue bay as a backdrop. Spiro Agnew was squinting in the sun.

"All life," he said, "is essentially the contributions that come from compromise." His voice was sleepy, his face without expression. The questions fit right in.

"It must have really been a thrill to have been picked for Vice President. Were you happy?"

"The ability to be happy is directly proportional to the ability to suffer," Agnew said. His tone indicated he might doze before finishing the sentence, "and as you grow older you feel everything less."

He stopped. There was silence on the film. Then the voice of the interviewer: "I see."

"Jesus Christ," someone said out loud in the dark little theater. Spiro Agnew's face kept moving in and out of focus.

"Is that the projector or the film?" Garment asked. The man who had made the film disappeared into the projection booth. The technical quality of the film did not improve.

"Loyalty is the most important principle," Agnew was saying, "when coupled with honesty, that is. And I think that such values are in danger when you hear people advocate violence to change situations which are intolerable . . . and most of the people who are cutting the United States up are doing so without offering a single concrete proposal to improve it."

"How did you become a Republican?"

"I became a Republican out of hero worship." Then Spiro Agnew went on to tell a long story about an old man in the law office where he had first worked as a clerk, and how the old man had been a Republican and how he had admired the old man so much that he had become a Republican too. There was more silence on the film. The focus was very bad.

"And . . . and . . . you just sort of went on becoming more and more Republican?"

"That's right," Spiro Agnew said. More silence. The sailboats moved slowly in the background. The water was very blue. Then the focus made everything a blur.

"What a heartbreak," the man who had made the films said, standing in the back of the theater.

"It looks like you're looking through a Coke bottle," Garment said.

"And he comes across as such an utter bore," Treleaven said. "I don't think the man has had an original observation in his life."

"He is rather non-dynamic," Garment said.

Frank Shakespeare was up now and pacing the back of the theater. "We can't use any of this," he said. "That picture quality is awful. Just awful. And Agnew himself, my God. He says all the wrong things."

"What we need is a shade less truth and a little more pragmatism," Treleaven said.

"I think Dexedrine is the answer," Garment said.


"I AM NOT going to barricade myself into a television studio and make this an antiseptic campaign," Richard Nixon said at a press conference a few days after his nomination. Then he went to Chicago to open his fall campaign. The whole day was built around a television show. Even when ten thousand people stood in front of his hotel and screamed for him to greet them he stayed locked up in his room, resting for the show.

Chicago was the site for the first of ten programs that Nixon would do in states ranging from Massachusetts to Texas. The idea was to have him in the middle of a group of people, answering questions live. Shakespeare and Treleaven had developed the idea through the primaries and now had it sharpened to a point. Each show would run for one hour. It would be live to provide suspense; there would be a studio audience to cheer Nixon's answers and make it seem to home viewers that enthusiasm for his candidacy was all but uncontrollable; and there would be an effort to achieve a conversational tone that would penetrate Nixon's stuffiness and drive out the displeasure he often seemed to feel when surrounded by other human beings instead of Bureau of the Budget reports.

One of the valuable things about this idea, from a political standpoint, was that each show would be seen only by the people who lived in that particular state or region. This meant it made no difference if Nixon's statements—for they were not really answers—were exactly the same, phrase for phrase, gesture for gesture, from state to state. Only the press would be bored and the press had been written off already. So Nixon could get through the campaign with a dozen or so carefully worded responses that would cover all the problems of America in 1968.

Roger Ailes, the executive producer of the Mike Douglas show, was hired to produce the one-hour programs. Ailes was twenty-eight years old. He had started as a prop boy on the Douglas show in 1965 and was running it within three years. He was good. When he left, Douglas's ratings declined. But not everyone he passed on his way up remained his friend. Not even Douglas. Richard Nixon had been a guest on the show in the fall of 1967. While waiting to go on, he fell into conversation with Roger Ailes.

"It's a shame a man has to use gimmicks like this to get elected," Nixon said.

"Television is not a gimmick," Ailes said.

Richard Nixon liked that kind of thinking. He told Len Garment to hire the man. Ailes had been sent to Chicago three days before Nixon opened the fall campaign. His instructions were to select a panel of questioners and design a set. But now, on the day of the program, only six hours, in fact, before it was to begin, Ailes was having problems.

"Those stupid bastards on the set-designing crew put turquoise curtains in the background. Nixon wouldn't look right unless he was carrying a pocketbook." Ailes ordered the curtains removed and three plain, almost stark wooden boards to replace them. "The wood has clean, solid, masculine lines," he said.

His biggest problem was with the panel of questioners. Shakespeare, Treleaven, and Garment had felt it essential to have a "balanced" group. First, this meant a Negro. One Negro. Not two. Two would be offensive to whites, perhaps to Negroes as well. Two would be trying too hard. One was necessary and safe. Fourteen percent of the population applied to a six- or seven-member panel equaled one. Texas would be tricky, though. Do you have a Negro *and* a Mexican-American, or if not, then which?

Besides the Negro, the panel for the first show included a Jewish attorney, the president of a Polish-Hungarian group, a suburban housewife, a businessman, a representative of the white lower middle class, and, for authenticity, two newsmen: one from Chicago, one from Moline.

That was all right, Roger Ailes said. But then someone had called from New York and insisted that he add a farmer. Roger Ailes had been born in Ohio, but even so he knew you did not want a farmer on a television show. All they did was ask complicated questions about things like parities, which nobody else understood or cared about. Including Richard Nixon. Besides, the farmer brought the panel size to eight, which Ailes said was too big. It would be impossible for Nixon to establish interpersonal relationships with eight different people in one hour. And interpersonal relationships were the key to success.

"This is the trouble with all these political people horning in," Ailes said. "Fine, they all get their lousy little groups represented but we wind up with a horseshit show."

There was to be a studio audience—three hundred people—recruited by the local Republican organization. Just enough Negroes so the press could not write "all-white" stories but not enough so it would look like a ball park. The audience, of course, would applaud every answer Richard Nixon gave, boosting his confidence and giving the impression to a viewer that Nixon certainly did have charisma, and whatever other qualities they wanted their President to have.

Treleaven and his assistant, Al Scott, came to the studio late in the afternoon. They were getting nervous. "Nixon's throat is scratchy," Treleaven said, "and that's making him upset." Al Scott did not like the lighting in the studio. "The lights are too high," he said. "They'll show the bags under RN's eyes."

Then there was a crisis about whether the press should be allowed in the studio during the show. Shakespeare had given an order that they be kept out. Now they were complaining to Herb Klein, the press-relations man, that if three hundred shills could be bussed in to cheer, a pool of two or three reporters could be allowed to sit in the stands.

Shakespeare still said no. No *newspapermen* were going to interfere with his TV show. Klein kept arguing, saying that if this was how it was going to start, on the very first day of the campaign, it was going to be 1960 again within a week. Treleaven and Ailes went upstairs, to the WBBM cafeteria, and drank vending-machine coffee from paper cups. "I agree with Frank," Ailes said. "It's not a press conference."

"But if you let the audience in . . ."

"Doesn't matter. The audience is part of the show. And that's the whole point. It's a television show. Our television show. And the press has no business on the set.

"Goddam it, Harry, the problem is that this is an electronic election. The first there's ever been. TV has the power now. Some of the guys get arrogant and rub the reporters' faces in it and then the reporters get pissed and go out of their way to rap anything they consider staged for TV. And you know damn well that's what they'd do if they saw this from the studio. You let them in with the regular audience and they see the warm-up. They see Jack Rourke out there telling the audience to applaud and to mob Nixon at the end, and that's all they'd write about. You know damn well it is." Jack Rourke was Roger Ailes's assistant.

"I'm still afraid we'll create a big incident if we lock them out entirely," Treleaven said. "I'm going to call Frank and suggest he reconsider."

But Shakespeare would not. He arranged for monitors in an adjacent studio and said the press could watch from there, seeing no more, no less, than what they would see from any living room in Illinois.

It was five o'clock now; the show was to start at nine. Ray Vojey, the makeup man borrowed from the Johnny Carson show, had arrived. "Oh, Ray," Roger Ailes said, "with Wilkinson, watch that perspiration problem on the top of his forehead."

"Yes, he went a little red in Portland," Ray Vojey said.

"And when he's off camera, I'd give him a treated towel, just like Mr. Nixon uses."

"Right."

Ailes turned to Jack Rourke, the assistant. "Also, I'd like to have Wilkinson in the room with Nixon before the show to kibitz around, get Nixon loose."

"Okay, I'll bring him in."

The set, now that it was finished, was impressive. There was a round blue-carpeted platform, six feet in diameter and eight inches high. Richard Nixon would stand on this and face the panel, which would be seated in a semicircle around him. Bleachers for the audience ranged out behind the panel chairs. Later, Roger Ailes would think to call the whole effect "the arena concept" and bill Nixon as "the man in the arena." He got this from a Theodore Roosevelt quote which hung, framed, from a wall of his office in Philadelphia. It said something about how one man in the arena was worth ten, or a hundred, or a thousand carping critics.

At nine o'clock, Central Daylight Time, Richard Nixon, freshly powdered, left his dressing room, walked down a corridor deserted save for Secret Service, and went through a carefully guarded doorway that opened on the rear of the set.

Harry Treleaven had selected tape from WBBM's coverage of the noontime motorcade for the opening of the show. Tape that showed Richard Nixon riding, arms outstretched, beaming, atop an open car. Hundreds of thousands of citizens, some who had come on their own, some who had been recruited by Republican organizations, cheered, waved balloons, and tossed confetti in the air. One week before, at the Democratic convention, it had been Humphrey, blood, and tear gas. Today it was Nixon, the unifying hero, the man to heal all wounds. Chicago Republicans showed a warm, assured, united front. And Harry Treleaven picked only the most magical of moments for the opening of his television show.

Then the director hit a button and Bud Wilkinson appeared on the screen, a placid, composed, substantial, reassuring figure introducing his close personal friend, a man whose intelligence and judgment had won the respect of the world's leaders and the admiration of millions of his countrymen, this very same man who had been seen entering Jerusalem moments ago on tape: Richard Nixon. And the carefully cued audience (for Jack Rourke had done his job well) stood to render an ovation. Richard Nixon, grinning, waving, *thrusting,* walked to the blue riser to receive the tribute.

It was warmly given. Genuine. He looked toward his wife; the two daughters; Senator Ed Brooke, the most useful Negro he had found; Charles Percy, the organization man; and Senator Thruston Morton, resigned if not enthusiastic. They sat in the first row together.

He was alone, with not even a chair on the platform for company, ready to face, if not the nation, at least Illinois. To communicate, man to man, eye to eye, with that mass of the ordinary whose concerns he so deeply shared, whose values were so totally his own. All the subliminal effects sank in. Nixon stood alone, ringed by forces which, if not hostile, were at least—to the viewer—unpredictable.

There was a rush of sympathy; a desire—a need, even—to root. Richard Nixon was suddenly human: facing a new and dangerous situation, alone, armed with only his wits. In image terms, he had won before he began. All the old concepts had been destroyed. He had achieved a new level of communication. The stronger his statement, the stronger the surge of warmth inside the viewer.

Morris Liebman, the Jewish attorney, asked the first question: "Would you comment on the accusation which was made from time to time that your views have shifted and that they are based on expediencies?"

Richard Nixon squinted and smiled. "I suppose what you are referring to is: Is there a new Nixon or is there an old Nixon? I suppose I could counter by saying: Which Humphrey shall we listen to today?"

There was great applause for this. When it faded, Richard Nixon said, "I do want to say this: There certainly is a new Nixon. I realize, too, that as a man gets older he learns something. If I haven't learned something I am not worth anything in public life. . . . I think my principles are consistent. I believe very deeply in the American system. I believe very deeply in what is needed to defend that system at home and abroad. I think I have some ideas as to how we can promote peace, ideas that are different from what they were eight years ago, not because I have changed but because the problems have changed.

"My answer is 'yes,' there is a new Nixon, if you are talking in terms of new ideas for the new world and the America we live in. In terms of what I believe in, the American view and the American dream, I think I am just what I was eight years ago."

Applause swept the studio. Bud Wilkinson joined in.

The farmer asked a question about farming. The Polish-Hungarian delivered an address concerning the problems of the people of Eastern Europe. His remarks led to no question at all, but no matter: Richard Nixon expressed concern for the plight of Eastern Europeans everywhere, including northern Illinois.

Then Warner Saunders, the Negro, and a very acceptable, very polite one he seemed to be, asked, "What does law and order mean to you?"

"I am quite aware," Richard Nixon said, "of the fact that the black community, when they hear it, think of power being used in a way that is destructive to them, and yet I think we have to also remember that the black community as well as the white community has an interest in order and in law, providing that law is with justice . . ."

John McCarter, the businessman, asked about Spiro Agnew. Nixon said, "Of all the men who I considered, Spiro Agnew had the intelligence, the courage, and the principle to take on the great responsibilities of a campaigner and responsibilities of Vice President."

McCarter came back later wanting to know if Nixon thought the Chicago police had been too harsh on demonstrators in the streets.

"It would be easy," Nixon said, "to criticize Mayor Daley and by implication Vice President Humphrey. But it wouldn't be right for me to lob in criticism. I am not going to get into it. It is best for political figures not to be making partisan comments from the sidelines."

The show went on like that. At the end the audience charged from the bleachers, as instructed. They swarmed around Richard Nixon so that the last thing the viewer at home saw was Nixon in the middle of this big crowd of people, who all thought he was great.

Treleaven plunged into the crowd. He was excited; he thought the show had been brilliant. He got to Nixon just as Nixon was bending down to autograph a cast that a girl had on her leg.

"Well, you've got a leg up," Treleaven said.

Nixon stood up and grinned and moved away.

"Gee, that was sure a funny look he gave me," Treleaven said. "I wonder if he heard me. I wonder if he knew who I was."

ORIGINALLY, TRELEAVEN HAD wanted David Douglas Duncan, the photographer, to make commercials. Duncan was a friend of Richard Nixon's but when Treleaven took him out to lunch he said no, he would be too busy. Then Duncan mentioned Eugene Jones. Treleaven wanted Duncan because he had decided to make still photography the basis of Richard Nixon's sixty-second television commercial campaign. He had learned a little about stills at J. Walter Thompson when he had used them for some Pan American spots. Now he thought they were the perfect thing for Nixon because Nixon himself would not have to appear. The words would be the same lines Nixon always used—the words of the acceptance speech. But they would all seem fresh and lively because a series of still pictures would flash on the screen while Nixon spoke. If it were done right, it would permit Treleaven to create a Nixon image that was entirely independent of words. Obviously, some technical skill would be required. David Douglas Duncan said Gene Jones was the man.

Treleaven met Jones and was impressed. "He's low-key," Treleaven said. "He doesn't come at you as a know-it-all."

Gene Jones, who was in his early forties, had been taking movies of wars half his life. He did it perhaps as well as any man ever has. Besides that, he had produced the *Today* show on NBC for two years and had done a documentary series on famous people called *The World of* — Billy Graham, Sophia Loren, anyone who had been famous and was willing to be surrounded by Jones's cameras for a month.

Jones understood perfectly what Treleaven was after. A technique through which Richard Nixon would seem to be contemporary, imaginative, involved—without having to say anything of substance. Jones had never done commercial work before but for $110,000, from which he would pay salaries to a nine-man staff, he said he would do it for Nixon.

A day or two later Jones came down to Treleaven's office to discuss details such as where he should set up a studio and what areas the first set of spots should cover. "This will not be a commercial sell," Jones said. "It will not have the feel of something a—pardon the expression—an agency would turn out. I see it as sort of a miniature *Project 20*. And I can't see anyone turning it off a television set, quite frankly."

That same day Jones rented two floors of the building at 303 East 53rd Street in Manhattan, one flight up from a nightclub called Chuck's Composite. Within three days, he had his staff at work. Buying pictures, taking pictures, taking motion pictures of still pictures that Jones himself had cropped and arranged in a sequence.

"I'm pretty excited about this," Jones said. "I think we can give it an artistic dimension."

Harry Treleaven did not get excited about anything but he was at least intrigued by this. "It will be interesting to see how he translates his approach into political usefulness," Treleaven said.

"Yes," Frank Shakespeare said, "if he can."

Gene Jones would start work at five o'clock in the morning. Laying coffee and doughnuts on his desk, he would spread a hundred or so pictures on the floor, taken from boxes into which his staff already had filed them. The boxes had labels like VIETNAM . . . DEMOCRATIC CONVENTION . . . POVERTY: HARLEM, CITY SLUMS, GHETTOS . . . FACES: HAPPY AMERICAN PEOPLE AT WORK . . .

He would select a category to fit the first line of whatever script he happened to be working with that day. He would select the most appropriate of the pictures, and then arrange and rearrange, as in a game of solitaire. When he had the effect he thought he wanted he would work with a stopwatch and red pencil, marking each picture on the back to indicate what sort of angle and distance the movie camera should shoot from and how long it should linger on each still.

"The secret is in juxtaposition," Jones said. "The relationships, the arrangement. After twenty-five years, the other things—the framing and the panning—are easy."

Everyone was excited about the technique and the way it could be used to make people feel that Richard Nixon belonged in the White House. The only person who was not impressed was Nixon. He was in a hotel room in San Francisco one day recording the words for one of the early commercials. The machine was turned on before Nixon realized it and the end of his conversation was picked up.

"I'm not sure I like this kind of a . . . format, incidentally," Nixon said. "Ah . . . I've seen these kind of things and I don't think they're very . . . very effective."

Still, Nixon read the words he had been told to read.

In the afternoons, Treleaven, Garment, and Shakespeare would go to Gene Jones's studio to look at the spots on a little machine called a Movieola. If they were approved, Jones would take them to a sound studio down the street to blend in music, but they never were approved right away. There was not one film that Garment or Shakespeare did not order changed for a "political" reason. Anything that might offend Strom Thurmond, that might annoy the Wallace voter whom Nixon was trying so hard for; any ethnic nuance that Jones, in his preoccupation with artistic viewpoint, might have missed: these came out.

"Gene is good," Treleaven explained, "but he needs a lot of political guidance. He doesn't always seem to be aware of the point we're trying to make."

Jones didn't like the changes. "I'm not an apprentice," he said. "I'm an experienced pro and never before in my career have I had anyone stand over my shoulder telling me to change this and change that. When you pull out a shot or two it destroys the dynamism, the whole flow."

The first spot was called simply VIETNAM. Gene Jones had been there for ninety days, under fire, watching men kill and die and he had been wounded in the neck himself. Out of the experience had come *A Face of War*. And out of it now came E. S. J. [for Eugene S. Jones] #1, designed to help Richard Nixon become President.

Harry Treleaven and Len Garment and Frank Shakespeare thought this commercial splendid.

"Wow, that's powerful," Treleaven said.

THE FOURTH OF the ten scheduled panel shows was done in Philadelphia. It was televised across Pennsylvania and into Delaware and New Jersey. Roger Ailes arrived in Philadelphia on Wednesday, September 18, two days before the show was to go on the air. "We're doing all right," he said. "If we could only get someone to play Hide the Greek." He did not like Spiro Agnew either.

The production meeting for the Philadelphia show was held at ten o'clock Thursday morning in the office of Al Hollender, program director of WCAU. The purpose was to acquaint the local staff with what Roger Ailes wanted to do and to acquaint Roger Ailes with the limitations of the local staff. Ailes came in ten minutes late, dressed in sweatshirt and sneakers, coffee cup in hand. He had a room at the Marriott Motor Hotel across the street.

"One problem you're going to have here, Roger," a local man said, "is the size of the studio. You've been working with an audience of three hundred, I understand, but we can only fit 240."

"That's all right. I can get as much applause out of 240 as three hundred, if it's done right, and that's all they are—an applause machine." He paused. "That and a couple of reaction shots."

"I'm more concerned," Ailes said, "about where camera one is. I've talked to Nixon twice about playing to it and I can't seem to get through to him. So I think this time we're going to play it to him."

"You ought to talk to him about saying 'Let me make one thing very clear' ten times every show," someone said. "It's driving people nuts."

"I have, and Shakespeare told me not to mention it again. It bugs Nixon. Apparently everybody has been telling him about it but he can't stop."

After half an hour, Roger Ailes left the meeting. "Those things bore me," he said. "I'll leave Rourke to walk around and kick the tires." He went across the street to the motel. The morning was clear and hot.

"The problem with the panels is that we need variety," Ailes said. "Nixon gets bored with the same kind of people. We've got to screw around with this one a little bit."

"You still want seven?" an assistant, supplied by the local Republicans, asked.

"Yes, and on this one we definitely need a Negro. I don't think it's necessary to have one in every group of six people, no matter what our ethnic experts say, but in Philadelphia it is. *U.S. News & World Report* this week says that one of every three votes cast in Philadelphia will be Negro."

"I know one in Philadelphia," the local man, whose name was Dan Boozer, said. "He's a dynamic type, the head of a self-help organization, that kind of thing. And he is black."

"What do you mean he's black?"

"I mean he's dark. It will be obvious on television that he's not white."

"You mean we won't have to place a sign around him that says, 'This is our Negro'?"

"Absolutely not."

"Fine. Call him. Let's get this thing going."

"Nixon is better if the panel is offbeat," Ailes was saying. "It's tough to get an articulate ditchdigger, but I'd like to."

"I have one name here," Boozer said. "Might be offbeat. A Pennsylvania Dutch farmer."

"No! No more farmers. They all ask the same dull questions."

The morning produced an Italian lawyer from Pittsburgh, a liberal housewife from the Main Line, and a Young Republican from the Wharton School of Finance and Commerce.

"Now we need a newsman," Roger Ailes said.

I suggested the name of an articulate reporter from the *Evening Bulletin* in Philadelphia.

"Fine. Why don't you call him?"

"He's a Negro."

"Oh shit, we can't have two. Even in Philadelphia. Wait a minute—call him, and if he'll do it we can drop the self-help guy."

But the reporter was unavailable. Then I suggested Jack McKinney, a radio talk-show host from WCAU. Ailes called him and after half an hour on the phone, McKinney, who found it hard to believe the show would not be rigged, agreed to go on. Then I suggested a psychiatrist I knew: the head of a group that brought Vietnamese children wounded in the war to the United States for treatment and artificial limbs.

"What's his name?"

"Herb Needleman."

Roger Ailes called him. Herb Needleman agreed to do the show. Roger Ailes was pleased. "The guy sounded tough but not hysterical. This is shaping up as a very interesting show."

A newsman from Camden, New Jersey, was added, and, at four o'clock, Ailes called Len Garment in New York to tell him the panel was complete.

". . . That's six," he was saying, "and then we've got a Jewish doctor from Philadelphia, a psychiatrist, who—wait a minute, Len, relax . . . I—yes, he's already accepted, he . . . Well, why not? . . . Are you serious? . . . Honest to God, Len? . . . Oh, no, I can get out of it, it'll just be a little embarrassing . . . No, you're right, if he feels that strongly about it . . ." Roger Ailes hung up.

"Jesus Christ," he said. "You're not going to believe this but Nixon hates psychiatrists."

"What?"

"Nixon hates psychiatrists. He's got this thing, apparently. They make him very nervous. You should have heard Len on the phone when I told him I had one on the panel. Did you hear him? If I ever heard a guy's voice turn white, that was it."

"Why?"

"He said he didn't want to go into it. But apparently Nixon won't even let one in the same room. Jesus Christ, could you picture him on a live TV show finding out he's being questioned by a shrink?"

There was another reason, too, why Herb Needleman was unacceptable. "Len says they want to go easy on Jews for a while. I guess Nixon's tired of saying 'balance of power' about the goddam Middle East."

So, at 4:15 P.M., Roger Ailes made another call to Dr. Needleman, to tell him that this terribly embarrassing thing had happened, that the show had been overbooked. Something about having to add a panelist from New Jersey because the show would be televised into the southern part of the state.

"You know what I'd like?" Ailes said later. "As long as we've got this extra spot open. A good, mean, Wallaceite cab driver. Wouldn't that be great? Some guy to sit there and say, 'Awright Mac, what about these niggers?' "

It was five o'clock in the afternoon. The day still was hot but Roger Ailes had not been outside since morning. Air conditioning, iced tea, and the telephone.

"Come on," Roger Ailes said. "Let's go find a cab driver." He stepped out to the motel parking lot and walked through the sun to the main entrance. The Marriott was the best place they had in Philadelphia. Eight cabs were lined up in the driveway. The third driver Roger Ailes talked to said that he was not really for Wallace, but that he wasn't really against him either.

"What's your name?" Roger Ailes said.

"Frank Kornsey."

"You want to go on television tomorrow night? Right across the street there, and ask Mr. Nixon some questions. Any questions you want."

"I've got to work tomorrow night."

"Take it off. Tell them why. We'll pay you for the hours you miss, plus your expenses to and from the studio."

"My wife will think I'm nuts."

"Your wife will love you. When did she ever think she'd be married to a guy who conversed with the next President of the United States?"

"I'll let you know in the morning," Frank Kornsey said.

Back in the motel room, the talk drifted to some of the curious associations into which Nixon seemed to fall. People he sought to align himself with, whose endorsement he was so pleased to accept, when even in political terms they probably did him more harm than good.

"That Wilkinson, for Christ's sake, he's like a marionette with the strings broken," Ailes's director said. The director had come over from the studio in midafternoon, after working on final placement of the cameras.

"Oh, Wilkinson's a sweet guy," Ailes said, "but he's got absolutely no sense of humor."

"If you're going to keep using him as a moderator, you should tell him to stop applauding all the answers."

"He's been told," Ailes said, "he's been told. He just can't help it."

Ailes got up from the table. "Let's face it, a lot of people think Nixon is dull. Think he's a bore, a pain in the ass. They look at him as the kind of kid who always carried a book bag. Who was forty-two years old the day he was born. They figure other kids got footballs for Christmas, Nixon got briefcases and he loved it. He'd always have his homework done and he'd never let you copy. Now you put him on television, you've got a problem right away. He's a funny-looking guy. He looks like somebody hung him in a closet overnight and he jumps out in the morning with his suit all bunched up and starts running around saying, 'I want to be President.' I mean this is how he strikes some people. That's why these shows are important. To make them forget all that."

# IN THE COUNTRY OF THE YOUNG, PART II

## (NOVEMBER 1969)

## *John W. Aldridge*

*" . . . If the young wish to make society over in the image of their idealism, they will need all the force of personality they can muster. They will need quite simply to be exceptional men, exceptional in mind, imagination, sensitivity, and courage."*

ONE CANNOT OBSERVE the student activist drama for very long without beginning to feel, with Marianne Moore, that "there are things that are important beyond all this fiddle." At one time we would not have needed to be reminded what those things are. But after nearly a decade of activist fiddle and at least two decades of being brainwashed by the doctrine that whatever is young is right, we have become ashamed to admit a truth we once thought too self-evident to need stating: that universities are not primarily rebel encampments, forums of political debate, or media for the distribution of pamphlets, but institutions whose first function is to train intelligence and preserve cultural standards.

It is perfectly true that historical precedent exists, particularly in Europe and South America, for both the activist and the educational roles of the universities. Very often in the past students have served as indispensable agents of public conscience, using their relative freedom from the pressures of expediency and compromise to impress upon the adult world the reality of moral issues on which there must be no compromise. But almost always in the past the two roles have existed in some sort of balanced relation to each other, and except in times of the most extreme ideological crisis, the one did not usurp, eclipse, or threaten to vitiate the authority of the other. Today, however, the activist role has become so inflated in our universities and the educational role so diminished, where not downright subverted, that we now accept it as customary to find students whose function on the campus is primarily that of agitation and only marginally that of becoming educated. Obviously, there are serious and intelligent students who are dedicated to activism. But since we can hardly assume that the many thousands or even millions of young people now engaged to one degree or another in campus agitation are *all* serious or intelligent enough to be dedicated political idealists, we must presumably seek elsewhere for an explanation of their behavior. In addition to the reasons I have already offered—the rather complicated psychological motives for confrontation, the need, among other things, to oppose, and be opposed by, adult authority in order to define personal identity—one might suggest that the present college population is so constituted that many of its members are bound to be drawn to activism simply because they are suited to no other role. This is, after all, the first student generation to be admitted to the universities on the principle that higher education is a right that should be available to all, and at the same time a necessity for anyone who hopes to achieve some measure of success in middle-class society. The result is that for the first time in our history the universities have had to accept large masses of students who may have proper credentials from the secondary schools—because those schools have themselves been obliged to lower their standards to accommodate the mediocre majority—but who possess neither the cultural interest nor the intellectual incentive to benefit from higher education. Such students, when confronted with complex ideas or stringent academic requirements, tend to sink into a protective lethargy or to become resentful because demands are being made on them which they are not equipped to meet and have no particular desire to meet. Most of them did not want to go to the universities in the first place but did so for reasons of practical expediency: parental pressure, fear of the draft, or the promise of a better job after graduation. But these motives, since they are imposed from without rather than generated from within, are not sufficient to sustain them through the rigors of their course work or give them a sense of purpose inside the structure of the university. Hence, their natural impulse is to try to compensate for their failure of ability or interest by involving themselves in some extracurricular activity which happens today to be political activism.

This kind of involvement has at least one important advantage over involvement in football and fraternity life: popular opinion has sanctified it as a worthy, even a heroic cause. Students with only marginal interests in anything else can, therefore, give themselves up to it not only without feeling guilty or frivolous, but with the pious conviction that they are doing something far more valuable—and certainly far more "relevant"—than training their minds, and something also which requires no special talent or mental capacity beyond a certain talent for indignation and the power to be vigorously inarticulate while trying to express it. Thus, they are afforded moral justification for not doing what they do not want to do, and at the same time an approved outlet for hostilities resulting from the pressures that are exerted upon them to do what they are not readily able to do.

But perhaps the most crucial factor of all is simply the boredom of the vast majority of students, a boredom which must be at least equal to, if not considerably worse than, that of the population as a whole. Without strongly internalized ambitions and interests that are satisfiable within the university system, average students, like average people everywhere, are entirely dependent upon outside stimuli to provide them with the distractions needed to make life bearable. The greater the intellectual vacuum, the greater the need for distraction, a vacuum in people being presumably even more abhorrent than it is in nature. Thus, run-of-the-mill students are especially vulnerable to the enticements of activism as well as to those of its soul-brother philosophy of hippyism. Activism supplies them not only with abundant opportunity to be active without having to think, but with a sense of concrete physical involvement in a kind of experience from which normally they feel rather tragically excluded. Here, after all, they are: young, vigorous, hairy, horny, not terribly bright, and aching for murder, and all the great occasions for challenge and adventure seem to have passed them by. They were born twenty years too late to have a part in that knightly crusade against tyranny which World War II now seems sentimentally to symbolize for their fathers. They did not even have the small but appealing satisfaction of going hungry in the Depression. And to make matters worse, the only available war is one they cannot morally accept and which they would consent to fight in only under the gravest duress. Obviously, there is a vacuum here more insidious than intellectual vacuum, an absence of the opportunity for therapeutic bloodshed, and for the really imperative confrontation between man and his fear of death.

The virtue of activism is that it provides a fair substitute for this lost opportunity. It restores the primitive connection between belligerent virility and a hostile environment, and, in so doing, makes it possible for the young to get a little of their own back from history. It allows them to fight their own morally acceptable war, carry on their own knightly crusade against tyranny, in brick-throwing street battles with the police and in stalwart confrontations of nerve with authorities old enough to be as enviably favored by history as Dad. They can taste blood in these encounters, and they can taste fear, and with a little luck they can contrive to become martyrs and spend a night or two in jail. The police may not be entirely satisfactory replacements for the Nazis (although there are differences of opinion on this score), but they can be as easily charged with brutality as the universities can be charged with corruption, and so can be conveniently transformed into enemies one can hate with a clear conscience and attack whenever one needs proof of one's courage or relief from one's boredom. Through activism, in short, life can become once again a frontier and a battlefield. The bland abstractedness of university life is canceled by violence and melodrama, and those who cannot function effectively on the frontier of ideas are brought back into touch with a reality they can understand.

The main difference between activism and hippyism—at least where the question of their attractiveness to the young is concerned—seems to be that hippyism appeals to an even more feckless and intellectually empty sector of the student population than activism does. In other respects they are very much alike, particularly in the respect that both offer powerful distractions from boredom and even more powerful rationalizations for that sensation of being without identity and purpose which afflicts so many mediocre students in the mass university society. If activism flatters the mediocre by allowing them to believe that their search for distraction is really a heroic political crusade, hippyism similarly flatters them by allowing them to believe that their ineffectuality is in fact a serious metaphysical position and connected in some portentous way with the power of positive feeling, courageous individualism, and the mystical wisdom of the East.

Thus, the hippie notion of complete freedom to do your own thing in your own way is attractively translatable into the notion that to be accepted by the group you don't have to have very much of a thing or be able to do very much with it. All that matters is that it is your own and *you* are doing it. Hence, you are free, and respected for being free, to be your own limp and aimless self. The ego dividends, furthermore, are enormous. In doing your own thing you are performing an act of spurious creativity and individuality entirely without cost to yourself. You are emulating the artist while enduring none of the agony and needing none of the talent of the artist, for the stipulation that you can do as you like relieves you of the necessity to produce anything interesting or important. The act is totally onanistic. It is for your benefit alone. Therefore, if doing your own thing happens in your case to be doing nothing but listening to your beard grow or sitting under a tree and plucking that old guitar or some other equally meditative activity, that is perfectly all right.

The hippie interest in uninhibited feeling has very much the same kind of appeal. Feeling, after all, is a private affair. Nobody can be sure what you are feeling or if, in fact, you are feeling anything. Also, the etiquette governing hippie feeling requires that you not talk about it or express it except in a grunt or almost any intestinal noise signifying ecstasy. Your only obligation toward feeling is to feel it. But the person of defective emotional equipment or limited vocabulary is protected on all counts. He does not have to describe what he feels, so if he feels nothing, nobody is the wiser.

THIS PHILOSOPHY, WHEN applied to sexual feeling, yields similar protective benefits. The hippie doctrine of more or less random, free-for-all sex would of course appeal irresistibly to any normal raunchy adolescent who has harbored the dream of one day discovering a paradise in which he could have a quick lay whenever he felt like it without having to worry about the girl or feel anything beyond the joy of ejaculation. Suddenly under the copulative offices of hippyism he is at least theoretically allowed to do just that, and what is even more delightful, he is allowed to do it on the very best of all possible moral terms. He can tell himself that while indulging in this form of coital masturbation he is actually performing a service to bourgeois society by helping to liberate it from its repressive sexual attitudes, and even that in the enjoyment of his freedom, he is attaining oneness with the Infinite, God in this case being, to update James Joyce, not a shout but a screw in the street. Thus, all the major pieties of the hippie moral canon—personal freedom, defiance of social convention, the sacramental nature of orgasm—are marshaled to the support of the urge for erotic anarchy among those of the young who have nothing on their minds but their groins.

It is also interesting to notice how much of the attraction of hippyism derives, like that of activism, from its power to provide an outlet for the nostalgia felt by the young for a past they were born too late to experience. If activism gives them an opportunity for violence and a sense of heroic mission emulative of the more adventurous moments of history, hippyism allows them to affect the manners and costumery which have become identified with the life-styles of past ages. Thus, one sees the hippie young wandering the streets dressed in the U.S. Army tunics of World War I, in the broad-brimmed hats and plunging sideburns of the Western plainsman, in the headbands of Comanche braves, in Edwardian suits, the smocks of French Bohemian painters, or the gaudy saris of guru-land.

One supposes that in itself there is no particular harm in this sort of masquerade. The young need to have something to do with their banality. But its social and psychological implications are depressing in the extreme. At the most serious level it is obviously meant to represent an act of rejection of the modern age and a declaration of preference for drama, individuality, and romance. The World War I uniform is presumably cherished as a sacred relic of a war fought according to the principles of a now-debased idealism. The Western plainsman, with or without his sideburns, enjoyed the distinction of being a loner, a law unto himself, the master of his manhood, and of using his strength in honorable contest with the primitive forces of nature, a kind of contest no longer possible in the denatured society of the present time. The Indian, of course, was the original American frontier Negro, the first victim of our corrupt bureaucratic system. He was also our first innocent, happy and free in his native Eden, until the white man conquered and brainwashed him so that he would be content to live miserably on a reservation. To emulate him is not only to remind the Establishment of its ancestral guilt. It is to suggest that the young too were once happy and free like the Indian and might have remained so if only they had been left alone by adults to do as they pleased.

All this is understandable, if rather infantile, regressivism. But the sad thing is that as a form of defiant self-assertion it is so singularly impotent, so utterly without force or originality, so lacking in the power to make a critical or even satirical point or disturb in any serious way the complacency of those it is supposedly intended to provoke. As social protest it is empty because it offers one kind of futility in ostensible rebuttal of another kind of futility. If modern life seems meaningless, it is absurd to attack it by resorting to an even more blatant meaninglessness. Walking around in that exhumed costumery of another age is no more interesting or daring than capitulating to the system and becoming a General Motors slave. In fact, the true radical

gesture these days would be to do just that. But both have equally little relation to the problem of how to achieve real identity and individuality in the modern world.

Yet this is undoubtedly just the point: the hippie young have no
interest whatever in achieving real identity, and the only individuality
they seem capable of is a most curious kind shared by thousands of
others to all appearances exactly like themselves. This corporate,
ready-to-wear idiosyncrasy is clearly their means of evading for as long
as possible the trauma of self-confrontation and the attendant trauma
of finding themselves gazing into the pit of their own bottomless
vacuity. So long as they enjoy the camouflage of interchangeable sarto-
rial decor, they will be protected from all encounters with the real and
with the self. They can become as children and exist forever in that
state of fantasy in which children dress up in the clothes of their parents and in so doing imaginatively take on the awesome mystery and
glamour of adults. But these particular children would not be caught
dead in the clothes of their parents, for the variety of death they most
abhor is adulthood. They prefer to remain at the stage of development
where role-playing, the amusing charade of the nursery, is an end in
itself, and where, through the costumes they put on and take off, they
can make and remake imaginary selves, secure in the knowledge that
nothing they do is real, that life is a fiction, that all is as it appears to
be, and everything appears to be something else.

All that I have said here may seem to be accurately descriptive only
of the dullest and least accomplished members of the student population. They are logically the most susceptible to boredom as well as sufficiently uncritical to be taken in by such mindless entertainments as
hippyism. Yet any sort of close contact with the young soon convinces
one that the tendencies dramatized so flamboyantly by the mediocre
can also be found among many of their more gifted and intelligent
contemporaries, whose distinction is perhaps that, being smarter, they
dramatize them not flamboyantly but with a kind of leaden self-righ-
teousness. But mediocre and gifted alike appear to share the same
compulsive need for diversion and excitement, the same indifference,
if not downright hostility, to ideas, the same horror of adulthood, the

same obsession with procedural questions and material solutions, and the same desire to inflate the role of student into a lifelong professional career.

IT IS A common experience in the universities to find students who, regardless of their capabilities, have absolutely no notion of what they want to do with their lives, and to whom the idea of doing anything beyond what they are already doing is tainted with the foul smell of compromise and, therefore, of corruption. Integrity for them appears to consist in the infinite refusal to commit themselves to any program of action that might challenge their moral presuppositions or force them to leave behind the protective sanctity of studentism. The worldly ambitions of earlier generations to become doctors, lawyers, businessmen, or artists—and the very best of these it was possible to become—are of course still occasionally to be found. Regressivism even among the young is not always infantile. But such ambitions are rare and they are suspect because as a rule the young are frightened both by what they consider the arrogance of any aspiration to excellence, and by the likelihood of having sooner or later to scale down whatever aspiration they may have in order to meet the requirements of expediency, the practical limits imposed by life and human weakness. It seems to them better not to aspire at all, and thus keep one's idealism intact, than to aspire in the face of almost certain compromise and be forced to settle for something less than absolute fulfillment. Their need for instant gratification demands that success be guaranteed before they will consent to try for it. Hence, it is the usual thing to find them describing the future in terms of self-protective negations and their plans for the future, if any, in terms of strategic withdrawals and postponements. One will try after graduation to go to Europe for a year and look around; one will apply to the Peace Corps; one will hitchhike out to Berkeley and do a little demonstrating and street-fighting; one will contrive to stay forever in graduate school.

It is easy to understand how anyone in his right mind might hesitate to embrace the joys of adulthood in a time like the present. The options open to the young for the pursuit of an adventurous or productive future may not actually be, but do certainly seem to be, far more limited than they were, and the chances are very good that before one has had time to discover what they are, one will get killed or maimed in a meaningless war. This is no country for young men right now, and it has never been a country for old men. But the failure of a sense of future in the young is not the result simply of adverse conditions peculiar to this age. They also suffer the handicap of having formed their impressions of adulthood largely on their parents, and it is obvious that the example of their parents has in most cases given them little except strongly negative attitudes toward the possibilities of adult life.

To the extent that they are certain of anything at all, they appear to be in agreement on one point: they do not want to become like Mother and Dad. The prospect of settling down in a dull job and a dull house, working to pay off the mortgage, seeking identity in reproduction, and then living for the children—with all that this implies in boredom, self-sacrifice, and generalized atrophy of the soul—fills them with a special kind of terror. Yet their experience of their parents has given them very little understanding of what the alternatives to this sort of life might be, and very little impulse to create their own alternatives. The best they seem able to do is lose themselves in their own form of middle-class anesthesia and live in the hope that some benevolent catastrophe will destroy adult society before they are obliged to enter it.

A large part of their problem is that their relation to both their parents' way of life and the social environment in general has been so lacking in abrasiveness that they have not been impelled to create their identities through opposition or insubordination. If, as I said earlier, this deficiency has given them a singular indifference to questions of quality and an overriding concern for procedural problems and material solutions, it has had an even more crippling effect on their power to think independently about the future and to initiate the kind of intensely personal rebellion *toward* the future which can only result from an intensely personal rebellion against a restrictive past.

Thus, it is not enough for the young simply to feel alienated from the way of life of their parents and to have no wish to emulate it. They must be *productively* alienated in the sense that they are stimulated or provoked into wanting to create for themselves a more vital and meaningful way of life. Unfortunately, the trouble with their particular form of alienation is that it is too complete to be productive in this way. It involves apparently a breakdown of understanding, sympathy, communication, and even mutual hostility so total that they are simply abstracted from their parents' world altogether and left stunned by the utter incomprehensibility of everything their parents represent. Hence, the effect of their alienation is not liberating but stultifying because it closes out every opportunity for effective connection with the home environment, and in particular the kind of connection that is produced by overt conflict. The generation gap is thus, contrary to middle-aged opinion, far more damaging to the young than it is to their parents, for the psychic health of the young can well depend on their being able to communicate with their parents, even if communication consists of shouting and screaming at them, so that they themselves can, if they so choose, create the gap on their own initiative and discover such freedom as they can in that ritual stroke of umbilical surgery. But when they are deprived of this possibility, the young tend to fall *into* the gap and to flounder there in a state of bewilderment, or they will simply desert from adult society without ever having belonged to it or declared war on it, and spend their time seeking ways—and usually the most insipid ways—to tranquilize their feelings of confusion and ineffectuality. For their need is, and must always be, to reach their parents, to be able to identify with them or do battle with them, and in so doing to define themselves.

This is to suggest that if the young had encountered genuine resistance from their parents, if their mothers had been strict disciplinarians rather than meekly permissive and their fathers had been domineering, bigoted, and hypercritical, thus becoming figures of influence, however negative, on the lives of their children, there might have been some real ground for confrontation, some palpable force to defy or overthrow. But the parents of this generation were evidently so often bland, tolerant, well-meaning, and anxiously solicitous of their children that the only possible response to them was one of indifference or sad contempt, neither of which offers a very sound basis for rebellion, self-definition, or even a usable Oedipus complex.

Such a basis has of course been provided to some degree by the universities, which represent for many of the young their first contact with a structured and potentially resistant environment, and, therefore, their first opportunity for the kind of confrontation denied them by their parents. But the trouble with the universities is that they provide this opportunity too late in a young person's psychological development to benefit him to any important extent, so late, in fact, that it more often than not does him important harm. By the time he has reached university age he should ideally have already formed the emotional and intellectual premises on which he will create his place in adult society. He should already have acquired the wounds and frustrations needed to propel him toward some goal of personal fulfillment. He should already have begun to convert his hostilities into determination and his sense of inadequacy into an ambition to excel. But if he has had to wait until university age to encounter an environment that will generate these compensatory impulses in him, he is likely to become arrested in the role of perpetual confrontation and reconfrontation of authority because his experience is, in effect, forcing him to regress to a stage of development which is inappropriate to his age. Instead of being free by that time to use the facilities of the university to train his mind and prepare himself for effective adulthood, he is compelled to use the university as an arena for the enactment of the parent-child conflict he never had, for getting rid of aggressions which he should have got rid of or learned how to turn to his own emotional advantage years before. Thus, the opportunity for rebellion provided the young by the universities is essentially an opportunity to remain adolescent, to carry forward the missed rebellion of their childhoods, and while so doing to stay safely within the benevolent protection of the institution, to make a fetish of concern for the deplorable conditions of university life—in the hope of course of making them seem repressive enough to deserve being rebelled against—and to exist in such a fever of indignation over the evils of adult society that they will seem morally justified in not joining it. In a very real sense the child is indeed the father of the man, and if the child does not have a chance to father the man at the right psychological moment, he is likely to remain a child forever.

IT IS NOTHING new to say that a little material hardship would also have had a liberating effect on the young. One does not wish to reanimate that ancient cliché with which self-made men used to browbeat their indolent sons, the one about getting up before dawn, milking six cows before breakfast, and walking four miles through hip-deep snow to the little red schoolhouse. This is our mythic apprenticeship for greatness, but it has turned far more fathers into bores than it has created heads of state.

Yet the human organism is so constructed that, left undisturbed, its natural tendency is to lie under a tree all day and pluck that old guitar. Some pressure of necessity or irritation, whether external or internal, is required to get it on its feet. It must hunger, thirst, lust, itch, or aspire, come into some abrasive relation with either its physical environment or its guilts, before it is motivated to go to work. Thus, the children of affluence and permissiveness have a double problem. They have been emotionally as well as intellectually impoverished because the irritant of necessity is missing from their physical environment and the irritant of guilt is missing from their psychological environment. They have been so heavily indulged by their parents, have been the recipients of such massive quantities of every kind of unearned largess, that they feel no need to ingratiate themselves with their parents in order to win their attention or approval. They already have more approval than they can stomach simply by virtue of being the marvelous creatures they are. If there is a burden of proof or reason to feel guilty, it belongs not to them but to their parents. They are the ones who must earn the approval of their children, for they, after all, bear the responsibility for having caused the children to be born into this dreadful world, and that is an offense for which no amount of atonement is excessive. In addition, they have caused their children to grow up with a sense of economic security so complete that the traditional obligation to do something or become somebody seems downright anachronistic. In the opinion of the young, it is absurd to spend one's life worrying about money when there is obviously so much of it around. And if parents continue in the face of this fact to spend their lives worrying about money, that only proves the truth of what the young have all along been saying: that the older generation has been corrupted by materialism and has lost touch with the things of the spirit, which of course can only be properly appreciated if one is relieved of the necessity of having to worry about money.

The great virtue of economic depression is that it combines a very low degree of opportunity with a very high degree of motivation. It creates limits within which one is forced to function and, in cutting down the range of available choices, it dispels the confusion about where best to apply one's energies. One *has* to apply them only where conditions permit, and one has to apply them in order to stay alive. Hence, one takes the available job and in time that job may become a career and an entire way of life. But if the pressure of economic necessity is missing, not only is motivation reduced to a minimum but one is confronted by such a plethora of possibilities for using one's energies that one may become paralyzed with indecision and end by doing nothing at all—or, like mice in an overly complicated maze, turn psychotic and simply sit down and goggle at the wall.

This is the kind of paralysis afflicting so many of the young at the present time. Affluence and their relative freedom from the motivations of guilt have allowed them to view dispassionately the possible choices of career open to them and to have very little compulsion to choose one over the other. The choice, if it is to be made at all, must be made more or less arbitrarily, as if they were trying to decide between two identical glasses of sour milk. They must simply pick a career and say to themselves that that is what they will do with their lives; if they have to become something, they might as well become that. Such an attitude is not likely to produce ambitious men, and it is certain not to produce dedicated men. What it does produce is a college generation and a young professional generation whose concern, when they select a career, is all with externals, who make a certain choice because it will enable them to live in California where they can go skin-diving, or because it provides high fringe benefits, or, in the case of teaching, because it offers security and long vacations. Their deepest interests, their most basic psychological drives, are not involved at all—indeed, cannot be involved since their work is neither an extension nor a vindication of themselves. They are not called, chosen, or compelled but are simply working because they are obliged somehow to fill up their time and get paid for it. Hence, they fill up their time not in making original contributions to their fields, not in the creative investigation of ideas, but with the busy work of professionalism. They camouflage their lack of genuine involvement by serving perpetually on committees, by becoming experts in the art of political intrigue, by analyzing the administrative policies of institutions, by showing extravagant concern for the methodology, but rarely the content, of university instruction—by engaging in the trivial backing-and-filling that represents the diversion of the intellectually uncommitted.

It is perhaps fortunate for such people that affluence has produced a particular social etiquette which tends to discourage self-fulfillment and to promote self-effacement. The uncommitted young are naturally obedient servants of this etiquette, and it is not surprising that they have inflated it into very nearly the proportions of a new world religion—since whatever their ineffectuality impels them to do they are inclined first to make holy. But one notices that as the economic and psychological pressures to distinguish themselves from others, whether through aspiration or achievement, have declined, new pressures are being exerted among the young to enforce cooperation with others and deference to the feelings of others. Subservience to the interests of the group has come to be regarded as the supreme virtue as well as the most valuable attribute of the ideal society, while competitiveness of any kind, like intolerance of any kind, is considered very bad form indeed and may result in one's expulsion from the group. To be gentle and unassuming, to be solicitous of one's peers and sensitive to the delicate shifts of their emotional temper—in particular, to project an image of oneself as having no personal being apart from the being one shares with others and which is their communal property before it is your private property—all this is to be not merely humane but to affirm one's membership in the universal brotherhood of man, which enfolds us all in a warm placenta of togetherness and makes us one flesh and one soul.

The rather cloying interest shown by the young in the phenomenon known as "communication" has its significance here. Communication is an experience which they value particularly highly not only because it is the ultimate expression of their other-directedness but because it frees them of the necessity to raise themselves above others through individual achievement. If you are devoting your energies to trying to communicate with others, your psychic eye is turned outward rather than inward, and you are counting on an intimate relationship with another person to supply you with the gratification you would otherwise be forced to create through the solitary cultivation of your own resources. Besides, the two interests are political opposites. The desire for self-fulfillment makes for unpleasant competitive tensions between people and is by nature aristocratic, since it presupposes that what you make of yourself is more important than what you make with others. Communication, on the other hand, democratizes in the sense that it necessarily takes place between people who wish to share themselves with each other and who are, therefore, equals rather than egotistical snobs. Hence, if you have no particular ambition to fulfill yourself or suspect that you have very little self to fulfill, it is a great comfort to be able to rationalize the deficiency by insisting that reaching others is actually far more socially valuable than self-fulfillment, that, in fact, it may even be the *highest form* of self-fulfillment.

It is also comforting that the kind of communication most favored by the young just happens to be the nonverbal kind, which can be neither described nor objectively evaluated. You can say that you are communicating with someone, and it is impossible to prove whether you are or not. The whole thing is beyond the power of mere language, and of course it is so beclouded by specious religiosity that to question it would be as gross an infringement of the right of worship as asking the devout to demonstrate the efficacy of prayer. It is all a matter of soul speaking to soul, lovers passionately sweating skin to skin, blown minds exchanging psychedelic mash notes—non-thoughts floating in non-words between nonentities.

ALL THIS MAY help to clarify one of the most fascinating paradoxes underlying the psychology of the young: the contrast between their collective vociferousness and their individual inarticulateness, their public militancy of manner and their personal limpness of manner. This is an incongruity which causes everything about them to exist in double focus and to take on more than a little flavor of high black comedy. It seems logical to assume, for example, that the violence of the obscenity-screaming, brick-throwing student mob would be a fairly reliable indication that the rioters are people of violent temperament, whose aggressive behavior as a mob accurately reflects their aggressive character as individuals. Yet all it appears to signify is that the young are schizoid. For once away from the barricades most of them behave so very differently that one suspects that their public belligerence has no relation whatever to their real natures but is simply a kind of ferocious costumery they put on in order to play a convincing role in the generational hostility rites. Apparently, they have a manner, just as they have various items of peculiar clothing, which they consider it appropriate to wear on ceremonial occasions and another which they keep for every day, and the two are as dissimilar as the faces of Eve.

In ordinary circumstances, when they are not operating as a Tartar horde, the great majority of the young seem to be creatures of remarkably flaccid personality. One senses in them a singular blandness, even a temperamental nullity. Where tics and crotchets ought to be, one finds vast reaches of spiritual moonscape, cold, sunless, as vacant as space. Talking to them is rather like talking into an electronic box that takes messages for people who are not at home. Part of the problem is that so many of them are so entirely without self-consciousness and idiosyncrasy that it is immensely difficult to get any clear impression of the person behind the face. It seems that the fashion now is to have not a face but a facade, a decor personality to go with the decor costumery and consisting of features that are equally standardized. But where the costumery is at least flamboyant, the personality is so colorless that one is obliged to describe it almost entirely in negatives. It is possible to say that it tends to be basically insensitive, often as if under some kind of sedation; intellectually untidy, perhaps because the capacity or the paranoia required for intellectual precision is simply not there; frequently discourteous, although seemingly more out of abstractedness than of any specific urge to be rude; as lacking in grace and guile as a child of two; yet poised, relaxed, urbane, and always completely self-assured. There is as much surface presence and internal absence in the type as one would expect to find in the most promising junior executive at General Motors. The electric, tense, exacting, cantankerous, abrasive, ambitious, and obsessively self-monitory personality so characteristic of past generations of rebels seems to have become as obsolete as the fat boy and the freckled-faced redhead with warts, and one very, very seldom encounters any longer a young person who is sufficiently maladjusted as to be shy, or who appears ever to have known what it is like to blush or tremble with stage fright when required to perform in public. The acting experience comes early these days, and whatever else the young may or may not be, they are the most confident and accomplished troupe of public performers in our history.

Their style of delivery is as much a piece of standardized decor as their style of personality. It may be that we have achieved, after years of painful evolution through steadily widening gyres of unselective breeding, a mode of speech that is the precise verbal expression of our democratic heritage. But the young have carried the evolutionary process forward—if that is the correct direction—into yet another phase, and in so doing have inevitably increased the number and variety of resources on which colloquial American is able to draw for its linguistic materials. The result is that their speech is a sort of patois of most of the major sounds ever uttered by human lips within their hearing: Mississippi Negro dialect, Appalachia hillbilly, the jargon of technology, the jargon of political science, the jargon of psychiatry, the jargon of the ghetto, the jargon of rock-music culture, the jargon of the dope addict, and the jargon of Madison Avenue—to name only those that come first to mind. Americans—perhaps because they have become deranged by the babble of so many parochial tongues—have always been the most lingually sloppy and tone-deaf people on earth. Listening to them talk, particularly after one has been away from the country long enough to have stopped taking the sound for granted, is like listening to parrots just coming out of ether. Our women are famous throughout the world for having voices which seem to proceed from some vengeful agitation of razor blades immediately behind the nose. And just as this sound must be symptomatic of some atonality of soul, the slack and derivative speech of the young seems to be the perfect idiom of their fecklessness.

Of course it takes no special knowledge of human psychodynamics to understand why the young are this way. If they are people of notably limp personalities, it is very probably because certain factors necessary to the development of strong personalities are missing from their experience. This is to say that strong personalities, like all neurotic disorders, are made rather than inherited, and they are made, as a rule, not by conditions of jolly good fellowship such as are enjoyed by the masses of the young, but by conditions of a far more stressful kind.

Essentially, it would seem that the factors required for strong personality are the same as those required for strong ambition: some degree of psychological isolation at the right moment in life and some productive relationship with an accessible but resistant environment. To define himself, to become aware of himself at all as an individual human being, a person needs to acquire what Henry James called the perspective of "otherness." This can only be acquired if he has the opportunity to be physically alone for extended periods during adolescence, and creatively alone in the sense that he is deprived of the usual social distractions and soporifics and therefore is forced to turn inward and seek satisfaction in the consciousness of his own powers, the cultivation of his own unique perceptions. In time, if the isolation is prolonged, a person will develop a powerful awareness of his own identity and a correspondingly powerful awareness of the very different identities of other people. He will take on the spectatorial attitude, the habit of seeing what is happening in the world of others as interesting or remarkable or preposterous just because it is happening to them and not to himself, because they are strangers or actors performing a play in which he has no part. It may even be that the role of the spectator is essential in a very basic sense to the development of perception, for conceivably we see only to the extent that our eye is attracted by the incongruous and unusual. If nothing within the range of our vision seems remarkable, we are likely not to notice it at all or we may simply register it unconsciously as normal and therefore as forgettable. On the other hand, the greater our sense of the incongruous, the greater will be our effective range of vision, for we will be like children perpetually seeing the world as if for the first time. Freudian psychology suggests that intelligence begins when the individual begins to separate himself from his environment, when through psychological isolation he ceases to perceive his environment as merely an extension of himself—and so, it seems, does personality begin.

BUT THE STATE of isolation, however valuable it may be for a certain period, is neither desirable nor supportable if continued for too long a time. It can only lead to permanent withdrawal, a distortion of the perspective of otherness into a sense of estrangement, and eventual immobilization of the psyche. Luckily, the tendency of healthy people is to try sooner or later to break out of their isolation and achieve some kind of productive relationship with others by impressing their personalities on them, perhaps through idiosyncrasy, emotional warmth, intellectual excellence, or creative accomplishment. It is necessary to confront the human community and to make use of the energy or wisdom acquired in isolation to earn one's membership in the community or to define one's differences from it. But for this to be possible, the social environment must be accessible, and it must also be at least initially resistant. It must put up barriers which will stimulate one to impress one's personality upon it and try to subdue it. This is why access to the small, provincial environment such as the neighborhood and town, or to an oppressive home environment, is so necessary to vital rebellion, just as it is necessary to creation of vital personality. One is goaded into self-definition by the pressure exerted by the environment to force one into conformity.

But the problem for the young is, as I have suggested, that so many of these essential influences are missing from their lives. They are, above all, a generation which seems never to have been alone; hence, they have never endured psychological isolation or been compelled to develop the perspective of otherness. The experience of the small, provincial environment is as historically and culturally remote from them as the English country-house life portrayed by Jane Austen, and they most assuredly show no signs of having suffered from an oppressive home environment. To most of them the social world has not been an arena of personal confrontation or conflict but the very embodiment of irrelevance, for they have always known the vast, vacant, structureless world of modern suburbia, which it is impossible to identify with and even more impossible to rebel against, which does not encourage the spectatorial attitude or provide one with a sufficient sense of incongruity even to see it as effectively *other*. Everything about it conspires to make one wish not to see it, to make one turn away from it, but turn not into the self—since that would only complete the process of estrangement—but frantically outward to the society of one's contemporaries. For it is undoubtedly because they have been unable to identify with the physical character of their social environment that the young have identified so completely with one another and sought in the society of one another the sense of human connection denied them by their environment. In fact, it would seem that the society of one another *is* their only accessible social environment, their only medium of satisfactory social experience.

Thus, it follows with sound Darwinian logic that their personalities should be perfect adaptations to the requirements of the collectivist society which they inhabit, that they should be self-effacing, colorless, politic, and free of all competitive tensions and idiosyncrasies. They have not needed to prove their worth or compete for the approval of the group because approval is instantly granted as a condition of generational membership. They have not needed to develop themselves intellectually because the group does not believe in ideas, only in actions. They have not needed to learn how to express themselves in language because the group has learned how to communicate without resorting to language. They have never felt estranged from one another, only from everybody else, so there is no question of their ever having had to impose their personalities upon their environment in order to provoke or subdue it. They already *are* their environment—and it is perhaps not a sufficiently militant irony to daunt their deadly earnestness that their qualities of personality are remarkably similar to the qualities of their physical surroundings, that they are just as bland, vacant, and structureless as the dreck culture with which they cannot identify but which now seems to have reclaimed them, as the jungle sooner or later reclaims even the most domesticated of its creatures, as its spiritual brothers and human counterparts.

All this bears rather strikingly on the character of their rebellion, and they do rebel of course if only to determine whether they are as irresistible to strangers as they are to one another. But it seems evident that if the young display individually little or none of the aggressiveness they display collectively, the reason must be that their emotions aren't engaged by the issues which they collectively support, that there is something impersonal about their public anger and programmatic about their zeal for reform. They are demonstrating, it would appear, in the name of abstractions and theoretical constructs of issues rather than the concrete specifics of issues, and one supposes they are doing so because they lack direct personal experience of those issues, because they are precisely as detached from the world in which those issues literally exist as they are from the realities of their social environment.

This is to say that their activism seems to be the result more of ideological commitment than of direct personal frustration and suffering, and perhaps that is why they cling to it so passionately—because it is what they have instead of personal involvement, because it is a structure of ideological intensity which has all the appearance of feeling without having been derived from feeling, and so is their only means of confronting experience in a dynamic way. They are very probably the first generation of American rebels not to have suffered to some degree personally as a result of the injustices and inequities which they seek to eradicate and this has created a crippling separation between their principles and their emotions, between their official idealism and their practical understanding. If they had ever actually been the victims of privation or persecution, if they had ever known the ugliness of discrimination, lived among the poor of Appalachia or Harlem, gone hungry, fought in a war, or tried to survive under Russian or Chinese Communism, they might have found a living basis for their outrage and discovered the terms of an effective personal rebellion. They might also have found a corrective for their tendency to romanticize the masses as well as the joys of life in a socialist republic. But affluence, American citizenship, and their favored or unfavored position in history have deprived them of these experiences and so left them physically and psychologically isolated from the objects of their official compassion and anger, theoretical in their concern for other people's realities.

This quality of abstractedness is revealed in the oddly obscure vocabulary they use to describe the evils which they wish to overthrow. They talk compulsively and ritualistically about *power structures, systems, establishments, bureaucracy,* and *technology,* and the vagueness of these words, their failure, when used singly, to describe specific conditions in a real world, is symptomatic of their function as empty pejorative metaphors for problems not personally engaged in by those who use them. It almost seems that such language is intended to invent a reality, or to lay false claim to the existence of a reality, which the young can then attack—as if they lack an objective correlative for their sense of grievance, sufficient justification for their impulse to revolt. By the same token, they appear to be far more interested in being militant about these verbal abstractions than they are in working to correct conditions that do have objective existence. They will demonstrate against *technology* but do nothing to help the technologically unemployed, against *oppression* but do nothing to help the real victims of oppression, who are most certainly not themselves, against *power structures* but do nothing to curb the abuses of their own power structure, which is rapidly becoming the most powerful and bureaucratic of them all. But the point, of course, is that the unemployed and oppressed are unreal to the young because they are outside the range of their specific experience, while the abstract catchwords of their dissent, the Newspeak of the very technology they profess to hate, give them the only sense of connection they have with experience beyond the society of one another. It would seem that to the abstracted only abstractions are real, just as modes of procedure are more real to them than concrete goals, and the administration of universities is more important than the content and quality of the ideas generated within them. Clearly, the young are suffering from a massive dissociation of sensibility, a loss of relationship with living realities.

IT MAY BE that it is just this isolation which has given the young the impetus for their rebellion. It may be that their militant actions represent an effort to bring about a confrontation not with authority but with reality, the kind of face-to-face confrontation they have been unable to achieve in any other way. But it is one of the many sadnesses of their predicament that their search for reality leads them inevitably back to authority, since, given their isolation, there is nothing else for them to confront. They are locked into the programmed circuits of mass bureaucratic society to such an extent that even their rebellion must be carried out within them. Just as technology can only be described and attacked by the young in the language of technology, so power structures can only be opposed by the erection against them of new power structures, those of revolution becoming finally as repressive of individual freedom as those they are intended to destroy.

But a far more poignant irony lies in the fact that the vision of the future so widely shared by the young is also the result of technological programming. For it would appear that their isolation from the specifics of experience inside the bureaucratic cage has given them such a horror of experience that they have incorporated into their image of the ideal society precisely the bureaucratic restrictions they now find restricting, and so project a society purified of risk, uncertainty, and every form of physical and intellectual challenge, the aim presumably being to make life safe from every possible intrusion of life. Their abstractedness, in short, has caused them to conceive of a paradise of abstractedness, to escalate the nightmare of their alienation into a dream of utopian alienation.

This is of course exactly the kind of society that technology has been endeavoring all along to bring into being, and it is a logical extension of the one the young are now demonstrating against. If left alone, our present society will naturally evolve into it, and if the reforms of the young are instituted, it will most certainly do so more quickly. But what is especially interesting is that this is also a more highly disinfected version of the society which their parents created for the young when they were growing up, one in which measures could always be taken and solutions could always be found and happiness consisted of discovering infinite distractions from the real. Thus, it is possible to wonder, when they envision a world without risk, whether the young are not in fact expressing their nostalgia for the secure, permissive, and instantly gratifying lost Eden of their childhoods, where every day was Christmas, and Mother and Dad were the Good Fairy and Santa Claus for one brief shining moment before they turned into ogres. Surely, the controlled environment which they anticipate for the future and which technology will inevitably provide is not so very different from the controlled environment of the nursery, and it is perfectly appropriate to the child's fear of the dark forces of contingency that seem, in his nighttime imagination, so monstrous and threatening. But these happen also to be the forces that give the adult life its edge of adventure and provide the only assurance we have that life is something more than a bubble of contentment drifting between the security of the nursery and the perfection of the grave.

Apparently the young are so abstracted from experience and so fearful of adulthood that they find this simple truth either incomprehensible or unbearable. Yet one supposes that a crucial event of adulthood is the discovery of virtue in the imperfect and the unexpected. However disturbing it may be to the emotionally delicate, however obstructive it may be of our progress toward sociological Godhead, there is excitement in the refusal of things to be safe, pure, rational, and predictable. The young, of all people, should know this, since it is because we have problems that they have been able to enjoy the excitement of agitating for their solution. Once they are solved, the young will have agitated themselves out of work and right back into boredom. Yet, paradoxically enough, this most rebellious and boreable of generations seems to be excited by problems without believing in them. They may derive their emotional sustenance from them at the present time, but they fail to see any value in them either for themselves or for the race in general, and their first act of legislative business when they come to create the ideal society of the future will evidently be to declare them illegal. Hence, they do not understand how there might be very real benefits to be derived from experiences that have nothing to recommend them except the fact that they are imperfect or expose one to uncertainty. There is, for example, that much excoriated phenomenon of their university careers, the bad professor, whose badness might be their only reliable gauge of what a good professor should be or simply prove so abrasive that some enterprising student will be goaded by it into becoming smarter in the field than he is. If, on the other hand, students are confronted by nothing but good professors, they are likely to become overawed by the proliferation of expertise and go away convinced that the best that is known and thought in the world has already been known and thought. It is quite possible that much of the current boredom of university students is the result of their not having encountered sufficient stupidity in their instructors. Sometimes there is no greater stimulus to intellectual ambition than a good dull mind.

The young also apparently find little exhilaration in those other hazards and dislocations of life which can often prove so challenging. They appear to dislike, and to do all they can to avoid, encountering people who are capricious, crotchety, intolerant, or just plain bigoted rather than reasonable, understanding, and colorless. They find no stimulus, regardless of the final cost, in the experience of economic uncertainty, in the risk of getting a girl pregnant, or flunking out of college, or choosing the wrong career, or being absolutely alone and against the crowd just because it *is* a crowd and all those people cannot possibly be right. At the moment they may seem to be taking their chances with the police, but they are taking them not as isolated individuals, not as rebel-outlaws, but as buck privates in a vast army of righteous orthodoxy, whose actions have all the choreographed daring of battle scenes in Vista-Vision. They are also taking their chances in the name of reforms ultimately aimed at the abolition of imperfection from the earth, the removal of all cause for even their own dissent.

THIS IS NOT quite to suggest that, in order to be worth living, life needs to be as dreadful or dangerous as possible. Yet it does seem to be true that difficulty brings more of our essential humanity into play than tranquillity does and so heightens our responsiveness to life, in very much the way that disease rallies the body's defenses or the eye works more energetically in the presence of varying intensities of light than it does in an all-white room. If, as T. S. Eliot said, "human kind cannot bear very much reality," it also cannot bear too little. We need the challenge of an untrustworthy and resistant environment to wake us from our psychic sleep and give us again the adrenal charge of panic that kept us alive in the jungle dark. We also need to be reminded, as imperfection and risk do remind us, of the possibilities of renewal, of comic surprise, the miracle of the fortuitous in nature. We need to be confirmed in our sense that life is individual and original, that we can dare to be lone guns at the shoot-out, that there is still an alternative to lockstep, some room left on the frontier of becoming.

But if imperfection and risk reopen the circuits connecting us with life, perfection, if it were attainable, would be a state of death, and a desire for it must be a desire to die. The solution of a problem, the eradication of some source of enigma or disharmony, represents one more instance in which we have relinquished our hold on the unpredictable, have capitulated to stasis, because we have entombed in some scheme of order, and so neutralized what was once capable of explosive and vital surprise. We necessarily reduce the possibilities of life in our struggle to make it coherent, and we also reduce the number of areas in which we can effectively engage it. In a sense we struggle not simply to understand our experience but to solve it so that it will no longer have the power to hurt us. The mystery becomes explicable; the dark is illuminated: we see that the shadow under the trees was not a tiger after all; and we are not frightened anymore. But we are also less alive.

The fear of life must be powerful in the young because nothing enrages them more than imperfection, the innate refusal of people and institutions to die into order, and nothing obsesses them more than the necessity to dissolve ambiguities, rectify inequities, and absorb all extremes into a normative condition of equilibrium. Such a desire, in the service of some ideal of creative liberation, could be heralded as the altogether inevitable and necessary urge of a new generation to free society from its paralysis in outmoded patterns of conduct by instituting new patterns more productive of growth. But it would seem that for this generation the precise opposite is the case. Their desire is apparently not to expand possibility but to contract it, to harness experience in its infinite and disturbing variety, to harness men in their infinite and disturbing individuality, to harness the contingent in the service of the safe—in short, to free society from the oppressions of adventure and make it eventually possible for the race to evolve to a point of security where it will be able to exist without having to suffer the pain of life.

It is only through a profound alienation from the dynamics of experience that the human mind can think in such coldly generalizing abstractions about experience, and I have already suggested that this kind of alienation is particularly common among the young at the present time. It appears to be responsible for their tendency to see society in terms of large masses of people rather than in terms of individuals, and to be concerned with issues rather than ideas, with quantitative rather than qualitative values, with political and economic reforms rather than the rehabilitation of the physical and cultural environment. It also seems to have produced in them a narrowing of sensibility, a decrease in emotional and intellectual responsiveness, a passivity in the face of challenge, and a rigidity in the face of the ambiguous. Just as the urban and rural landscape has been uglified as a result of the materialism and environmental insensitivity of the men who exploit it, so personality has become trivialized by this same insensitivity to the qualities of existence beyond the material, by its inability to relate to the world except in the abstract, from the stand-point of social theories and technological programs.

All this is particularly unfortunate because if the young wish to make society over in the image of their idealism, they will need all the force of personality they can muster. They will need quite simply to be exceptional men, exceptional in mind, imagination, sensitivity, and courage. But the praiseworthy effort to provide all men with the opportunity for a decent life—and the social philosophy usually responsible for such an effort—is not always congruous with either the need for or the production of exceptional men. We can attempt to save the masses of people only at the risk of destroying the unique and individual. We can become so concerned about rights that we forget about privileges and responsibilities. In trying to abolish unfair distinctions we can wash out distinction. The quality of life can be diminished for all in the effort to raise the standard of living for all. We can easily produce—and may, in fact, have already produced—a society in which more and more people have less and less, and fewer and fewer have really enough. And of course the more we concentrate on providing for the security and sustenance of the whole population, the more sterilized of uncertainty and risk life will become. For a collectivist utopia must above all be bureaucratically organized and efficiently run, and every action must be judged on the basis not of its originality and daring but of its value in promoting the greatest good for the greatest number.

Nevertheless, before the young can create such a utopia, they must somehow manage to become original and daring themselves. If they expect to be the custodians of its conscience, as they have tried to be of ours, they had better acquire some direct knowledge of the specifics of moral experience, and this they cannot do without exposing themselves to hazards rather more potent than those they have so far confronted at the campus barricades. If they expect it to embody a revised and liberated American sensibility, they had first better become men of sensibility. If they wish it to be free of materialism, they had better stop thinking so exclusively in materialistic terms. They had also better begin now to develop human resources to put in place of the abolished materialism, resources which will enable them to survive in a world from which not merely materialism but all imperfections will presumably have been abolished—survive *and* create a civilization that will have the power to preserve the quality of the individual life at the same time that it guarantees the tranquillity of the collective life.

Yet this is just where the young seem to be singularly ill-equipped to be the administrators of a trouble-free society, for they have left out of account one vital factor: their own inability to live in such a society without going out of their minds. With no more problems to be solved, with no more injustices to demonstrate against, with no more repressive authorities to confront, they would need precisely the dedication to ideas, the interest in aesthetic values, in creative expression, in intellectual analysis, in the amenities of the leisured, affluent life which their preoccupation with solving material problems has prevented them from developing. Thus, in the long hard winters of utopia, they would have complete freedom to do their own thing and nothing to do but face the vacuum in themselves. They would be able to smoke pot all day and all night, pluck their guitars under every tree, screw on every street corner, and go naked whenever and wherever they pleased. But even the young can be diverted only so long by their diversions, by the soporifics that dull, by the psychedelics that substitute a chemical intensity for a life of meaning. Even the naked body grows familiar in time and becomes one more experience of life which is canceled out, which even the most assiduous voyeur is finally abstracted from, through boredom. It is possible that hang-ups would, in the process, be eradicated, and that would represent the achievement of one of the most vital social goals of the young. People would then be liberated from guilt as well as from imperfection and be free at last to feel absolutely nothing.

Undoubtedly, a society of this kind would eventually become polarized by two extreme psychological types, both of which would be mutations of types that are now rather familiar. There would be the catatonic, and there would be the berserk: the passive vegetable man and the violent mechanical man, opposites in their modes of behavior but identical in their paralysis of feeling. The catatonic would have ceased long ago to strive or respond, for all irritants would have disappeared from his sphere of consciousness. He would have no needs that were not supplied, no desires that were not instantly gratified. For days or weeks on end he would simply stare at walls or watch, fascinated, the copulation of insects. Having been relieved of the struggle of becoming, he would exist simply to be. The berserk type, on the other hand, would react very differently to the absence of irritants. He would become nervous and disoriented, would roam the streets with mayhem in his heart and nothing behind his eyes except perhaps a baby-blue look of death. Unable to discharge his hatreds in socially approved skirmishes with the police, he would periodically tear up the pavements and throw bricks through store windows and shout obscenities at the sky. It would be violence for its own sake, in the name of no cause except his need to remind himself of feeling, of the way it used to feel to be alive. In between these two extremes there would of course be the millions of normal people like ourselves, people going about their business as usual, seeing nothing amiss, finding nothing remarkable, being tolerant and forgiving, having learned long ago how to live tranquilly together in this best of all possible worlds.

# Voices from the Silent Majority

## Silent Majority

### Nixon's Elusive Constituency Speaks Up

#### (April 1970)

## Joseph C. Goulden

*And so—to you, the great silent majority of my fellow Americans—I ask for your support. Let us be united for peace. Let us also be united against defeat. Because let us understand: North Vietnam cannot defeat or humiliate the United States. Only Americans can do that.*
            —President Nixon to the nation, November 3, 1969

WE WERE RIDING through downtown Aurora, Illinois, in William G. Mitchler The Real Estate Man's brand-new Cadillac automobile. "Damn it, Mitchler," said Bobby Moga The Township Supervisor, "if you ever get into politics you're going to have to sell this thing. Who'd vote for a man who rides around in a car this big?" "I earned this car," replied William G. Mitchler, whose shoulders filled about half the front seat. "Give me a choice between the office and the car, and I think I'll keep on driving around."

Moga twisted sidewise in the seat to talk to me, the visiting journalist, in Aurora in quest of Mr. Nixon's Silent Majoritarians. Over the phone a few nights earlier I had explained to Moga that I had

249

obtained, from Herb Klein's office in the White House, a sampling of letters written to the President after the November 3 speech, that I intended to do an article on some of the persons who wrote them, and that I would like to visit with him.

The attention pleased Moga, a stocky fellow of thirty-seven with thinning hair, a firm grip, and a metal American flag in his lapel. "You mean that Mr. Nixon The President actually sat down and read my letter?" he asked when I arrived in his office. That I did not know, I said, only that the White House bureaucracy, upon request, disgorged his letter as "representative" of the 400,000-odd received the week following the address. "Think of that," Bobby Moga said. "You write the President, and they listen to you."

Now we were driving through Aurora, and talking about its attitude toward the war. Aurora is forty miles and two counties due west of Chicago, originally farming, now light industrial; population (Chamber of Commerce estimate) 100,000; but still far enough from The City to avoid what Moga called "the kooky stuff." "Most patriotic place in the whole country," Bobby Moga said. He pointed to a hardware store that rambled most the length of a city block. "Fellow there, on patriotic occasions, he furnishes flags for this entire section of the street. Good people here, none of that mess you have in Chicago or New York.

"This is a cute little incident that happened during the Moratorium. We have some of those damned people here, even in a decent town like Aurora. Some get out here from Chicago, some of them are homegrown, those damned hippies. But nobody pays much attention to them.

"Anyway, this guy with greasy long hair and those granny glasses—a ridiculous-looking creep, I get mad just looking at them—anyway, he came into the township building and he started setting up a card table and some signs.

"I got red. God but I got mad. I walked over to him and I didn't even read his sign. I knew what the hell he was all about. I said to him, What's your problem, pal? What's with you, pal? I kept calling him pal every second breath, that's the way to keep those bastards off balance.

"I said to him, You ain't setting up nothin' like that in here, pal, let's get movin', pal.

250

"Oh, hell yes, he started protesting, he was saying Nazi Germany and civil rights and freedom of speech and how I was no better than a German storm trooper, and I started getting madder.

"I reached out and grabbed him under my left arm, got a good hold on him, just like this"—and Moga turned in the seat and gripped himself under the arm to demonstrate his hold—"and I was holding him real tight, and he was hollering. And with my other arm, my right one—I'm right-handed, too, you know—I picked up his lousy stinking card table and his goddamned sign and I pulled the whole mess right through the door and pitched his ass out on Water Street. Don't bring that sort of crap into this building, pal, and don't make me mad, I told him. That's the only way to handle jerks like that—hustle'm right on outside. I'm not letting any goddamned hippie jerk of a demonstrator use my office for that sort of thing."

SANDUSKY, OHIO, IN early December is a place of raw, cheek-chilling cold, where gulls peck stupidly at the ice of Lake Erie, two blocks north of downtown, wondering what happened to the water; and even the locals hurry when out of doors. Economically, Sandusky is part of the Detroit-Pittsburgh industrial sprawl, with auto factories of each of the Big Three, foundries, and metals-fabricating plants. Geographically, Sandusky just misses the beaten path—too far north of the Ohio Turnpike to attract motorists without specific business there; too far west of Cleveland (126 miles) for a comfortable one-day trip; lacking even that most esteemed merit badge of contemporary boosterism, scheduled commercial airline service. Jean Gast, a pleasant, fortyish housewife and mother of four, has lived in Sandusky all her life, and the last twenty-three years, those of her marriage, in the same house her Irish-descended family occupied when she was a child. She isn't exactly bored, for she has her children, her bowling (trophies dominate a shelf at one end of the living room), her sewing (she is good enough to have a faithful clientele for her dresses), and her church work—but Jean Gast does recognize that her town isn't the intellectual center of the Western world.

"Sandusky is a stick-in-the-mud community," she volunteered after we had chatted awhile. "There's no tendency for people to take off and live elsewhere. You tend to associate with your high-school friends; the same people you grew up with you see the rest of your life. People may move out into the housing developments outside of town, but most stay right here."

But Jean Gast tries. Last year she did volunteer work at a neighborhood opportunities center, financed by OEO, attempting to bring a fifth-grade child up from third-grade reading level. After several months of tutoring he improved dramatically. "He began to do extra reading. You know, some of these children had never been to a public library. Lynn was so proud when he did well on his tests." But because of budget cuts the center closed, and Jean Gast is more than a little miffed with the Nixon Administration.

Jean Gast paid little attention to the war until her eldest son became a senior in high school. "I really became concerned about it then, when it began to get close to home." Her understanding of the war is limited to what she gleans from casual reading of daily newspapers and newsmagazines. "Lot of it I don't feel we will ever understand—I think we more or less drifted into it. But we made a pact with them (the South Vietnamese); when you do that, make a pact, you should honor it." Pause. "I don't feel we have enough information to know whether policies are right or not. Leave it to the leader."

Bob Gast, a heavy-bellied man in a work jacket, works at a General Motors plant. He drifted in to join our conversation. Does he hear much discussion of the war at work or among friends? "I'm afraid not. We have a pretty well-established group at the plant, men who've been there, and in the union, for twenty years or more. They're comfortable, very little bothers them."

Mrs. Gast listened to the President's speech in her living room—alone, because Bob Gast was working that night. Afterwards, she sat down at her portable typewriter and wrote Mr. Nixon a letter which said, in part:

> We did not vote for you in the last election, but now I wish there would be a place on the ballot to give you a vote of confidence, so that you would know we are 100% behind you. . . .We have quite a stake in your peace plan as we have

two boys in the service now. One is stationed in this country and the other is flying supplies into Da Nang. Also, we have a sixteen-year-old boy who is rapidly approaching draft age. . . . Stick to your guns and stand firm, not only with the enemy, but also with the dissenters and troublemakers who give aid and comfort to the enemy by tearing us apart from within. If only the quiet ones would raise their voices, they would drown out the protesters and let the Communists know we are still a united people.

Jean Gast mailed the letter at the corner at midnight while going to pick up her husband at the factory. "I had never written to a President before, but that night I felt he had the odds against him, and he needed someone to say they were with him. I really felt sorry for him, struggling against large odds and betting on the outcome."

BOBBY MOGA WAS especially pleased that I had come to Aurora on December 8, a Monday. "The combined service clubs are having a luncheon over at the YMCA today commemorating the Jap attack on Pearl Harbor. Let's go over there—it will give you an idea of what a helluva town this is, and how we get together behind the right ideas." Soon I found myself standing in line with several score Aurorans on a basketball court, awaiting a paper plate of fried chicken and stuffed cabbage. Bobby Moga's brother, John, shook my hand and gave me a red plastic comb embossed: MAKE JOHNNY MOGA THE PLUMBER YOUR PLUMBER.

Moga tugged at my arm. "Come on. We're putting you at the head table." I insisted I'd just as soon sit among the citizens at the long common tables. "No, no," Moga said, propelling me to the platform and a wooden folding chair next to a Marine major general. "Let's make sure I got your name right from Moga," said the toastmaster. He handed me a slip of paper on which was printed: MR. GOLDEN, REPRESENTING THE WHITE HOUSE.

My first horrified impulse was to snatch away the paper and swallow it. Posing as Captain Joe Golden, head of the Philadelphia Police Department's homicide squad, and as Joe Dealey, publisher of the *Dallas News,* are stunts I have performed under the impulsiveness of reportorial license, each time capitalizing upon someone's misintroduction. But as an agent of the Nixon Administration—"God no," I said. "I'm just a writer, here to do a story." "But Moga said Herb Klein sent you." "No, no, I got Moga's *letter* from Klein's office. I don't work for Klein." This intelligence disappointed the man, and I thought for a moment I would be sent to the kitchen to eat with the help. A few minutes later he said to four hundred assembled Aurorans: "And also with us at the head table today is Mr. Gordon from Herb Klein's office in the White House." I said something *sotto voce* that brought an alarmed glance from the Marine general, and I continued eating my fried chicken.

The luncheon was the idea of Dr. Stanley Parks, a dentist who is president of the Aurora Navy League, a quasi-official organization which lobbies for bigger Navy appropriations and warns the public against the Soviet naval menace. Parks said he had been questioned "as to why we would want to remember this day; are we trying to open up old wounds?" Something more was involved than honoring the 2,400 Americans who died at Pearl Harbor: "We remember that Americans reacted to the shocking attack with a unity that has never been expressed in the history of our country. . . . Americans weren't ashamed to profess their loyalty and their patriotism. . . . *Yes, patriotism stood at a high ebb.*" Now, Parks lamented, "loyalty and patriotism are regarded cynically as being left to the squares, and it is really something 'cool' to criticize and protest. The Constitutional right of dissent has degenerated to an excuse to undermine. From the Senate floor, the college campus, sensationalist picture magazines, and other such media, sanctimonious hypocrites would castigate the men who loyally serve our country . . ." Rising applause. ("Dammit, let's make sure Senator Percy gets a copy of Doc's speech," I heard a man say later. "Or better yet, let's send Doc to Washington and bring Percy home for a rest.")

Nine Pearl Harbor survivors from Aurora and the vicinity sat at round tables-of-honor with their wives—self-consciously excited about an event almost three decades distant, now revived to bring them unaccustomed attention. Police Captain Alex Puscas spoke for them. How sad it was, Puscas said, to hear taps sounded over soldiers' graves. "Will taps ever be sounded for the last time? Will America ever die? Not so long as its people do as we are doing at this moment—*Remember Pearl Harbor!*"

A local music teacher closed the proceedings with "The Battle Hymn of the Republic," truly a song for all seasons—Andy Williams sang it, agonizingly low and slow, the sad June morning when Bobby Kennedy's body was borne from the heavy gloom of St. Patrick's Cathedral; the Republicans sang it in Miami Beach two months later, then nominated Richard Nixon for the Presidency; now the Silent Majoritarians sang it in anthem rhythm, finding in Mr. Lincoln's song a soulful bond to the American tradition: quasi-religious verses that bring tears to the eyes and send them back to their insurance offices and grain stores and drug counters with the satisfied feeling one gets from a good Methodist sermon or a close football victory.

"These are real people," Bobby Moga said as we left the YMCA. "Did you ever see anything like this in Washington?"

THE RECESS CLUB is a luncheon recluse for auto executives in north downtown Detroit, a dim, comfortable place that smells faintly of bourbon and old leather. It is devoid of Automobia's chrome and fintails, the only place in the neighborhood (General Motors' headquarters are across the street) where Roosevelt-era styling is acceptable.

My host looked vaguely like Johnny Carson—nervous smile, neat short haircut, an open sincere face, eager eyes that keep right on you. He wants you to like him, *he does,* and he wants to like you. But he was restrained the first few minutes of our conversation; something bothered him, and we couldn't get beyond pleasantries. He finally said, "Do you intend to identify me by name?" I said I hoped so, that one purpose of my article was to give flesh-and-blood identity to the Silent Majoritarians. This disturbed my host. "I live in Birmingham, Michigan. Birmingham has the reputation of . . . well, being an all-white community, that sort of thing. I'm afraid I might be labeled a racist, you know what I mean? I don't want to be the target of crank mail." He would not be swayed: no anonymity, no interview. When I acquiesced, my host—let's call him Morrow, although that is not his name—relaxed.

255

"Because the world is divided into power blocs, and always has been so, war is going to be with us until man's nature changes. I recall my father saying to me, 'Your war will come.' Well, this was in the Thirties, and I said the same thing to my sons in the Fifties. Sure enough, their war did come.

"My oldest is a helicopter pilot, a big handsome guy six-five and more than two hundred pounds. His attitude is absolutely beautiful; the tapes we get from Vietnam would tear you up, the pride he takes in doing his job. Now my brother isn't so lucky. I was at their place early this fall, and their daughter, who's in college, had this hippie type with her. Man, what a mess—long hair, granny glasses, work clothes. And what ignorance! His mind was closed. America is imperialistic. America is in a warmongering stage. America doesn't believe in justice. Closed mind, I couldn't touch him. I mentioned Pearl Harbor. They were blank—they'd never heard of it.

"What do I read? I'm up at 5:45 A.M. every day, an old habit of mine. I start with the *Detroit Free Press.* Then *Life, Newsweek, Harper's, Look,* a golf magazine, the *Dan Smoot Report.* I think a lot of Smoot. He has good insight into what's going on in the country—he's an ex-FBI agent, you know.

"No, I don't have time for books, but I do get to some. For instance. Eddie Rickenbacker's *Incredible Victory* [*sic*], about Midway. That's what I'm doing now. On Vietnam? No, can't say that I have. Are there any books on Vietnam? Bernard Fall? No, haven't run across him . . .

"On the networks, I start with Cronkite. I'll get pissed off with him, and turn to Huntley-Brinkley, and turn back to Cronkite. TV news is too much nonsense and not enough empirical fact.

"I kind of agree with Agnew on news control. As an experiment once, a friend and I sat down with a Michigan newspaper and marked out all the syndicated news on the front page. Why, there wasn't anything left. That shows you the news is controlled by a few people. There's something else I'll tell you. We found a situation in a chain of Michigan newspapers—I'm not going to give you their name—where a word was being deleted from these syndicated stories, or a line transposed, so that the entire meaning was changed. The net result was to disseminate a distinctively Communist line. Well, we took care of it. We found out who was responsible, and we took care of it."

How?

A smile. "Oh, let's not get into that. But the doctoring of news stopped. All I wanted to point out is that there *are* people who will distort the news for ulterior motives."

Morrow didn't give a thought to voting for Hubert Humphrey because he detests union "feather-bedding and inflation" (asserting labor wrecked a small company he once owned). "I was fifty-fifty when the campaign started, between Our Friend George and Nixon. I turned to Nixon, who had always been pretty straight. Besides, I was afraid Wallace might turn fascist . . ."

Morrow was traveling the night of Nixon's speech, and he wrote his letter on Holiday Inn stationery from Erie, Pennsylvania:

> Your speech tonight reaffirms my faith in you as our President. I agree one hundred percent with your position. . . . It is my opinion also that there would be a bloodbath of all opponents to Communism in South Vietnam if we should pull out of that country overnight.
>
> My son is there and tells us by letters and tapes that he feels he *should* be there. My wife and I are, of course, concerned about his safety, but we both agree that we have a commitment to the future that our son is there to protect.

On Moratorium weekend Morrow visited his youngest son's fraternity at Michigan State University. "We had the football game, a nice buffet, and the next day, films of last year's Notre Dame game. It was a fine program, all weekend long. But do you know, fifteen of the kids were missing. I asked where they were, and found they had gone to Washington to demonstrate. Can you imagine such a thing—to go off and march when we had such a nice program at Lansing for them?"

"I THINK THE time has come," said Major General Francis S. Greenleaf, deputy director of the Pentagon's National Guard Bureau, in a directive to state Guard commandants in November 1969, "for all of us to awaken to the difficulties misguided activities create for our nation's efforts to bring about an honorable peace. . . . It's time for Americans to unite behind a move that will demonstrate true majority opinion in this country. . . . I urge that we encourage all National Guardsmen, as citizens . . . to (1) fly the American flag at their homes and businesses; (2) drive their automobiles with the headlights turned on and turn their porch lights on at home."

> I am a member of the Ohio National Guard. . . . At our monthly Guard meeting this past weekend we were each given a copy of a letter in support of President Nixon's policy on the Vietnam war. We were requested to sign the letters and give them to the commander or mail them personally to the President. . . . Although the signing was supposedly voluntary, a report was to be made as to the number of men who participated.
> —Constituent's letter to Senator Stephen Young (Democrat, Ohio)

ROBERT R. MOGA is classifiable as a Silent Majoritarian solely because until November 1969 he had never undertaken to tell a President of the United States what he thought about a subject. But he has long been an activist. As a Jaycee he originated Keep Illinois Beautiful, a statewide cleanup campaign. But Moga didn't share the chronic Jaycee proclivity for foolishness. At a state convention he was reading a report on his beautification work when Jaycees from East St. Louis trooped in with a giant Budweiser can, hoping their town's famed beer would attract next year's meeting. "I got disgusted. The chairman rapped for order, but nobody would listen. They all stood up and yelled about the beer can. I walked off the platform. That ended it with me and the Jaycees." Aurorans knew Moga as the sometime basketball announcer for a local radio station—and he says unabashedly he was a good one. Moga dropped into his broadcaster's voice to demonstrate his technique, telling how he described "a scuffle between two colored boys" at a tourney. "Come on, Peaches, give 'em some skin and let's get this show on the road." Moga laughed. "I didn't have to say they were colored . . . everybody knew it when I said it that way . . . folks here were laughing about it for days."

Moga entered politics almost by impulse. Five years ago he was working for an Aurora trucking firm. One morning factory workers were slow unloading one of his trucks, and he went over to speed them along. Moga gave the men cigars and joshed to a bystander that he hoped "the hillbillies"—an Aurora term for Southern immigrants—would work faster. The shop steward, who was also a local elected official, objected to the term and ordered the men off the truck. When Moga returned there was a bitter confrontation. The steward accused Moga of prejudice and called him "a hunky bastard from Pigeon Hill," referring to Moga's Romanian ancestry and the East Aurora neighborhood where he was born. There were no fisticuffs. But Moga made an instant decision: "I'm going into politics, I said. Here was a man whose family had run a goddamned whorehouse—that's where all his money came from—here was this kind of man representing the people of Aurora. The only way to get his kind out of office was for people like me to run for office. So I did." Moga didn't challenge the shop steward directly; what he did was run for County Board, and win handily. (Johnny Moga The Plumber met the steward later at a wedding reception on Pigeon Hill and told him he didn't like the term "hunky bastard." The conversation continued: "You going to leave, and you going to leave now—by the door or through the wall. Now which you prefer?")

After four years on the County Board—a part-time job—Moga bucked the Republican organization to become Township Supervisor. His principal duty is administering the welfare program, in some of which he takes a personal interest because, as he says, "I'm one of the biggest homeowning taxpayers in East Aurora," paying $1,200 per year on his house. "Animals," Moga calls his welfare clients. "They breed like animals, live like animals; they do things your wife, my wife, wouldn't do." He gave me examples: A caseworker visited a welfare recipient just released from the hospital. "She had to go through this living room where three or four big colored bucks were sitting drinking. I told her never to go in a house like that again. Now there's a case for you—a $360 hospital bill. They ain't a-never gonna pay that—the taxpayers are going to pay it. . . . All they do is take—they never put."

Moga chuckled at his ingenuity in disposing of cases. "We had a woman come in here who had family in Peoria. She wanted money. I asked if the family would take care of her if she got to Peoria, and she said yeah. So I called a gas station and said give her a tank so she could get out of town. That's one we don't worry about no more."

We switched suddenly to the war, for Moga's opinions on proper family conditions, which make welfare anathema, are in large part responsible for his views on Vietnam. Indeed, Moga asserted, the fact that Aurora is heavily Romanian and Hungarian is responsible for the town's militancy. He lowered his voice, as if he didn't want to appear to be indulging in ethnic boasting. "Certain kinds of boys from certain backgrounds are more patriotic than others. They learn to jump at the sound of an order. Discipline. There's discipline in these homes. Percentage-wise, of all the Aurora boys in the war, the highest number was from the Hungarian and Romanian communities, Pigeon Hill, where I was raised. The same for the dead—go over to the cemetery, look at the tombstones. Most of the names, Hungarian, Romanian. When a guy is in the trench and the lieutenant blows the whistle and says, Let's go, there's always a percentage that stays behind. Boys with *background* are the ones who go."

We crossed the street to the Woolworth's store for coffee. School had ended, and teenagers crammed the lunch counter. We found stools in the corner.

"Look," Bobby Moga muttered. "Just look at them. You ever see anything like that in your life?"

Pea jackets. A few peace medallions. Natural hairdos on several of the black girls, no bras on several of the white ones. The boys' hair appreciably longer than Moga's thinning locks.

*While driving into Aurora that morning from Chicago I listened to a radio station in Gary, Indiana, and jotted down a line from the mid-morning commodities report, not knowing how or when I would ever use it: "Slaughter sheep plentiful, pork bellies firm."*

SOUTH OF HOUSTON the coastal prairie degenerates swiftly into a marsh inhabitable only by the most hardy of waterfowl and the petrochemical industry; a land with an aesthetically scatological horizon, its borders the phallic towers of Shell and Monsanto and Phillips, ejaculating flame and smoke and heavy, clinging oil-scent into the evening sky. ("Boy, what you smellin' is money," Texans tell themselves to justify the spoilage.) A highway café across the marsh from Galveston Bay, tar paper nailed over a frame of pine two-by-fours and chicken wire. BROWN PIGS COLD BEER TRUCKS WELCOME OPEN 24 HRS. DON'T PARK ON SHOULDER GO TO REAR and Bobby Bare from the jukebox: *God Bless America again, you must know the trouble that she's in, wash her pretty face, dry her eyes, and then, God Bless America again.* A drunk wants to talk. "Why doesn't she like me?" he says of the barmaid. Wall sign: "State law prescribes a maximum penalty of five years imprisonment for carrying weapons where alcoholic beverages are sold, consumed, or served."

You wouldn't find Diane Hicks in a roadside beer joint. She is a lady, a precise, self-confident one. She is twenty-seven years old. She is a teacher, civics and American history, in La Porte, Texas, High School. She attended Southwest Texas State Teachers College, Lyndon Johnson's alma mater, for one year, then finished at Mary Hardin-Baylor College. She marched with the SWTSTC band in Kennedy's inaugural parade. She hasn't done anything for a Democrat since, and she is about as silent as the jukebox on the highway. "I've written seven letters since September," Diane Hicks says, "to the President, to Senators, to Congressmen. I dictate them to girls in the vocational education class at school, and they type them. Golly gee, I think I'm a *vocal majority.*" Her letter after November 3 expressed the same idea: "I was pleased and proud to hear your speech. . . . Thank you for speaking to the 'silent majority.' I'm far from silent, but perhaps I've spoken too softly. I feel your Vietnam policy is the *best possible,* and I'm behind you 100%."

Diane Hicks continues: "The President did a good job of telling the American people not what they *wanted* to hear, but what they *needed* to hear. Johnson, I always felt he was holding back. It's like . . . golly gee, it's like having a doctor when you are sick. I'd rather have a doctor tell me the truth. 'Mrs. Hicks, you are going to die,' rather than 'Mrs. Hicks, you are getting a little better.' He [Johnson] was holding back information; you tend to be discouraged when someone is not telling you the truth.

"I grew up in the Cold War generation. I believe that if you don't fight Them there, you will fight Them here. Their basic doctrine is that all the world will be Communist.

"South Vietnam invited us in. My position there—I believe in fighting Them in South Vietnam and winning an honorable peace. Golly gee, all our men and equipment are there, in working order. You'd have to move all the equipment and manpower that you have stashed away, move it to Cambodia or Laos. No, I don't believe in the domino theory. The whole world is a domino, when you are fighting Communists. You know, you can't win militarily against a Communist. It is impossible, period. Golly gee, Communism is an ideology. You can't win unless you chop off a head."

Mrs. Hicks's husband, Bruce, sat with us at the kitchen table, drinking coffee and listening. "I'm much stronger than she is. I don't believe in Americans getting killed for a stalemate. There are not all that many heads to roll. They [the Communists] have said they are going to shovel dirt in our face—I want to do some shoveling myself."

We talked about the media. Diane Hicks: "TV news has gotten to the point where . . . well, golly gee, it presents one side, boy, and that's it. I agree with Agnew all the way. I wrote a letter to him saying, 'The only thing I can say to you, sir, is Sock It To Them.' TV has to compete with sex movies, that's why it's so awful. I don't like to see the dead and dying on TV news. I want to know what's going on, not see blood and guts spread all over the living room. It's not in the best interests of the people for the commentators to *stand* there, and you not be able to talk back to them; golly gee, at least you can write a letter to a newspaper.

"Pressure groups, the vocal ones, they are the ones who get their ideas presented. But the pendulum will swing the other way when the media realize what the country wants. The sponsors and the networks—they leave it to subordinates, and who the ding-dong are they? The sponsors could care less. They are fat and sitting on the Riviera or somewhere else. *Time* and *Life,* even, are getting mucky. They present their side, that's all; why, golly gee, they've already got Lieutenant Calley tried, convicted, and before the firing squad."

On Moratorium Day, she said, "some of the students dashed around with their little armbands. This made me unhappy." Why?

"They said we should get out. I was surprised. I thought they were very well informed. That is when I required them to read the Sunday newspapers. If they came into class, and didn't know what they were talking about, I made them take the armbands off. . . . What do they know about the war? From last year to this year, that's all. Sure, they think about it . . . they are next up in the draft."

What is her own background on the war? "I read *U.S. News & World Report, Time, Newsweek, Life,* the *Houston Chronicle* most of the time. Books? No, none on Vietnam; what are some?"

"Oh, yes, one thing more—our debate subject this year is on unilateral intervention, and I have this book of source material; you know, magazine articles, things like that, pro and con; it's put out by the government. What articles? Oh, I don't know offhand, but good articles."

*The* Houston Post *editorial page the next morning contained Art Buchwald, Joe Alsop, and Joseph Kraft, the same fare I find at home in the* Washington Post. *I turned to the letters. A citizen was angry about a* Post *story which stated that an analysis of moon dust found "the moon is billions of years old." The citizen deposed: "God says in the King James Bible that he made the sun, moon, stars, and Adam, practically 6,000 years ago within seven days, the moon having been made on the fourth day. I was afraid when our boys found the moon . . . that there would be some wisenheimer . . . to try to prove the word of God wrong, and try to tear down the facts . . . God . . . tried so faithfully to convey to all of us." The* Post *replied that the questioned article contained no statement "that anyone was trying to prove the word of God wrong."*

Fire base Kien, South Vietnam, Jan. 2 (AP)—Vice President Agnew, visiting what GIs call the boonies, told American troops here yesterday the people back home are "darned proud of what you are doing" in Vietnam. He said the troops have the public's 100 percent support. "Don't be alarmed by what you may see or read in certain publications," Agnew told a group of about 75 soldiers . . .
— *Washington Post,* January 2, 1970

SATELLITE BEACH, FLORIDA, is a community of convenience—an incorporated real-estate development, cinder-block homes nestled in culs-de-sac bulldozed through the sand dunes of the Cape south of the

Air Force's Eastern Test Range at Patrick Air Force Base, part of the Cape Kennedy complex. A proud display on A-l-A, the main coastal highway that serves as Satellite Beach's spine, tells what the area is all about: Polaris Poseidon Hawkeye Bull-pup Thor Atlas Terrier Tartar Talos, the fire-tailed monsters that roar aloft from Patrick to splash into the Atlantic twenty, two hundred, two thousand miles away. Drugstore shout from an extraordinarily beautiful woman in slacks and curlers: "Did you hear how The Shot went this morning?" Her friend: "Beautiful Shot, it worked beautiful. . . . They're all real excited. Will we be seeing you Saturday night?" The Beautiful Shot, the papers said the next morning, was the first launch from a submarine of a multiple individually targetable re-entry vehicle, the MIRV, a quantum jump in nuclear weaponry.

Tom Frey, forty-three, an electrical engineer, is a civilian employee at Patrick, as are most of his neighbors, and he is archetypical of the technocrats who keep Modern America working more or less as it should. Soon after graduation from the University of Illinois, Frey worked for a St. Louis brewery, installing a new plant, then for the Ralston Purina Company. The transition from beer and Wheat Chex to missiles was nothing more than a change of jobs. He is decidedly unsympathetic to things out of the ordinary. And one who doesn't want to be misunderstood, even by association. "We fell out with Huntley and Brinkley several years ago when they did a special on our area. They interviewed mostly prostitutes and showed bars and cocktail lounges. They could have presented the Cape Kennedy area in a better vein." I remarked that some of my friends in the aerospace industry had said Cape Kennedy and environs was a swinging area. "That may be," Frey said. "We don't smoke, we don't drink, so that leaves out parties for us."

Huntley and Brinkley notwithstanding, Frey considers TV his prime source of news. "Frankly, I've become disillusioned with the papers. You read a speech, and the stories don't say the same thing you heard when the man said it on television." Both Frey and his wife described themselves as busy readers—he prefers spy novels, she historical novels—but they haven't gotten around to any books on the war. ("I think it [the war] is strictly Communistic," Tom Frey said. "The Communists took North Vietnam, and now they want to take South Vietnam.") Barbara Frey, nineteen, a college student, had been listening to us. "*Are* there any Vietnam books?" she asked. Before I left she came in with pad and pencil and asked for some titles. She also mentioned students who participated in Moratorium activities. "I thought they were kind of stupid. Why, they were even standing on desks. I think people who make laws know more about what is happening than we do."

Tom Frey, who has worked around the Air Force the past six years, thinks it should have been permitted to bomb Haiphong and Hanoi—"get in there and get it over with, quick." Political realities being what they are, he knows this is not now to happen. But he is most willing to leave the war in Mr. Nixon's hands; as he wrote the President: "It is understandable that we can not be told everything. . . . Since you have more insight into all our country's problems, perhaps you could explain to us why the dissenting group in this country seems to be made up of people who have the most to lose if we do not help keep the world free . . ."

HOME. A BRICK rancher, the driveway curving through the snow to a three-car parking area, basketball goal, and the ice-crusted tracks of a snowplow. "They don't work as good as a shovel, do they?" Moga said. A thirty-six-foot flagpole on the front lawn. "Didn't cost me a thing. I welded it myself, even got the ball and the eagle at the top." Moga stopped. "I hope I'm never in the vicinity of a crowd where somebody burns an American flag." Why? "I don't think I could control myself. I think I'd do something awful to the people—kick the hell out of them, even kill them. I don't think anybody could hold me back."

Joyce Moga, a pretty brunette who smiles and blushes easily, was ironing in the kitchen. We joke about husbands who don't warn they are bringing company home, and about wives who don't like to be caught wearing curlers while they are ironing.

The living room. Family history. Bobby Moga's Uncle Jack was a city policeman whose ferocity alarmed even his colleagues, inclined to end tavern quarrels by banging the relevant heads until the noise ended. "In the old days there were no squad cars. At the end of a shift each officer walked his prisoners to the station house. One snowy morning Uncle Jack was checking doors in an alley when he saw an officer with a prisoner fall. Uncle Jack started after the prisoner, and the officer yelled, 'No, Jack, no, he didn't do anything; I slipped and fell.' " Moga smiled. "The policeman knew good and well that Uncle Jack would have killed that prisoner with his bare hands for hitting an officer."

Many of Moga's stories had this undercurrent of violence. The Romanian community once played the Aurora Swedes in baseball, a social event replete with cheering women and kegs of beer behind the screen, and gradually escalating enthusiasm for victory. There was an argument at home plate while Uncle Sam Moga was batting, and he turned and lifted the mask from the Swede catcher. "They had to call an ambulance to haul the Swede away when Sam finished him," Bobby Moga laughed, as did his eight-year-old son, sitting with us.

Moga's brother Romulus. "Rome, we call him, he was the fifth in a row to have the name." Rome was killed in the Battle of the Java Sea in 1942, and a boy brought the telegram on Sunday morning. "We decided to keep the word from Mom until we knew for sure. We did this for two weeks. She heard. There were four Aurora boys on the USS *Houston,* and two of them were killed. She heard from a reporter."

A TV news show from Chicago. Bert Quint of CBS narrates a film of a South Vietnamese soldier putting cigarettes into the mouth of a dead North Vietnamese, clowning and smiling for onlookers and the camera. "That's the sort of thing that shouldn't be shown," Moga said. "It depresses you."

Sources of information on the war? "I read books, magazines, everything. I can't sit down without reading, even on the throne. The car radio, television. No, no books. I don't have time, no. See, I get calls out of the house all the time—people in trouble, that sort of thing. I'm a very busy man, a public official. Why, the other night I got a call from a guy who had been in a stabbing at a club. A

Republican committeeman, and I had to take care of it, get him out on recognizance. All sorts of things like that . . ."

*The newspaper in which Bobby Moga and other Aurorans read about the war and Nixon policies is the* Aurora Beacon-News, *owned by the Copley Press, Inc., chain. Although the* Beacon *was the first Copley newspaper (Ira C. Copley, sometime colonel, natural-gas entrepreneur and Aurora resident, bought it in 1905), the editorial tone of the fiercely conservative chain is set by the flagship paper, the* San Diego Union, *which Herb Klein edited for ten years. During my visit the* Beacon *was publishing a series on the Moratorium by Francis J. McNamara, longtime staff director of the House Un-American Activities Committee. "The most important fact about the demonstrations," McNamara wrote for the twenty-six Copley papers and the 340 newspaper clients of the Copley news service, "was the revelation of a weakness in U.S. ability to deal effectively with internal Communist subversion.*

MRS. HUGH ARMSTRONG lives in Jessup, in the turpentine and pulpwood country of southern Georgia. What she said to Mr. Nixon, and why, is best expressed in her letter itself, which she decided could be published after an hour's consultation with the son she discusses in it:

Just one year ago today the War Department sent us a telegram saying our son Tony was burned over 50% of his body, arms, face, and legs. He was a Cobra pilot in the 1st Air Cav and a good one—he won two distinguished flying crosses. For 5 1/2 months he was in Yokohama, Japan, and Brooke Gen. Hosp. in Texas—14 skin grafts. He'll never have the use of his right hand, the bones were too badly burned, he'll also wear rubber hose on his legs for the better part of his life—but thank God he came home and cheered us up. . . .

Now what I want to say, your speech was a "good one." My husband and I both feel it's the only honorable way. Every time we see our friends' sons leave for Vietnam our hearts bleed for them, and we pray they never know the anxiety we suffered.

Tony's back in college now, he's learned to do with his left hand, and never has said one unkind thing about his condition.

This letter was not meant to be a tear jerker, just wanted to say I'm glad you are in. God bless you and guide you in all the rough times ahead, and the decisions you are having to make.

AURORA DOWNS, A trotting track, celebrated its grand opening that night, and as a township official Bobby Moga had gratis clubhouse tickets—gold cardboard affairs entitling the bearer to free admission, free dinner, free drinks, and free access to pari-mutuel lines where he could bet the contents of his wallet on the horses puffing clouds of steam during warm-ups. Joyce Moga bright-eyed and smiling in a new dress, excited about a night out. Hard-frozen snow pushed into the infield, mid-twenties temperatures. "This was a drafty old barn last year," Moga said. "But Johnny my brother put in a new heating system. Feels pretty good, eh? Johnny has it heated up real nice."

Aisle table. Bobby did some politicking. "Hi-ya Hallie boy, any of these horses been telling you how fast they can run?" He bounced around the chair, looking into the stands and behind us for friends and acquaintances and for people who should see him in the honored guest area.

Bobby was serious about the trotters, and after we ordered prime ribs he excused himself for the first of many whispered consultations with assorted insiders. His brother-in-law, a track faithful, had talked to a trainer who knew a jockey and who knew something special about a race. (The horse lost.) "I think all of this is silly," Joyce Moga said. We bet—and lost—the first of three races, following faithfully Ambassador Annenberg's form sheets. "Let's use my system," Joyce Moga said. "It makes as much sense." She held her pencil at arm's length above the table and dropped it on the program. "Number Six. Hit it right on the nose. That's our horse." We split a two-dollar bet. And glorious joy, Number Six took a quick lead, led by three lengths at the halfway mark, by four at the three-quarters post, and by five no less than fifty yards from the finish—saliva-blowing, snorting ferocity, but we aurally antiseptic behind the plate glass that kept us snug in the clubhouse. One glimpsed, but could not hear (and thus emphatically feel) the wrrrHACKkkkkkkk of the crop; muscles and neck veins pulsating in glistening ridges.

Number Six stumbled in the stretch, broke stride, and went from first to seventh quicker than we could moan our disappointment. "Horses," said Joyce Moga. Bobby Moga threw a pile of pari-mutuel slips on the table and we went home.

After midnight I tried to find something to read before going to sleep. The bookcase in the Mogas' guest room contained William Shirer's *Berlin Diary,* a world atlas, a collected works of Shakespeare, the *Dell Crossword Dictionary, The Day Christ Died* by Jim Bishop, *The Exciting Story of the White Sox* (about their pennant year), and the *Handbook of Beauty.* I sat down on the bed and read Bobby Moga's letter again.

> We watched you on television, address the Nation on the Viet-Nam situation. We wholeheartedly support your position, and think that ninety per cent of Americans do too.
>
> Funny thing, I've always considered our young educated people to be the strength of our Nation. Much to everyone's surprise the so called intellectuals strangely enough are a weakness. They can not see the students in Czechoslovakia, trying to tell the world about Russia, and Communism.
>
> I honestly, think that what some of these younger people need, is a callused hand, wheeled by a strict father, or a boot camp Master Sergeant, to bring a full appreciation of our beautiful Country.
>
> Both of my parents, were born in Romania, and when I asked my Dad recently, whether he would like to visit his birth place he said, and I quote "what for, sixty-seven years ago I ran away from that place."
>
> Also, I want to tell you that our family supports you even though, we lost our older brother, in World War II in the Battle of the Java Sea, in 1942. In 1945 another brother was wounded on Okinawa. I myself, served in 1950 to 1952 in the Korean War.
>
> I can guarantee you that our family is ready, and will always be ready to fight for our beautiful Flag.
>
> Yours very truly,
> Robert R. Moga
> Township Supervisor

# OPEN LAND: GETTING BACK TO THE COMMUNAL GARDEN

## (JUNE 1970)

### Sara Davidson

*Wheeler Ranch: free land—live-in, drop-in.*
—Commune Directory

THE FRONT WHEELS drop and the car thuds down a wet, muddy ravine. Thick night fog, raining hard. The car squishes to a stop, front end buried in clay and the right rear wheel spinning. I get out and sink to my ankles. No flashlight. No waterproof gear. Utter blackness, except for the car's dulled lights under the dirt. I climb back in, but because of the 45-degree angle, I'm pitched forward against the dashboard. Turn on the radio. Only eight o'clock—a long wait until daylight. Am I anywhere near Wheeler Ranch? Haven't seen another car or a light anywhere on this road. I start honking the horn. Cows bellow back from what seems very close range. I imagine angry ranchers with shotguns. Tomorrow is Sunday—eight miles back to the nearest town, and nothing will be open. Is there an AAA out here? Good God, I'll pay anybody anything! If they'll just get me out of this.

I HAD STARTED north from San Francisco in late afternoon, having heard vague descriptions of a commune called Wheeler's that was

271

much beloved by those who had passed through it. The commune had had trouble with local police, and no one was sure whether the buildings were still standing or who was there. At sunset, a storm came up, and rather than turn back, I continued slowly along narrow, unlit country roads, my headlights occasionally picking up messages like "Stop War," painted on the side of a barn, and "Drive slowly, no M.D. around," on a fence post. When I reached the woodsy, frontier town I knew to be near Wheeler's, I stopped in a bar to ask directions. Heads turned. People froze, glasses in hand. A woman with an expressionless, milky face said, "Honey, there isn't any sign. You just go up the road six miles and there's a gate on the left. Then you have to drive a ways to git to it. From where I live, you can see their shacks and what have you. But you can't see anything from the road."

After six miles, there was a gate and a sign, "Beware of cattle." I opened it and drove down to a fork, picked the left road, went around in a circle and came back to the fork, took the right and bumped against two logs in the road. I got out and moved them. Nothing could stop me now. Another fork. To the left the road was impassable—deep ruts and rocks; to the right, a barbed-wire fence. Raining harder, darker. This is enough. Get out of here fast. Try to turn the car around, struggling to see . . . then the sickening dip.

I got into my sleeping bag and tried to find a comfortable position in the crazily tilted car. My mood swung between panic and forced calm. At about 5:00 A.M., I heard rustling noises, and could make out the silhouettes of six horses which walked around the car, snorting. An hour later, the rain let up, and a few feet from the car I found a crude sign with an arrow, "Wheeler's." I walked a mile, then another mile, through rolling green hills, thinking, "If I can just get out of here." At last, around a bend were two tents and a sign, "Welcome, God, Love." The first tent had a light burning inside, and turned out to be a greenhouse filled with boxes of seedlings. At the second tent, I pushed open the door and bells tinkled. Someone with streaked brown hair was curled in a real bed on two mattresses. There was linoleum on the floor, a small stove, a table, and books and clothes neatly arranged on shelves. The young man lifted his head and smiled. "Come in."

I was covered with mud, my hair was wild and my eyes red and twitching. "I tried to drive in last night, my car went down a ravine and got stuck in the mud, and I've been sleeping in it all night."

"Far out," he said.

"I was terrified."

The young man, who had gray eyes set close together and one gold earring, said, "Of what?"

"There were horses."

He laughed. "Far out. One of the horses walked into Nancy's house and made a hole in the floor. Now she just sweeps her dirt and garbage down the hole."

My throat was burning. "Could we make some coffee?"

He looked at me sideways. "I don't have any." He handed me a clump of green weeds. "Here's some yerba buena. You can make tea." I stared at the weeds.

"What's your name?" I asked.

"Shoshone."

"Mine's Sara."

"Far out."

He got dressed, watered the plants in the greenhouse, and started down a path into the bushes, motioning for me to follow. Every few feet, he would stop to pick yerba buena, listen to birds, watch a trio of pheasants take off, and admire trees that were recently planted—almond, Elberta peach, cherry, plum. They were all in blossom, but I was in no mood to appreciate them. After every ten minutes of walking, we would come to a clearing with a tent or wooden shack, wake up the people in their sorry sleeping bags and ask them to help push the car out. The dwellings at Wheeler's are straight out of Dogpatch—old boards nailed unevenly together, odd pieces of plastic strung across poles to make wobbly igloos, with round stovepipes poking out the side. Most have dirt floors, though the better ones have wood. In one tent, we found a young man who had shaved his head except for one stripe of hair down the center, like a Mohican. He grinned with his eyes closed. "In an hour or so, I might feel like helping you." We came to a crooked green shack with a peace sign on the door and the inside papered with paintings of Krishna. Nancy, a blonde former social worker, was sleeping on the floor with her children, Gregory, eight, and Michelle, nine. Both have blond hair of the same length and it is impossible to tell at first which is the girl and which the boy. At communities like this, it is common for children to ask each other when they meet, "What are you?" Nancy said, "Don't waste your energy trying to push the car. Get Bill Wheeler to pull you out with his jeep. What's your hurry now? Sunday's the best day here. You've got to stay for the steam bath and the feast. There'll be lots of visitors." She yawned. "Lots of food, lots of dope. It never rains for the feast."

Shoshone and I walked back to the main road that cuts across the 320-acre ranch. The sun had burned through the fog, highlighting streaks of yellow wild flowers in the fields. Black Angus cows were grazing by the road. People in hillbilly clothes, with funny hats and sashes, were coming out of the bushes carrying musical instruments and sacks of rice and beans. About a mile from the front gate we came to the community garden, with a scarecrow made of rusty metal in the shape of a nude girl. Two children were chasing each other from row to row, shrieking with laughter, as their mother picked cabbage. A sign read, "Permit not required to settle here."

BILL WHEELER WAS working in his studio, an airy, wood-and-glass building with large skylights, set on a hill. When Bill bought the ranch in 1963, looking for a place to paint and live quietly, he built the studio for his family. Four years later, when he opened the land to anyone who wanted to settle there, the county condemned his studio as living quarters because it lacked the required amount of concrete under one side. Bill moved into a tent and used the studio for his painting and for community meetings.

Bill is a tall, lean man of thirty with an aristocratic forehead, straight nose, deep-set blue eyes, and a full beard and flowing hair streaked yellow by the sun. His voice is gentle with a constant hint of mirth, yet it projects, like his clear gaze, a strength, which is understood in this community as divine grace. Quiet, unhurried, he progresses with steady confidence toward a goal or solution of a problem.

He is also a voluptuary who takes Rabelaisian delight in the community's lack of sexual inhibitions and in the sight of young girls walking nude through the grass. He lives at the center of the ranch with his third wife, Gay, twenty-two, and their infant daughter, Raspberry. His humor and self-assurance make it easy for those around him to submit to the hippie credo that "God will provide," because they know that what God does not, Bill Wheeler will.

Bill promises to rescue my car after he has chopped wood and started a fire for the steam bath. "Don't worry," a friend says, patting me on the back. "Bill's saved people who've given up hope, lost all confidence." A grizzly blond called Damian says, "Why don't you let me pull her out?" Bill says, "Damian, I love you, but I wouldn't trust you with any of my vehicles." Later, we pass Damian on the road, into which he is blissfully urinating. "Ha," Bill says, "the first time I met Damian he was peeing."

With the jeep and a chain, Bill pulls out the car in less than two minutes, and as it slides back onto secure road, I feel my tension drain away. Maybe I should stay for the feast. Maybe it really is beautiful here. I park the car at the county road, outside the first gate, and walk the three miles back to Wheeler's. The access road cuts across property owned by James G. Kelly, a breeder of show cattle and horses, who is enraged at the presence of up to a hundred itinerant hippies on the ranch adjacent to his. He has started court action to block Wheeler from using the access road, and his hired hands walk around with guns slung over their shoulders and their faces pinched with bilious hate.

On a bluff behind Wheeler's garden, the steam bath is set to go. Red-hot rocks are taken from the fire into a plastic tent that can be sealed on all sides. Shifts of eight or nine people undress and sit on the mud floor, letting out whoops, chanting and singing. Gallon wine jugs filled with water are poured on the rocks, and the tent fills up with steam so hot and thick that the children start coughing and no one can see anyone else. After a few minutes, they step out, covered with sweat, and wash off in a cold shower. The women shampoo their hair and soap up the children. The men dig out ticks from under the skin. Much gaiety and good-natured ogling, and then, as the last shift is coming out, a teenage visitor carrying the underground *Berkeley Tribe* wanders in and stops, dumbfounded, staring with holy-fool eyes, his mouth open and drooling, at all that flesh and hair and sweat.

The garden, like a jigsaw puzzle whose pieces have floated together, presents the image of a nineteenth-century tableau: women in long skirts and shawls, men in lace-up boots, coveralls, and patched jeans tied with pieces of rope, sitting on the grass playing banjos, guitars, lyres, wood flutes, dulcimers, and an accordion. In a field to the right are the community animals—chickens, cows, goats, donkeys, and horses. As far as the eye can see, there are no houses, no traffic, nothing but verdant hills, a stream, and the ocean with whitecaps rising in the distance. Nine-year-old Michelle is prancing about in a pink shawl and a floppy hat warbling, "It's time for the feast!" Nancy says, "The pickins are sort of spare because tomorrow is welfare day and everybody's broke." She carries from the outdoor wood stove pots of brown rice—plain, she says, "for the purists who are on George Ohsawa's ten-day brown-rice diet"—and rice with fruit and nuts for everyone else; beans, red and white; oranges and apples; yogurt; hash; pot; acid; mescaline. A girl says there are worms in the green apples. Another, with a serious voice and glasses, says, "That's cool, it means they were organically grown. I'd rather eat a worm than a chemical any day." They eat with their fingers from paper plates, and when the plates are gone, directly from the pot. A man in his forties with red-spotted cheeks asks me if I have any pills. "I'll take anything. I'm on acid now." I offer him aspirin. He swallows eight.

Everyone who lives at Wheeler's ranch is a vegetarian. By some strange inversion, they feel that by eating meat they are hastening their own death. Vegetarianism is, ironically, the aspect of their lifestyle that aggravates even the most liberal parents. ("What? You won't eat meat? That's ridiculous!") Bill Wheeler says that diet is "very central to the revolution. It's a freeing process which people go through, from living on processed foods and eating gluttonous portions of meat and potatoes, to natural foods and a simple diet that is kinder to your body. A lot has to do with economics. It's much cheaper to live on grains and vegetables you can grow in your garden. When Gay and I moved here, we had to decide whether to raise animals to slaughter. Gay said she couldn't do it. Every Thanksgiving, there's a movement to raise money to buy turkeys, because some people think the holiday isn't complete without them. But an amazing thing happens when carrion is consumed. People are really greedy, and it's messy. The stench and the grease stay with us for days."

Gravy, roast beef, mashed potatoes, Parker House rolls, buttered peas—the weekly fare when Bill was growing up in Bridgeport, Connecticut. His father, a lawyer who speculated famously in real estate, told Bill he could do anything with his life as long as he got an education. So Bill, self-reliant, introspective, who loved the outdoors, went to Yale and studied painting. After graduating, he came to San Francisco to find a farmhouse where he could work. When he saw the 320-acre ranch which was then a sheep and Christmas-tree farm, he felt, "I've got to have it. This is my land." He bought it with his inheritance, and still has enough money to live comfortably the rest of his life. "My parents would be shocked out of their gourds if they saw the land now," Bill says. "They died before I opened it."

THE IDEA OF open land, or free land, was introduced to Bill by Lou Gottlieb, a singer with the pop folk group The Limelighters who, in 1962, bought a thirty-two-acre piece of land called Morning Star about ten miles from Wheeler Ranch. Gottlieb visits Wheeler's every Sunday for the feast; when I met him, he was walking barefoot with a pink blanket wrapped around him like a poncho and fastened with a giant safety pin. A man of soaring height with crow eyes and a dark, silky beard, he talks in sermonettes, rising on his toes with enthusiasm. Gottlieb and a friend, Ramon Sender, decided in 1966 to start a community at Morning Star with one governing precept: access to the land would be denied to no one. With no rules, no organization, they felt, hostilities would not arise, and people could be reborn by living in harmony with the earth. Gottlieb deeded the land to God, and, shortly, a woman sued God because her home had been struck by lightning. "Now that God owns property," her lawyer argued, "He can be sued for natural disasters." It was not until 1967, Gottlieb says, that hippies began to patronize open land.

"From the first, the land selected the people. Those who couldn't work hard didn't survive. When the land got crowded, people split. The vibration of the land will always protect the community." Gottlieb points to the sky. "With open land, *He* is the casting director." What happens, I ask, if someone behaves violently or destructively? Gottlieb frowns. "There have been a few cases where we've had to ask people to go, but it's at terrible, terrible cost to everyone's soul that this is done. When the land begins to throw off people, everyone suffers." He shakes his body, as if he were the land, rejecting a germ. "Open land has no historical precedent. When you give free land, not free food or money, you pull the carpet out from under the capitalist system. Once a piece of land is freed, 'no trespassing' signs pop up all along the adjoining roads."

Bill Wheeler refers to his ranch as "the land," and talks about people who live on the land, babies that are born on the land, music played on the land. He "opened the land," as he phrases it, in the winter of 1967, after Sonoma County officials tried to close Morning Star by bulldozing trees and all the buildings except Gottlieb's house. Some Morning Star people moved to Wheeler's, but others traveled to New Mexico, where they founded Morning Star East on a mesa near Taos owned by another wealthy hippie. The Southwest, particularly northern New Mexico and Colorado, has more communes on open land than any other region. The communes there are all crowded, and Taos is becoming a Haight-Ashbury in the desert. More land continues to be opened in New Mexico, as well as in California, Oregon, and Washington. Gottlieb plans to buy land and deed it to God in Holland, Sweden, Mexico, and Spain. "We're fighting against the territorial imperative," he says. "The hippies should get the Nobel Prize for creating this simple idea. Why did no one think of it before the hippies? Because hippies don't work, so they have time to dream up truly creative ideas."

IT WAS SURPRISING to hear people refer to themselves as "hippies"; I thought the term had been rendered meaningless by overuse. Our culture has absorbed so much of the style of hip—clothes, hair, language, drugs, music—that it has obscured the substance of the movement with which people at Morning Star and Wheeler's still strongly identify. Being a hippie, to them, means dropping out completely and finding another way to live to support oneself physically and spiritually. It does not mean being a company freak, working nine to five in a straight job and roaming the East Village on weekends. It means saying no to competition, no to the work ethic, no to consumption of technology's products, no to political systems and games. Lou Gottlieb, who was once a Communist party member, says, "The entire Left is a dead end." The hippie alternative is to turn inward and reach backward for roots, simplicity, and the tribal experience. In the first bloom of the movement, people flowed into slums where housing would be cheap and many things could be obtained free—food scraps from restaurants, secondhand clothes, free clinics and services. But the slums proved inhospitable. The hippies did nothing to improve the dilapidated neighborhoods, and they were preyed upon by criminals, pushers, and the desperate. In late 1967, they began trekking to rural land where there would be few people and life would be hard. They took up what Ramon Sender calls "voluntary primitivism," building houses out of mud and trees, planting and harvesting crops by hand, rolling loose tobacco into cigarettes, grinding their own wheat, baking bread, canning vegetables, delivering their own babies, and educating their own children. They gave up electricity, the telephone, running water, gas stoves, even rock music, which, of all things, is supposed to be the cornerstone of hip culture. They started to sing and play their own music—folky and quiet.

Getting close to the earth meant conditioning their bodies to cold, discomfort, and strenuous exercise. At Wheeler's, people walk twenty miles a day, carrying water and food, gardening and visiting each other. Only four-wheel-drive vehicles can cross the ranch, and ultimately Bill wants all cars banned. "We would rather live without machines. And the fact that we have no good roads protects us from tourists. People are car-bound, even police. They could never come in here without their vehicles." Although it rains a good part of the year, most of the huts do not have stoves and are not waterproof. "Houses shouldn't be designed to keep out the weather," Bill says. "We want to get in touch with it." He installed six chemical toilets on the ranch to comply with county sanitation requirements, but, he says, "I wouldn't go in one of those toilets if you paid me. It's very important for us to be able to use the ground, because we are completing a cycle, returning to Mother Earth what she's given us." Garbage is also returned to the ground. Food scraps are buried in a compost pile of sawdust and hay until they decompose and mix with the soil. Paper is burned, and metal buried. But not everyone is conscientious; there are piles of trash on various parts of the ranch.

Because of the haphazard sanitation system, the water at Wheeler's is contaminated, and until people adjust to it, they suffer dysentery, just as tourists do who drink the water in Mexico. There are periodic waves of hepatitis, clap, crabs, scabies, and streptococcic throat infections. No one brushes his teeth more than once a week, and then they often use "organic toothpaste," made from eggplant cooked in tinfoil. They are experimenting with herbs and Indian healing remedies to become free of manufactured medicinal drugs, but see no contradiction in continuing to swallow any mind-altering chemical they are offered. The delivery of babies on the land has become an important ritual. With friends, children, and animals keeping watch, chanting, and getting collectively stoned, women have given birth to babies they have named Morning Star, Psyche Joy, Covelo Vishnu God, Rainbow Canyon King, and Raspberry Sundown Hummingbird Wheeler.

The childbirth ritual and the weekly feasts are conscious attempts at what is called "retribalization." But Wheeler Ranch, like many hippie settlements, has rejected communal living in favor of a loose community of individuals. People live alone or in monogamous units, cook for themselves, and build their own houses and sometimes gardens. "There should not be a main lodge, because you get too many people trying to live under one roof and it doesn't work," Bill says. As a result, there are cliques who eat together, share resources, and rarely mix with others on the ranch. There was one group marriage between two teenage girls, a forty-year-old man, and two married couples, which ended when one of the husbands saw his wife with another man in the group, pulled a knife, and dragged her off, yelling, "Forget this shit. She belongs to me."

With couples, the double standard is an unwritten rule: The men can roam but the women must be faithful. There are many more men than women, and when a new girl arrives, she is pounced upon, claimed, and made the subject of wide gossip. Mary Cordelia Stevens, or Corky, a handsome eighteen-year-old from a Chicago suburb, hiked into the ranch one afternoon last October and sat down by the front gate to eat a can of Spam. The first young man who came by invited her to a party where everyone took TCP, a tranquilizer for horses. It was a strange trip—people rolling around the floor of the tipi, moaning, retching, laughing, hallucinating. Corky went home with one guy and stayed with him for three weeks, during which time she was almost constantly stoned. "You sort of have to be stoned to get through the first days here," she says. "Then you know the trip." Corky is a strapping, well-proportioned, large-boned girl with a milk-maid's face and long blond hair. She talks softly, with many giggles: "I love to run around naked. There's so much sexual energy here, it's great. Everybody's turned on to each other's bodies." Corky left the ranch to go home for Christmas and to officially drop out of Antioch College; she hitchhiked back, built her own house and chicken coop, learned to plant, do laundry in a tin tub with a washboard, and milk the cows. "I love dealing with things that are simple and direct."

Bill Wheeler admires Corky for making it on her own, which few of the women do. Bill is torn between his desire to be the benefactor-protector and his intolerance of people who aren't self-reliant. "I'm contemptuous of people who can't pull their own weight," he says. Yet he constantly worries about the welfare of others. He also feels conflict between wanting a tribe, indeed wanting to be chieftain, and wanting privacy. "Open land requires a leap of faith," he says, "but it's worth it, because it guarantees there will always be change, and stagnation is death." Because of the fluidity of the community, it is almost impossible for it to become economically self-sufficient. None of the communes have been able to live entirely off the land. Most are unwilling to go into cash crops or light industry because in an open community with no rules, there are not enough people who can be counted on to work regularly. The women with children receive welfare, some of the men collect unemployment and food stamps, and others get money from home. They spend very little—perhaps $600 a year per person. "We're not up here to make money," Bill says, "or to live like country squires."

When darkness falls, the ranch becomes eerily quiet and mobility stops. No one uses flashlights. Those who have lived there some time can feel their way along the paths by memory. Others stay in their huts, have dinner, go to sleep, and get up with the sun. Around 7:00 P.M., people gather at the barn with bottles for the late milking. During the week, the night milking is the main social event. Corky says, "It's the only time you know you're going to see people. Otherwise you could wander around for days and not see anyone." A girl from Holland and two boys have gathered mussels at a nearby beach during the day, and invite everyone to the tipi to eat them. We sit for some time in silence, watching the mussels steam open in a pot over the grate. A boy with glassy blue eyes whose lids seem weighted down starts to pick out the orange flesh with his dirt-caked hands and drops them in a pan greased with Spry. A mangy cat snaps every third mussel out of the pan. No one stops it . . .

Nancy, in her shack about a mile from the tipi, is fixing a green stew of onions, cabbage, kale, leeks, and potatoes; she calls to three people who live nearby to come share it. Nancy has a seventeen-year-old, all-American-girl face—straight blond hair and pink cheeks—on a plump, saggy-stomached mother's body. She has been married twice, gone to graduate school, worked as a social worker and a prostitute, joined the Sexual Freedom League, and taken many overdoses of drugs. Her children have been on more acid trips than most adults at the ranch. "They get very quiet on acid," she says. "The experience is less staggering for kids than for adults, because acid returns you to the consciousness of childhood." Nancy says the children have not been sick since they moved to Wheeler's two years ago. "I can see divine guidance leading us here. This place has been touched by God." She had a vision of planting trees on the land, and ordered fifty of exotic variety, like strawberry guava, camelia, and loquat. Stirring the green stew, she smiles vacuously. "I feel anticipant of a very happy future."

With morning comes a hailstorm, and Bill Wheeler must go to court in Santa Rosa for trial on charges of assaulting a policeman when a squad came to the ranch looking for juvenile runaways and Army deserters. Bill, Gay, Gay's brother Peter, Nancy, Shoshone, and Corky spread out through the courthouse, peeling off mildewed clothes and piling them on benches. Peter, a gigantic, muscular fellow of twenty-three, rips his pants all the way up the back, and, like most people at Wheeler's, he is not wearing underwear. Gay changes Raspberry's diapers on the floor of the ladies' room. Nancy takes off her rain-soaked long johns and leaves them in one of the stalls.

It is a tedious day. Witnesses give conflicting testimony, but all corroborate that one of the officers struck Wheeler first, leading to a shoving, running, tackling, pot-throwing skirmish which also involved Peter. The defendants spend the night in a motel, going over testimony with their lawyer. Bill and Corky go to a supermarket to buy dinner, and wheel down the aisle checking labels for chemicals, opening jars to take a taste with the finger, uhmmm, laughing at the "obsolete consciousness" of the place. They buy greens, Roquefort dressing, peanut butter, organic honey, and two Sara Lee cakes. The next morning, Nancy says she couldn't sleep with the radiator and all the trucks. Gay says, "I had a dream in which I saw death. It was a blond man with no facial hair, and he looked at me with this all-concealing expression." Bill, outside, staring at the Kodak blue swimming pool: "I dreamed last night that Gay and I got separated somehow and I was stuck with Raspberry." He shudders. "You know, I feel love for other people, but Gay is the only one I want to spend my life with."

The jury goes out at 3:00 P.M. and deliberates until 9:00. In the courtroom, a mottled group in pioneer clothes, mud-spattered and frizzy-wet, are chanting, "Om." The jury cannot agree on four counts, and finds Bill and Peter not guilty on three counts. The judge declares a mistrial. The county fathers are not finished, though. They are still attempting to close the access road to Wheeler's and to get an injunction to raze all buildings on the ranch as health hazards. Bill Wheeler is not worried, nor are his charges, climbing in the jeep and singing, "Any day now . . ." God will provide.

> *We must do away with the absolutely specious notion that everybody has to earn a living. . . . We keep inventing jobs because of this false idea that everybody has to be employed at some kind of drudgery because, according to Malthusian-Darwinian theory, he must justify his right to exist. . . . The true business of people should be to . . . think about whatever it was they were thinking about before somebody came along and told them they had to earn a living.*
>
> —R. Buckminster Fuller

HIGHWAY 101 RIBBONING down the coast: narcotic pastels, the smell of charbroiled hamburgers cooking, motels with artificial gas-flame fireplaces. Total sensory Muzak. California banks now print their checks in salmon and mauve colors with reproductions of the Golden Gate Bridge, the High Sierras, the Mojave Desert, and other panoramas. "Beautiful money," they call it. As I cross the San Rafael Bridge, which, because the clouds are low, seems to shoot straight into the sky and disappear, Radio KABL in San Francisco is playing "Shangri-la."

South of the city in Menlo Park, one of a chain of gracious suburbs languishing in industrial smoke, Stewart Brand created the *Whole Earth Catalog,* and now presides over the Whole Earth Truck Store and mystique. Brand, a thirty-year-old biologist who was a fringe member of Ken Kesey's Merry Pranksters, put out the first catalog in 1968 as a mail-order source book for people starting communes or alternative life-styles. The success of the catalog—it is selling a thousand copies a day—indicates it is answering needs that cut across age and philosophical gaps. One of these is the need to regain control over the environment, so that when the refrigerator breaks, or the electric power goes out, you don't have to stand around helplessly waiting for repairmen, middlemen, and technical "experts" to fix things at your expense. The *Whole Earth Catalog* lists books and tools that enable one to build furniture, fix cars, learn real-estate law, raise bees for honey, publish your own books, build houses out of foam, auto tops, or mud, and even bury your own dead so that the rites of passage are simple and meaningful. The *Catalog* also speaks to the need to break out of the inflationary cycle of higher earning and higher spending. It offers books such as *How to Get Out of the Rat Race and Live on $10 a Month* and *How to Live on Nothing,* and suggests *The Moonlighters' Manual* for people who want to earn subsistence money with minimum commitment of psyche.

Brand says, "I admit we encourage starting from scratch. We don't say it will be easy, but education comes from making mistakes. Take delivering babies at home. That's hazardous! We carry books that tell how hazardous it is. People have lost babies that way, but it won't hit the fan until we lose a few mothers. When it works, though, it's glorious." Brand, with oversized blue eyes and gaunt cheeks, breaks into infectious laughter as he describes his fantasies. "The city-country pull is behind everything going on now. An anthropologist Cherokee we know feels the cycle goes like this: a kid grows up, has talent, goes to the city to fulfill himself, becomes an ideologue, his personality deteriorates, and to recuperate, he goes back to the land." The impulse to return to the land and to form "intentional communities," or communes, is being felt in the sudden demand for publications like *The Green Revolution,* founded in the 1940s to promote rural revival, and *The Modern Utopian,* produced by Alternatives! Foundation in Sebastopol, California, which also runs a commune matching service.

Brand says there are few real alternative life-styles right now: "There's black pride, and the long-haired run for the hills. That's it. What we want are alternative economies and alternative political systems. Maybe alternative ecologies. You can't do this with six people." Brand points out that new social programs "are always parasitic, like newborn babies. They feed off the parent culture until they're strong enough to be self-sustaining." The communes in New Mexico, he says, can eventually develop their own economy by trading goods and services and paying in tokens, "like the casinos in Las Vegas. The climate is great for experiments now. There's no end of resources for promising ideas. But people had better hurry, because the avenues will start being closed off." He laughs, thrusting his chin up. "Things are getting weirder and weirder."

> *No society racing through the turbulence of the next several decades will be able to do without [some] form of future-shock absorber: specialized centers in which the rate of change is artificially depressed. . . . In such slow-paced communities, individuals who needed or wanted a more relaxed, less stimulating existence could find it.*
> —Alvin Toffler, "Coping with Future Shock"

ROADS ACROSS THE upper Northwest are flat and ruler-straight, snowbound for long months, turning arid and dusty in the summer. At an empty crossing in a poor, wheat-growing county, the road suddenly dips and winds down to a valley filled with tall pines and primitive log cabins. The community hidden in this natural canyon is Freedom Farm, founded in 1963. It is one of the oldest communes to be started on open land. The residents—about twenty-four adults and almost as many children—are serious, straightforward people who, with calculated bluntness, say they are dropouts, social misfits, unable or unwilling to cope with the world "outside." The community has no rules, except that no one can be asked to leave. Because it predates the hippie movement, there is an absence of mystical claptrap and jargon like "far out." Only a few are vegetarians. Members do not want the location of the farm published for fear of being inundated with "psychedelic beggars."

I drove to the canyon in the morning and, having learned my lesson, left the car at the top and walked down the steep, icy road. The farm is divided into two parts—80 acres at the north end of the canyon and 120 acres at the south. The families live separately, as they do at Wheeler's, but their homes are more elaborate and solidly built. The first house in the north end is a hexagonal log cabin built by Huw Williams, who started the farm when he was nineteen. Huw is slight, soft-spoken, with a wispy blond beard. His face and voice are expressionless, but when he speaks, he is likely to say something startling, humorous, or indicative of deep feeling. When I arrived, he was cutting out pieces of leather, wearing a green-and-brown lumberman's shirt and a knife strapped to his waist. His wife, Sylvia, was nursing their youngest son, while their two-year-old, Sennett, wearing nothing but a T-shirt, was playing on the floor with a half-breed Norwegian elkhound. The cabin was snugly warm, but smelled faintly of urine from Sennett peeing repeatedly on the rug. There was a cast-iron stove, tables and benches built from logs, a crib, an old-fashioned cradle, and a large bed raised off the floor for warmth and storage space. On the wall there was a calendar opened to January, although it was March.

I asked Huw how the community had stayed together for seven years. He said, deadpan, "The secret is not to try. We've got a lot of rugged individualists here, and everyone is into a different thing. In reflection, it feels good that we survived. A lot of us were from wealthy backgrounds, and the idea of giving it all up and living off the land was a challenge." Huw grew up on a ranch 40 miles from the canyon. "I had everything. When I was fourteen, I had my own car, a half-dozen cows, and $600 in the bank." When he was fifteen, his house burned down and he saw his elaborate collections—stamps, models, books—disappear. He vowed not to become attached to possessions after that, and took to sleeping outdoors. He remembers being terrified of violence, and idolized Gandhi, Christ, and Tolstoy. At seventeen, he became a conscientious objector and began to work in draft resistance. While on a peace walk from New Hampshire to Washington, D.C., he decided to drop out of the University of Washington and start a nonviolent training center, a community where people could live by sharing rather than competing. He persuaded his mother to give him 80 acres in the canyon for the project, rented a house, called the Hart House, and advertised in peace papers for people to come and share it with him.

The first summer, more than fifty came and went and they all lived in the Hart House. One of the visitors was Sylvia, a fair-skinned girl with long chestnut hair and warm wistful eyes that hint of sadness.

They were married, and Huw stopped talking about a peace center and started studying intentional communities. He decided he wanted a community that would be open to anyone, flexible, with no prescribed rules to live by. Work would get done, Huw felt, because people would want to do it to achieve certain ends. "It's a Western idea. You inspire people by giving them a goal, making it seem important; then they'll do anything to get there." If people did not want to work, Huw felt, forcing them would not be the answer.

The results were chaotic. "Emotional crises, fights over everything. A constant battle to get things done. A typical scene would be for one guy to spend two hours fixing a meal. He had to make three separate dishes—one for vegetarians, one for nonvegetarians, and one for people who wouldn't eat government-surplus food. He would put them on the table, everybody would grab, and if you stood back you got nothing. When people live that close together, they become less sensitive, and manners go right out the window. It was educational, but we knew it wasn't suitable for raising children." The group pooled resources and bought another 120 acres two miles away. Huw and Sylvia built their own cabin and moved out of the Hart House; another couple followed. Then around 1966, the drug scene exploded and the farm was swamped with speed freaks, runaways, addicts, and crazies. A schism grew between the permanent people and the transients. The transients thought the permanents were uptight and stingy. The permanents said the transients were abusing the land. When most of the permanents had built their own cabins, they began talking about burning down the Hart House. I heard many versions of the incident. Some say a man, whom I shall call George, burned it. Some say everyone did it. Some said they watched and were against it but felt they should not stop it. Afterwards, most of the transients left, and the farm settled into its present pattern of individual families tending their own gardens, buying their own supplies, and raising their own animals. Each family has at least two vehicles—a car and a tractor, or a motorcycle or truck. Huw says, "We do our share of polluting."

The majority at Freedom live on welfare, unemployment compensation, and food stamps. A few take part-time jobs picking apples or wheat, one does free-lance writing, and some do crafts. Huw makes about $50 a month on his leather work, Ken Meister makes wall hangings, Rico and Pat sell jewelry to psychedelic shops, and Steve raises rabbits. Huw believes the farm could support itself by growing organic grains and selling them by mail order, but he hasn't been able to get enough cooperation to do this. "It's impossible to have both a commune, where everyone lives and works collectively, and free land, where anyone can settle," he says. "Someday we might have a commune on the land, but not everyone who lived on the land would have to join it."

The only communal rituals are Thanksgiving at the schoolhouse and the corn dance, held on the first full moon of May. Huw devised the corn dance from a Hopi Indian ceremony, and each year it gets wilder. Huw builds a drum, and at sundown everyone gathers on a hillside with food, wine, the children in costumes, animals, and musical instruments. They take turns beating the drum but must keep it beating until dawn. They roast potatoes, and sometimes a kid, a pig, or a turkey, get stoned, dance, howl, and drop to sleep. "But that's only once a year," one of the men says. "We could have one every month, and it would hold the community together." Not everyone wants this solidarity, however. Some are like hermits and have staked out corners of the canyon where they want to be left alone. The families who live nearby get together for dinners, chores, and baby-sitting. At the north end, the Williamses, the Swansons, and the Goldens pop in and out constantly. On the day I arrive, they are having a garden meeting at the Swansons' to decide what to order for spring planting.

The Swansons, who have three young children, moved into the canyon this year after buying, for $1,000, the two-story house a man called Steve had built for his own family. Steve had had a falling-out with Huw and wanted to move to the south acres. The Swansons needed a place they could move into right away. The house has the best equipment at the farm, with a flush toilet (sectioned off by a blanket hung from the ceiling), running water, and electricity that drives a stove, refrigerator, and freezer. Jack Swanson, an outgoing, ruddy-faced man of thirty-five, with short hair and a moustache, works on a newspaper 150 miles away and commutes to the farm for weekends. His wife, Barbara, twenty-four, is the image of a Midwestern college girl: jeans cut off to Bermuda length, blouses with Peter Pan collars, and a daisy-printed scarf around her short brown hair. But it is quickly apparent that she is a strong-willed nonconformist. "I've always been a black sheep," she says. "I hate supermarkets—everything's been chemically preserved. You might as well be in a morgue." Barbara is gifted at baking, pickling, and canning, and wants to raise sheep to weave and dye the wool herself. She and Jack tried living in various cities, then a suburb, then a farm in Idaho, where they found they lacked the skills to make it work. "We were so ill-equipped by society to live off the earth," Jack says. "We thought about moving to Freedom Farm for three or four years, but when times were good, we put it off." Last year their third child was born with a lung disease which required months of hospitalization and left them deep in debt. Moving to the farm seemed a way out. "If we had stayed in the suburbs, we found we were spending everything we made, with rent and car payments, and could never pay off the debts. I had to make more and more just to stay even. The price was too high for what we wanted in life," Jack says. "Here, because I don't pay rent and because we can raise food ourselves, I don't have to make as much money. We get help in farming, and have good company. In two or three months, this house is all mine—no interest, no taxes. Outside it would cost me $20,000 and 8 percent interest."

A RAINSTORM HITS at midnight and by morning the snow has washed off the canyon walls, the stream has flooded over, and the roads are slushy mud ruts. Sylvia saddles two horses and we ride down to the south 120. There are seven cabins on the valley floor, and three hidden by trees on the cliff. Outside one of the houses, Steve is feeding his rabbits; the mute, wiggling animals are clustering around the cage doors. Steve breeds the rabbits to sell to a processor and hopes to earn $100 a month from the business. He also kills them to eat. "It's tough to do," he says, "but if people are going to eat meat, they should be willing to kill the animal." While Steve is building his new house, he has moved with his wife and four children into the cabin of a couple I shall call George and Liz Snow. George is a hefty, porcine man of thirty-nine, a drifter who earned a doctorate in statistics, headed an advertising agency, ran guns to Cuba, worked as a civil servant, a mason, a dishwasher, and rode the freights. He can calculate the angles of a geodesic dome and quote Boccaccio and Shakespeare. He has had three wives, and does not want his name known because "there are a lot of people I don't want to find me."

Steve, a hard-lived thirty-four, has a past that rivals George's for tumult: nine years as an Army engineer, AWOL, running a coffeehouse in El Paso, six months in a Mexican jail on a marijuana charge, working nine-to-five as chief engineer in a fire-alarm factory in New Haven, Connecticut, then cross-country to Spokane. Steve has great dynamism and charm that are both appealing and abrasive. His assertiveness inevitably led to friction in every situation, until, tired of bucking the system, he moved to the farm. "I liked the structure of this community," he says. "Up there, I can't get along with one out of a thousand people. Here I make it with one out of two." He adds, "We're in the business of survival while the world goes crazy. It's good to know how to build a fire, or a waterwheel, because if the world ends, you're there now."

Everyone at Freedom seems to share this sense of imminent doomsday. Huw says, "When the country is wiped out, electricity will stop coming through the wires, so you might as well do without it now. I don't believe you should use any machine you can't fix yourself." Steve says, "Technology can't feed all the world's people." Stash, a young man who lives alone at the farm, asks, "Am I going to start starving in twenty years?"

Steve: "Not if you have a plot to garden."

Stash: "What if the ravaging hordes come through?"

Steve: "Be prepared for the end, or get yourself a gun."

There is an impulse to dismiss this talk as a projection of people's sense of their own private doom, except for the fact that the fear is widespread. Stewart Brand writes in the *Whole Earth Catalog*: "One barometer of people's social-confidence level is the sales of books on

291

survival. I can report that sales on *The Survival Book* are booming; it's one of our fastest moving items."

Several times a week, Steve, Stash, and Steve's daughter Laura, fourteen, drive to the small town nearby to buy groceries, visit a friend, and, if the hot water holds out, take showers. They stop at Joe's Bar for beer and hamburgers—40 cents "with all the trimmings." Laura, a graceful, quiet girl, walks across the deserted street to buy *Mad* magazine and look at rock record albums. There are three teenagers at the farm—all girls—and all have tried running away to the city. One was arrested for shoplifting, another was picked up in a crash pad with seven men. Steve says, "We have just as much trouble with our kids as straight, middle-class parents do. I'd like to talk to people in other communities and find out how they handle their teenagers. Maybe we could send ours there." Stash says, "Or bring teenage boys here." The women at the farm have started to joke uneasily that their sons will become uptight businessmen and their daughters will be suburban housewives. The history of utopian communities in this country has been that the second generation leaves. It is easy to imagine commune-raised children having their first haute cuisine meal, or sleeping in silk pajamas in a luxury hotel, or taking a jet plane. Are they not bound to be dazzled? Sylvia says, "Our way of life is an overreaction to something, and our kids will probably overreact to us. It's absurd. Kids run away from this, and all the runaways from the city come here."

In theory, the farm is an expanded family, and children can move around and live with different people or build houses of their own. In the summer, they take blankets and sleeping bags up in the cliffs to sleep in a noisy, laughing bunch. When I visited, all the children except one were staying in their parents' houses. Low-key tension seemed to be running through the community, with Steve and Huw Williams at opposite poles. Steve's wife, Ann, told me, We don't go along with Huw's philosophy of anarchy. We don't think it works. You need some authority and discipline in any social situation." Huw says, "The thing about anarchy is that I'm willing to do a job myself, if I have to, rather than start imposing rules on others. Steve and George want things to be done efficiently with someone giving orders, like the Army."

At dinner when the sun goes down, Steve's and George's house throbs with goodwill and festivity. The cabin, like most at the farm, is not divided into separate rooms. All nine people—Steve, Ann, and their four children, the Snows and their baby—sleep on the upstairs level, while the downstairs serves as kitchen, dining, and living room. "The teenagers wish there were more privacy," Steve says, "but for us and the younger children, it feels really close." Most couples at the farm are untroubled about making love in front of the children. "We don't make a point of it," one man said, "but if they happen to see it, and it's done in love and with good vibrations, they won't be afraid or embarrassed."

While Ann and Liz cook hasenpfeffer, Steve's daughters, Laura and Karen, ten, improvise making gingerbread with vinegar and brown sugar as a substitute for molasses. A blue jay chatters in a cage hung from the ceiling. Geese honk outside, and five dogs chase each other around the room. Steve plays the guitar and sings. The hasenpfeffer is superb. The rabbits have been pickled for two days, cooked in red wine, herbs, and sour cream. There are large bowls of beets, potatoes, jello, and the gingerbread, which tastes perfect, with homemade apple sauce. Afterwards, we all get toothpicks. Liz, an uninhibited, roly-poly girl of twenty-three, is describing how she hitchhiked to the farm, met George, stayed, and got married. "I like it here," she says, pursing her lips, "because I can stand nude on my front porch and yell, fuck! Also, I think I like it here because I'm fat, and there aren't many mirrors around. Clothes don't matter, and people don't judge you by your appearance like they do out there." She adds, "I've always been different from others. I think most of the people here are misfits—they have problems in communicating, relating to one another." Ann says, "Communication is ridiculous. We've begun to feel gossip is much better. It gradually gets around to the person it's about, and that's okay. Most people here can't say things to each other's face."

I walk home—I'm staying in a vacant cabin—across a field, with the stars standing out in brilliant relief from the black sky. Lights flicker in the cabins sprinkled through the valley. Ken Meister is milking late in the barn. The fire is still going in my cabin; I add two logs, light the kerosene lamps, and climb under the blankets on the high bed. Stream water sweeps by the cabin in low whooshes, the fire sputters. The rhythm of the canyon, after a few days, seems to have entered my body. I fall asleep around ten, wake up at six, and can feel the time even though there are no clocks around. In the morning light, though, I find two dead mice on the floor, and must walk a mile to get water, then build a fire to heat it. It becomes clear why, in a community like this, the sex roles are so well-defined and satisfying. When men actually do heavy physical labor like chopping trees, baling hay, and digging irrigation ditches, it feels very fulfilling for the woman to tend the cabin, grind wheat, put up fruit, and sew or knit. Each depends on the other for basic needs—shelter, warmth, food. With no intermediaries, such as supermarkets and banks, there is a direct relationship between work and survival. It is thus possible, according to Huw, for even the most repetitive jobs such as washing dishes or sawing wood to be spiritually rewarding. "Sawing puts my head in a good place," he says. "It's like a yogic exercise."

IN ADDITION TO his farming and leather work, Huw has assumed the job of teacher for the four children of school age. Huw believes school should be a free, anarchic experience, and that the students should set their own learning programs. Suddenly given this freedom, the children, who were accustomed to public school, said they wanted to play and ride the horses. Huw finally told them they must be at the schoolhouse every day for at least one hour. They float in and out, and Huw stays half the day. He walks home for lunch and passes Karen and another girl on the road. Karen taunts him, "Did you see the mess we made at the school?"

"Yes," Huw says.

"Did you see our note?"

Huw walks on, staring at the ground. "It makes me feel you don't have much respect for the tools or the school."

She laughs. "Course we don't have any respect!"

"Well, it's your school," Huw says softly.

Karen shouts, "You said it was your school the other day. You're an Indian giver."

Huw: "I never said it was my school. Your parents said that." Aside to me he says, "They're getting better at arguing every day. Still not very good, though." I tell Huw they seem to enjoy tormenting him. "I know. I'm the only adult around here they can do that to without getting clobbered. It gives them a sense of power. It's ironic, because I keep saying they're mature and responsible, and their parents say they need strict authority and discipline. So who do they rebel against? Me. I'm going to call a school meeting tonight. Maybe we can talk some of this out."

In the afternoon I visit Rico and Pat, whose A-frame house is the most beautiful and imaginative at the farm. It has three levels—a basement, where they work on jewelry and have stored a year's supply of food; a kitchen-living-room floor; and a high sleeping porch reached by a ladder. The second story is carpeted, with harem-like cushions, furs, and wall hangings. There are low tables, one of which lifts to reveal a sunken white porcelain bathtub with running water heated by the wood stove. Rico, twenty-five, designed the house so efficiently that even in winter, when the temperature drops to 20 below zero, it is warm enough for him to lounge about wearing nothing but a black cape. Pat and Rico have talked about living with six adults in some form of group marriage, but, Pat says, "there's no one here we could really do it with. The sexual experiments that have gone on have been rather compulsive and desperate. Some of us think jealousy is innate." Rico says, "I think it's cultural." Pat says, "Hopefully our kids will be able to grow up without it. I think the children who are born here will really have a chance to develop freely. The older children who've come here recently are too far gone to appreciate the environment."

In the evening, ten parents and five children show up at the school, a one-room house built with eighteen sides, so that a geodesic dome can be constructed on top. The room has a furnace, bookshelves and work tables, rugs and cushions on the floor. Sylvia is sitting on a stool in the center nursing their son. Two boys in yellow pajamas are running in circles, squealing, "Ba-ba-ba!" Karen is drawing on the blackboard—of all things, a city skyscape. Rico is doing a yoga headstand. Steve and Huw begin arguing about whether the children should have to come to the school every day. Steve says, in a booming voice, "I think the whole canyon should be a learning community, a total educational environment. The kids can learn something from everyone. If you want to teach them, why don't you come to our house?" Huw, standing with a clipboard against his hip, says, "They have to come here to satisfy the county school superintendent. But it seems futile when they come in and say I'm not qualified to teach them. Where do they get that?"

Steve says, "From me. I don't think you're qualified." Huw: "Well, I'm prepared to quit and give you the option of doing something else, or sending them to public school."

Steve says, "Don't quit. I know your motives are pure as the driven snow . . ."

Huw says, "I'm doing it for myself as well, to prove I can do it. But it all fits together."

They reach an understanding without speaking further.

Steve then says, "I'd like to propose that we go door-to-door in this community and get everyone enthused about the school as a center for adult learning and cultural activity first, and for the kiddies second. Because when you turn on the adults, the kids will follow. The school building needs finishing—the dome should be built this summer. Unless there's more enthusiasm in this community, I'm not going to contribute a thing. But if we get everybody to boost this, by God I'll be the first one out to dig."

Huw says, "You don't think the people who took the time to come tonight is enough interest? I may be cynical, but I think the only way to get some of the others here would be to have pot and dope."

Steve: "Get them interested in the idea of guest speakers, musicians, from India, all over. We can build bunk dorms to accommodate them."

Huw: "Okay. I think we should get together every Sunday night to discuss ideas, hash things over. In the meantime, why don't we buy materials to finish the building?"

On the morning I leave, sunlight washes down the valley from a cloudless sky. Huw, in his green lumberman's shirt, rides with me to the top road. "My dream is to see this canyon filled with families who live here all the time, with lots of children." He continues in a lulling rhythm: "We could export some kind of food or product. The school is very important—it should be integrated in the whole community. Children from all over could come to work, learn, and live with different families. I'd like to have doctors here and a clinic where people could be healed naturally. Eventually there should be a ham radio system set up between all the communities in the country, and a blimp, so we could make field trips back and forth. I don't think one community is enough to meet our needs. We need a world culture."

Huw stands, with hands on hips, the weight set back on his heels—a small figure against the umber field. "Some day I'm going to inherit six hundred more acres down there, and it'll all be free. Land should be available for anybody to use like it was with the Indians." He smiles with the right corner of his mouth. "The Indians could no more understand owning land than they could owning the sky."

> *We've got to get ourselves back to the garden.*
> —Joni Mitchell, from the song "Woodstock"

LAST HALLOWEEN IN Jemez, New Mexico, the squidlike "rock-drug-alternative-culture" underground gathered itself together to discuss what to do with the energy manifested at Woodstock. How can we use that power, they asked, and prevent it from being sickened and turned as it was at the Rolling Stones Free Concert in Altamont? The answer seemed to generate itself: buy land, throw away the deed, open it to anyone, and call it Earth People's Park. Hold an earth-warming festival and ecological world's fair—all free. A nonprofit corporation was formed to collect money and handle legal problems. But there would be no authorities and no rules in Earth People's Park. Paul Krassner, Tom Law, Milan Melvin, Ken Kesey, Mama Cass Elliot, and the Hog Farm traveling communal circus led by Hugh Romney fanned out to sell the idea. They asked everyone who had been at Woodstock in body or spirit to contribute a dollar. At first, they talked of buying 20,000 acres in New Mexico or Colorado. In a few months, they were talking about 100,000 acres in many small pieces, all over the country. They flooded the media with promises of "a way out of the disaster of the cities, a viable alternative." Hugh Romney, calling himself Wavy Gravy, in an aviator suit, sheepskin vest, and a Donald Duck hat, spoke on television about simplicity, community, and harmony with the land. The cards, letters, and money poured in. Some were hand-printed, with bits of leaves and stardust in the creases, some were typed on business stationery. One, from a young man in La Grange, Illinois, seemed to touch all the chords:

*Hello. Maybe we're not as alone as I thought. I am 24, my developed skills are as an advertising writer-producer-director. It seems such a waste. I have energy. I can simplify my life and I want to help. I am convinced that a new lifestyle, one which holds something spiritual as sacred, is necessary in this land. People can return to the slow and happy pace of life that they abandoned along with their understanding of brotherhood. Thank you for opening doors.*

*P.S.—Please let me know what site you purchase so I can leave as soon as possible for it.*

# ABOUT THE AUTHORS

Eric F. Goldman (1916–1989) is the author of *Rendezvous with Destiny: A History of Modern American Reform* and *The Tragedy of Lyndon B. Johnson,* among other works. He was Rollins Professor of History at Princeton University.

Priscilla Johnson McMillan (1928– ) is a fellow at the Russian Research Center at Harvard University. She is the author of *Marina and Lee,* a book based on her interviews with Lee Harvey Oswald. She is currently at work on a book about J. Robert Oppenheimer and the hydrogen bomb.

Eric Larrabee (1922–1990) was an associate editor at *Harper's Magazine* from 1946 to 1958. He is the author of *Commander in Chief—Franklin Delano Roosevelt: His Lieutenants and Their War.*

George Plimpton (1927– ) is the editor of *The Paris Review* and a contributing editor to *Harper's Magazine.* He is the author of numerous books, including *Paper Lion, The Bogey Man,* and *The X-Factor.*

Richard Hofstadter (1916–1970) won Pulitzer Prizes for his books *The Age of Reform: From Bryan to FDR* and *Anti-Intellectualism in American Life.* He was DeWitt Clinton Professor of American History at Columbia University.

Louis E. Lomax (1913–1970 ) is the author of *When the Word Is Given: A Report on Elijah Mohammed, Malcolm X and the Black Muslim World.*

Walker Percy (1916–1990) won the National Book Award for his novel *The Moviegoer*. His other works include the novel *The Last Gentleman* and *The Message in the Bottle,* a collection of essays.

C. Vann Woodward (1908– ) is Sterling Professor Emeritus of History at Yale University. He has written numerous books, including *Origins of the New South: 1877–1913* and *Thinking Back: The Perils of Writing History.*

Richard Todd (1940– ) is an editor at Houghton Mifflin. He has contributed to a variety of publications, including *The Atlantic Monthly* and *Worth.*

Tom Wicker (1926– ) was the Washington bureau chief and a columnist for *The New York Times.* He is the author of *Unto This Hour* and *One of Us: Richard Nixon and the American Dream,* among other books.

David Halberstam (1934– ) is a Pulitzer prize–winning writer whose books include *The Making of a Quagmire: America & Vietnam During the Kennedy Era, The Best & The Brightest,* and *The Reckoning.* He was a correspondent for *The New York Times* and a contributing editor to *Harper's Magazine.*

Robert Kotlowitz (1924– ) is an editorial adviser to WNET/ Channel Thirteen. He is the author of several books, including *Sea Changes* and *His Master's Voice.*

Ward S. Just (1935– ) is currently at work on his eleventh novel. He is the author of *The Congressman Who Loved Flaubert & Other Stories, Jack Gance,* and, most recently, *Ambition & Love.*

Stephen Minot (1927– ) teaches creative writing at the University of California, Riverside, and is a contributing editor to *The North American Review.* He is the author of *Chill of Dusk* and *Surviving the Flood,* among other books.

John Corry (1933– ) is the author of *The Manchester Affair, The Golden Clan,* and, most recently, *My Times: Adventures in the News Trade.* He is a monthly columnist for *The American Spectator* and was a contributing editor to *Harper's Magazine* from 1968 to 1971.

Joe McGinniss (1942– ) is the author of several works of fiction and nonfiction, including *The Selling of the President, The Dream Team, Fatal Vision,* and *Cruel Doubt.*

John W. Aldridge (1922– ) is the author of *After the Lost Generation, The American Novel & The Way We Live Now,* and *In Search of Heresy: American Literature in an Age of Conformity,* among other books.

Joseph C. Goulden (1934– ) is the author of numerous books, including *The Curtis Paper, Korea: The Untold Story of the War,* and, most recently, *Fit to Print: A. M. Rosenthal & His Times.*

Sara Davidson (1943– ) is the author of several books, including *Loose Change.* She was co-executive producer for the television program *Dr. Quinn Medicine Woman* and is currently at work on a novel.

# ACKNOWLEDGEMENTS

Each of the articles in this book was originally published by *Harper's Magazine* and is protected by copyright © in the name of *Harper's Magazine,* with the exception of the following articles: "Good-By to the Fifties—and Good Riddance," © 1960 by Eric F. Goldman. Published by permission of the Estate of Eric F. Goldman. "The Paranoid Style in American Politics," © 1964 by Richard Hofstadter. "Turned On and Super-Sincere in California," © 1967 by Richard Todd. "George Wallace: A Gross and Simple Heart," © 1967 by Tom Wicker. "Return to Vietnam," © 1967 by David Halberstam. "Vietnam Notebook," © 1968 by Ward S. Just. Reprinted by permission of the author. "On Aiding and Abetting: The Anguish of Draft Counseling," © 1968 by Stephen Minot. "The Selling of the President 1968," © 1969 by Joe McGinniss. Reprinted by permission of Sterling Lord Literistic, Inc. "Voices from the Silent Majority," © 1970 by Joseph C. Goulden. Reprinted by permission of Brandt & Brandt Literary Agents, Inc. "Open Land: Getting Back to the Communal Garden," © 1970 by Sara Davidson.

# THE AMERICAN RETROSPECTIVE SERIES

## VOICES IN BLACK & WHITE:
Writings on Race in America from *Harper's Magazine*

## TURNING TOWARD HOME:
Reflections on the Family from *Harper's Magazine*

## THE WORLD WAR TWO ERA:
Perspectives on All Fronts from *Harper's Magazine*